THE SEVEN TABLETS

OF

CREATION,

OR THE BABYLONIAN AND ASSYRIAN LEGENDS
CONCERNING THE CREATION OF THE WORLD
AND OF MANKIND.

EDITED BY

L. W. KING, M.A., F.S.A.,

ASSISTANT IN THE DEPARTMENT OF EGYPTIAN AND ASSYRIAN ANTIQUITIES, BRITISH MUSEUM.

VOL. II.

London:
LUZAC AND CO.
1902.

Enuma Elish: Vol. 2
ISBN 1-58509-042-5

Also Available:

Enuma Elish: Vol. 1
ISBN 1-58509-041-7

Enuma Elish: Vol. 1 & 2 (combined)
ISBN 1-58509-043-3

Published by
The Book Tree
Post Office Box 724
Escondido, CA 92033

ENUMA ELISH: The Seven Tablets of Creation

VOLUME TWO
FOREWARD

The *Enuma Elish* is receiving renewed interest from modern researchers delving into the origins of mankind, the earth, and the solar system. It is a story first written down by the ancient Sumerians thousands of years ago. Over the centuries a copy ended up in the library at Nineveh in the 7th century B.C., and was uncovered by archaeologists in the late 1800s. Written in cuneiform text and preserved on seven clay tablets, the entire story was called "The Seven Tablets of Creation." After being translated the story revealed how the planets were to be aligned, how a cosmic catastrophe affected the earth, how mankind came upon the scene, and how the "gods" played a role in all of it.

Before there was man it would seem obvious that other witnesses were needed in order to tell the story (provided that the story is actually true). Those witnesses were the gods. The words enuma elish actually mean "when above," and this is the detailed story of the gods before, and after, coming to earth. They had human-like personalities and were described in human form, coming to the earth, settling it, and ultimately manipulating and ruling over mankind. In other words, this was an advanced race of human-like beings having enough advanced technology and know-how to get here, to the degree that simple humans (us) considered them as "gods." Later advances in our own sciences, especially in biology and genetics, have revealed clues to our past and how we may have been influenced by those with higher knowledge.

If such beings never existed, how does one explain this incredible story? Read it first, and then decide if it is nothing more than myth, or if such events may in fact have happened. Traditional archaeologists reject the pioneering views of men like Zecharia Sitchin and Neil Freer, but the general public, in all walks of life, have exploded with interest. We want to know where we *really* came from and where we are going, and traditional explanations provided by the basic theory of evolution and/or our religious institutions just don't hold water any more for millions of people—at least enough to provoke a serious exploration. These people are, in general, highly intelligent and have come to the realization that if they want to achieve real answers, they must search for them on their own without taking anyone else's word for it. The *Enuma Elish: The Seven Tablets of Creation* contains a wealth of information and is a great place to start.

In this supplemental volume, L.W. King has provided us with other accounts of creation stories which can be used in comparison to the *Enuma Elish*. Researchers will find many interesting parallels and similar versions also coming from ancient Sumeria. These include references to the creation of the moon and sun, the slaying of the dragon, and the creation of the world by the god Marduk.

Some Assyrian commentaries which were also discovered have been included, as well as ancient Assyrian legends of the temptation of man and the Tower of Babel. Ancient astrological literature which relates to the creation stories is also included, plus a fascinating prayer to the goddess Ishtar.

The last section displays exact duplicates of each of the original tablets, front and back, making this work invaluable to the most serious of researchers. This two volume set by King is still considered the best translation and rendition of these rare tablets to date.

Paul Tice

Contents.

PAGE

PLATES :—

SUPPLEMENTARY TEXTS.

II.

Other Accounts of the History of Creation.

I. Another Version of the Dragon-Myth.[1]

OBV.

1. *i-ta - an - ḫu alāni*^{pl} *nišē*^{pl} *d[a - . . . .]*
2. *in - da - ṭa - a nišē*^{pl} *e - [. . . . . . .]*
3. *a - na ik - kil - li - ši - na ul [. . . . . . .]*
4. *a - na rim - ma - ti - ši - na ul i - ṣab - [. . . .]*

5. *man - nu - um - ma ṣiru [. . . . . . .]*
6. *tam - tu - um - ma ṣiru [. . . . . . .]*
7. *ilu Bēl ina šamē(e) i - te - ṣir [. . . . . . .]*
8. *L kas - pu mu - rak - šu I kas - p[u . . . . .]*[3]

[1] For the text, see *Cuneiform Texts*, part xiii, pl. 33 f., Rm. 282; for a previous publication, cf. Delitzsch, *Assyrisches Wörterbuch*, p. 390 f.; translations have been given by Zimmern in Gunkel's *Schöpfung und Chaos*, pp. 417 ff., and by Jensen in Schrader's *Keilins. Bibl.*, vi, pp. 44 ff. Strictly speaking, the text is not a creation legend, though it gives a variant form of the principal incident in the history of creation according to the version *Enuma eliš*. In the tablet Rm. 282 the fight with the dragon did not precede the creation of the world, but took place after men had been created and cities had been built; see further the Introduction.

[2] The form of the name here used is *Tāmtu*, "the Sea."

[3] The *kaspu* is the space that can be covered in two hours travelling, i.e., about six or seven miles. These general dimensions of the size of the dragon are in accordance with the statement made in l. 8 f. of the reverse to the effect that after the dragon had been slain his blood flowed for more than three years. The

II.

Other Accounts of the History of Creation.

I. Another Version of the Dragon-Myth.[1]

OBV.

1. The cities sighed, men [. . . . .],
2. Men uttered lamentation, [they . . . . . .],
3. For their lamentation there was none [to help],
4. For their grief there was none to take [them by the hand].
5. Who was the dragon [. . . . .]?
6. Tiamat[2] was the dragon [. . . . .]!
7. Bēl in heaven hath formed [. . . . . . .].
8. Fifty kaspu in his length, one kaspu [his height],[3]

---

second measurement in the line is taken by Zimmern to refer to the dragon's breadth, but, as Jensen points out, this is not consistent with the measurement of the mouth given in the following line. Even Zimmern's readings of 60 GAR in l. 10 and 65 GAR in l. 11 do not explain, but render still more anomalous, the ⅓ GAR in l. 9. Without going into the question of the probable length of the Babylonian cubit, it is obvious that the dragon's breadth can hardly have been given as so many miles, if its mouth only measures so many feet. This difficulty can be got over by restoring *ṣīrūtišu* in place of the suggested *rupussu* at the end of l. 8. We then have a consistent picture of the dragon as a long thin snake, rearing his head on high; his coils might well have been believed to extend for three hundred or three hundred and fifty miles, and the raising of his head in the air to a height of six or seven miles would not be inconsistent with the measurement of his mouth as six cubits, i.e., some ten feet or more across.

9. ½ GAR *pi - i - šu* I GAR [. . . . .]
10. *I* GAR *li - ma - a - ti ša u[z -* . . . .]
11. *ana*[1] *V* GAR *iṣ - ṣu - ri i - [* . . . .]
12. *i - na mē*^{pl} *IX ammatu i - šad - da - [ad* . . .]
13. *u - še - ik - ki zi - im - bat - su i - [* . . . . . .]
14. *ilāni ša šamē(e) ka - li - šu - nu* [. . . . . .]
15. *ina šamē(e) ilāni*^{pl} *ka-an-šu ana pān* [. . . .]

16. *u ša* ^{ilu}*Sin ina ulinni - šu ur - ru - [* . . . . .]

17. *man - nu il - lak - ma lab - b[i* . . . . . .][2]
18. *ma - a - tum ra - pa - aš - tum u - še - iz - [* . . . .]
19. *u šarru - u - ti ip - pu - u[š* . . . .]
20. *a - lik* ^{ilu}*Tišḫu*[3] *lab - bi d[u -* . . . . . .]
21. *ma - a - ta ra - pa - aš - ta šu - zi - b[a* . . . . .]
22. *u šarru - u - ta e - pu - uš* [. . . . . .]
23. *taš-pu-ra-an-ni be-el dal-ḫu-ut*[4] *nāri* [. . . . .]

24. *ul i - di - e - ma ša lab - bi* [. . . . .]

[The rest of the Obverse and the upper part of the Reverse of the tablet is wanting.[5]]

---

[1] See Jensen, *Keilins. Bibl.*, vi, p. 364; Zimmern takes the upright wedge as part of the number, cf. the preceding note.

[2] Lines 17–19 are the appeal of the gods to the Moon-god; ll. 20–22 contain the address of the Moon-god to Tišḫu; and ll. 23 ff. give Tišḫu's answer to the Moon-god.

[3] For this value of the sign SUḪ, cf. Brünnow, No. 3,013, and Jensen, *Keilins. Bibl.*, vi, p. 365.

9. Six cubits is his mouth, twelve cubits [his . . . .],
10. Twelve cubits is the circuit of his [ears . . . .];
11. For the space of[1] sixty cubits he [. . . .] a bird;
12. In water nine cubits deep he draggeth [. . . .].
13. He raiseth his tail on high [. . . . .];
14. All the gods of heaven [. . . . .].
15. In heaven the gods bowed themselves down before [the Moon-god . . . .];
16. The border of the Moon-god's robe they hasti[ly grasped]:
17. "Who will go and [slay] the dragon,[2]
18. "And deliver the broad land [from . . . . .].
19. "And become king [over . . . .]?"
20. "Go, Tišḫu,[3] [slay] the dragon,
21. "And deliver the broad land [from . . . . .],
22. "And become king [over . . . .]!"
23. "Thou hast sent me, O lord, [to . . . . .] the raging (creatures)[4] of the river,
24. "But I know not the [. . . .] of the Dragon!"

[The rest of the Obverse and the upper part of the Reverse of the tablet are wanting.[5]]

---

[4] Jensen, *ri-ḫu-ut*, which he renders as "moisture." The plural, *dalḫūti*, may perhaps be explained by supposing that, according to this version also, the dragon had other creatures to help her in the fight.

[5] Of ll. 25 and 26 the following traces are preserved: (25) [. . . . .] *maḫ-r[a- . . . . .]*, (26) [. . . . .] *mē*[pl] [. . . . .].

REV. . . . .

1. [. . .] *pa-a-šu i-pu-uš-ma a-na* ilu[1][. . .]

2. *šu-uš-ḫi-it ur-pa mi-ḫa-a* [. . . . . .]

3. *ku-nu-uk-ku na-piš-ti-ka i-na pa-ni-ka* [. . .]

4. *us-kam-ma lab-ba du-*[. . . . . .]

5. *u-ša-aš-ḫi-it ur-pa mi-ḫa-a* [. . . . .]

6. *ku-nu-uk-ku na-piš-ti-šu ina pa-ni-šu* [. . . . .]

7. *is-su-kam-ma lab-bi* [. . . . . .]

8. *III šanāti*pl *III arḫē*pl *ūmu I* KAN *u* [. . . . .][2]

9. *ša lab-bi il-la-ku da-mu-šu* [. . . . .][3]

---

[1] Jensen suggests the restoration ilu *B*[*ēl*], which he deduces from the traces upon the tablet as published by Delitzsch; for, as he states, the only other restoration possible would be ilu *I*[*štar*], and this is rendered unlikely by the masculine form of the imperatives in ll. 2 and 4. This would prove that the slayer of the dragon was Bēl, or Marduk, in both the versions of the story. As a matter of fact, the traces are incorrectly given by Delitzsch; they represent the sign AN and not the conflate sign AN + EN (cf. *Cun. Txts.*, pt. xiii, pl. 34), and it is not possible to conclude from the text who is the hero of this version.

[2] Jensen suggests the restoration *u*[. KAS-PU], i.e., "for three years, three months, a day and [. hours]." The trace of the

REV. . . . .

1. [And . . . .] opened his mouth and [spake] unto the god[1] [. . . . .]:
2. " Stir up cloud, and storm [and tempest]!
3. " The seal of thy life [shalt thou set] before thy face,
4. " Thou shalt grasp it, and thou shalt [slay] the dragon."
5. He stirred up cloud, and storm [and tempest],
6. He [set] the seal of his life before his face,
7. He grasped it, and [he slew] the dragon.
8. For three years and three months, one day and [one night][2]
9. The blood of the dragon flowed [. . . . .].[3]

---

next character after *u* is the single diagonal wedge (cf. *Cun. Txts.*, pt. xiii, pl. 34); according to Jensen's restoration this sign can only be the number "10," i.e. X KAS-PU, "twenty hours," a not very probable reading. The diagonal wedge is more probably the beginning of the sign MI, i.e. *mūšu*, and the end of the line may be restored as *umu I^KAN u* [*mūšu I^KAN*]; this may be rendered "one day and one night," or possibly, as Zimmern in his translation suggests, "day and night."

[3] Line 9 is the last line of the text. The lower part of the tablet is taken up with the common colophon found upon tablets from Ašur-bani-pal's palace.

II. A reference to the Creation of the Cattle and the Beasts of the Field.[1]

1. *e-nu-ma ilāni*^{pl} *i-na pu-uḫ-ri-šu-nu ib-nu-u* [. . .][2]

2. *u-ba-aš-šim-mu* [*bu*]*-ru-mi iḳ-ṣu-*[*ur* . . . . .][3]

3. *u-ša-pu-u* [*šik-na*]*-at na-piš-ti* [. . . . . . .]

4. *bu-ul ṣēri* [*u-ma-a*]*m ṣēri u nam-maš-še-e* [. . . . .][4]

5. *u*[*l*]*-tu*[5] [. . . .] *a-na šik-na-at na-piš-ti* [. . . .]

6. [. . . .][6] *ṣēri u nam-maš-še-e ali u-za-'-*[*i-zu* . . .]

7. [. . . *pu-u*]*ḫ-ri nam-maš-ti gi-mir nab-ni-ti* [. . . .]

8. [. . . .] *ša i-na pu-uḫ-ri kim-ti-ia š*[*e-* . . . .]

---

[1] For the text, see *Cuneiform Texts*, part xiii, pl. 34, D.T. 41; for a previous publication, cf. Delitzsch, *Assyrische Lesestücke*, 3rd ed., p. 34 f.; and for previous translations, see George Smith, *The Chaldean Account of Genesis*, p. 76 f., Zimmern in Gunkel's *Schöpfung und Chaos*, and Jensen in Schrader's *Keilins. Bibl.*, vi, p. 42 f. This fragment, which George Smith suggested might be part of the Seventh Tablet of the Creation Series, does not belong to that series; it contains the introduction or opening lines of a text, and describes the creation of two small creatures by Nin-igi-azag,

II. A reference to the Creation of the Cattle and the Beasts of the Field.[1]

1. When the gods in their assembly had made [the world],[2]
2. And had created the heavens, and had formed [the earth],[3]
3. And had brought living creatures into being [. . . .],
4. And [had fashioned][4] the cattle of the field, and the beasts of the field, and the creatures [of the city],—
5. After[5] [they had . . . .] unto the living creatures [. . . .],
6. [And between the beasts][6] of the field and the creatures of the city had divided [. . . .],
7. [And had . . . .] all creatures, the whole of creation [. . . .],
8. [And had . . . .], which in the whole of my family [. . . .],

"The lord of clear vision." The reference to the creation of cattle and beasts of the field is merely incidental; it occurs in the long opening sentence and indicates the period at which the two small creatures were made; see further the Introduction.

[2] Possibly restore *kullatu* at the end of the line.

[3] Possibly restore *irṣiti*; Jensen suggests *dan-ni-nu* (cf. p. 108, l. 115).

[4] Probably restore *ali ibnū* at the end of the line.

[5] The reading *u*[*l*]-*tu* is certain from the traces on the tablet.

[6] Probably restore the beginning of the line as *ana būl*.

9. [. . . .][1] *-i-ma* [ilu] *Nin-igi-azag šinā ṣu-ḫa-*[*ri* . . . .]

10. [. . . *pu*]*-uḫ-ri nam-maš-ti uš-tar-ri-i*[*ḫ* . . . .][2]

11. [. . . . [ilu]] *Gu-la ḫa-ma-a-ni ir*[. . . . .]
12. [. . . . . . .] *iš-ḳa pi-ṣi* [*u ṣa-al-mi* . . . .]

13. [. . . . . .] *iš-ḳa pi-ṣi u ṣa-*[*al-mi* . . . . .]

14 [. . . . . . .][3] *- ṣi i - n*[*am -* . . . .]

[The rest of the text is wanting.]

III. A reference to the Creation of the Moon and the Sun.[4]

I. UD[5] AN - NA (DINGIR) EN - LIL - LA (DINGIR) EN - KI DINGIR - [E - NE][6]

---

[1] Possibly restore the verb as [*ib-ni*]*-i-ma*; Jensen suggests the restoration [*i-te-li*]*-i-ma* and adds *ib-na-a* at the end of the line.

[2] Restore *ina* at the beginning of the line; at the end of the line Jensen suggests the reading *nab-nit-su-un*.

[3] The traces of the character before *ṣi* are those of *pa* or *ú*; we cannot, therefore, read [. . . *pi*]*-ṣi i-n*[*am bi*], "[. . . .] he calleth the white one by name [. . . .]." It is probable, however, that the second section of the text also dealt with the two small creatures whose creation is described in the first paragraph.

[4] The text is taken from the obverse of the tablet 82–7–14, 4,005, which is published in vol. ii, pl. xlix. The tablet is one of the so-called "practice-tablets," or students' exercises, and contains on the obverse an extract from a Sumerian composition (ll. 1–7), an extract from a Babylonian composition (ll. 8–14) very similar to the Sumerian extract which precedes it, and on the lower part

9. [Then did] Nin-igi-azag [fashion][1] two small creatures [. . . .],
10. [Among] all the beasts he made [their form][2] glorious
11. [. . . . .] the goddess Gula . . [. .]
12. [. . . . .] . . one white [and one black . . . . .]
13. [. . . . .] . . one white and one black [. . . . .]

14. [. . . . . .][3] . . . . [. . . . .]

[The rest of the text is wanting.]

III. A reference to the Creation of the Moon and the Sun.[4]

1. When[5] the gods[6] Ana, Enlil, and Enki

---

of the tablet a number of grammatical notes arranged in three columns and referring to the extracts given above. The first word of l. 8 is broken, but the traces suggest the word *š[a]-n[i]-[e]*, which may be rendered "version." Lines 8–14 are not, however, a literal translation of ll. 1–7, though they appear to have been taken from a somewhat similar Babylonian text. It is clear that the extracts formed the opening lines of the compositions to which they belonged, and that the scribe has written them out for comparison, adding notes on some of the expressions which occur.

[5] That both the Sumerian and Babylonian extracts are to be taken as single sentences, and not broken up into separate phrases, is proved by the note in l. 15. Here the scribe equates UD with *e-nu-ma*, and to *e-nu-ma* adds the grammatical note *iš-tu šu-ta-mu-u mal-ma-liš*, "corresponding to *šutamū*."

[6] The end of the line should possibly be restored as DINGIR-[GAL-GAL-LA], "the great gods."

2. (MAL + GAR)[1]-NE-NE-GI-NA-TA ME[2]-GAL-GAL-LA-[TA]

3. MA-TU[3] (DINGIR) EN-ZU-NA MU-UN-GI-NE-E[Š]
4. U-SIR SIR-SIR-DA[4] ITU U-TU-UD-DA

5. U-ITI[5] AN-KI-A MU-UN-GI-NE-EŠ
6. MA-TU[6] AN-NA IM-PA-UD-DU ŠA-A-NE
7. ŠAG AN-NA IGI-BAR-RA TA-UD-DU

8. *š[a]-n[i]-[e]*[7] *e-nu-ma*[8] ^{ilu}*A-num* ^{ilu}*Bēl* ^{ilu}*E-a*
9. *ilāni*^{pl} *rabūti*^{pl} *ina mil-ki-šu-nu ki-i-nu*
10. *uṣurāti*^{pl} *šamē(e) u irṣitim(tim) iš-ku-nu*
11. *a-na ḳātē*^{II} *ilāni*^{pl} *rabūti*^{pl} *u-kin-nu*
12. *u-mu ba-na-a arḫa ud-du-šu ša inaṭṭalū*^{pl}

13. *a-me-lut-tum* ^{ilu}*Šamaš*[9] *ina libbi bāb aṣī-šu i-mu-ru*

14. *ki-rib šamē(e) u irṣitim(tim) ki-niš uš-ta-mu-u*[10]

---

[1] Cf. Brünnow, No. 5,525.

[2] Cf. Br., No. 10,374.

[3] The group MA-TU occurs in the Cylinder Inscription of Tiglath-pileser I, col. i, l. 6, in the expression *ša-ḳu-u* MA-TU, applied to Sin; and, from the occurrence of the parallel expression *ša-ḳu-u nam-ri-ri* on the obelisk of Shalmaneser II, l. 6, MA-TU is rendered *namriru*, "brightness." In l. 17 of the text the scribe furnishes the new equation MA-TU = ^{ilu}ŠEŠ-KI-RU, and at the end of the line he adds the explanation RU = *e-di-šu*. MA-TU, therefore, signifies the brightness of the New Moon, and in the present passage may be translated "renewal."

[4] The group SIR-SIR = *banū* (Br., No. 4,304), *aṣū* (No. 4,302),

2. Through their sure counsel[1] and by their great commands[2]
3. Ordained the renewal[3] of the Moon-god,
4. The reappearance of the moon,[4] and the creation of the month,
5. And ordained the oracle[5] of heaven and earth,
6. The New Moon[6] did Ana cause to appear,
7. In the midst of heaven he beheld it come forth.

8. [Version].[7] When[8] Anu, Bēl and Ea,
9. The great gods, through their sure counsel
10. Fixed the bounds of heaven and earth,
11. (And) to the hands of the great gods entrusted
12. The creation of the day and the renewal of the month which they might behold,
13. (And) mankind beheld the Sun-god[9] in the gate of his going forth,
14. In the midst of heaven and earth they duly created (him).[10]

---

and *napāḫu* (No. 4,327); in l. 18 the scribe equates U-SIR with *ar-ḫa*, but, as ITU occurs in the second half of l. 4, it is preferable to take U-SIR as referring to the moon itself (cf. Br., No. 7,860).

[5] Cf. Br., No. 9,426.

[6] See above, note 3.

[7] See above, p. 125, note 4.

[8] See above, p. 125, note 5.

[9] It is interesting to note that in the Semitic version the creation of the sun is substituted for that of the moon, although in the preceding line the renewal of the month is referred to.

[10] The reverse of the tablet, which is badly preserved (see vol. ii, pl. L), is inscribed with some grammatical and astrological notes.

IV. An Address to the River of Creation.[1]

1. *šiptu at - ti*[2] *nāru banat(at)*[3] *ka - l[a - mu]*
2. *e - nu - ma iḫ - ru - ki ilāni*[pl] *rabūti*[pl]
3. *ina a - ḫi - ki*[4] *[iš - ku - nu] dum - ḳa*[5]
4. *ina libbi-ki* [ilu]*E-a šar ap-si-i ib-na-[a šu-bat-su]*[6]

5. *a - bu - ub la ma - ḫar ka - a - ši iš - ruk - [ku]*[7]
6. *i - ša - tum uz - za na - mur - ra - ti pu - luḫ - t[i]*
7. [ilu]*E - a u* [ilu]*Marduk*[8] *iš - ru - ku - nik - kim - ma*
8. *d[i] - ni te - ni - še - e - ti ta - din - ni at - ti*[9]
9. *nāru rabīti(ti) nāru ṣir - ti nāru eš - ri - e - ti*[10]

---

[1] This mystical river of creation was evidently suggested by the Euphrates, on the waters of which the fertility of Babylonia so largely depended; for a comparison of similar conceptions of a river of creation both in Egyptian and in Hebrew mythology, see the Introduction. The text forms the opening words of an incantation and is taken from the reverse of S. 1,704, with restorations and variant readings from the obverse of 82–9–18, 5,311 (cf. Appendix II). A translation of the former tablet has been given by Sayce, *Hibbert Lectures*, p. 403.

[2] 82–9–18, 5,311, *at-ta.*

[3] 82–9–18, 5,311, *ba-na-a-t[um].*

[4] 82–9–18, 5,311, *ina a-ḫi-ka.*

[5] 82–9–18, 5,311, *dum-ki*; the division of ll. 2–4 in the text is taken from 82–9–18, 5,311.

[6] 82–9–18, 5,311, *ina kir-bi-ka* [ilu]*Ea* (AN-BAT) *šar apsī ib-na-a šu-bat-su*; it is possible that the line in S. 1,704 read *dum-ḳa ina libbi-ki* [ilu]*E-a šar ap-si-i ib-na-[a].*

IV. An Address to the River of Creation.[1]

1. O thou River, who didst create all things,
2. When the great gods dug thee out,
3. They set prosperity upon thy banks,[5]
4. Within thee Ea, the King of the Deep, created his dwelling,[6]
5. The deluge they sent not before thou wert![7]
6. Fire, and wrath, and splendour, and terror
7. Have Ea and Marduk[8] presented unto thee!
8. Thou judgest the cause of mankind!
9. O River, thou art mighty! O River, thou art supreme! O River, thou art righteous![10]

---

[7] Upon 82–9–18, 5,311, ll. 5–7 read as follows: (5) *iš-ru-uk-ku im-ma uz-zu na-mur-tum pu-luḫ-tum* (6) *a-bu-bu la maḫ-ri ka-a-šu im-bi-ka* (7) [*p*]*i-ki* ^{ilu}*Ea* (AN.BAT) *u* ^{ilu}*Marduk* (AN.ASAR.LU.ŠAR) *iš-ru-ku im-ma*. It may be noted that the duplicate in l. 5 reads *im-ma*, "daylight," for *i-ša-tum*, "fire," and for l. 7 gives the interesting variant reading "At thy word did Ea and Marduk bestow the daylight."

[8] AN.ASAR.LU.ŠAR.

[9] 82–9–18, 5,311 reads [. .]-*nu te-ni-še-e-tum ta-dan-nu al-ta*.

[10] 82–9–18, 5,311 omits l. 9, and from this point onwards it seems probable that the tablets ceased to be duplicates. The invocation to the river ceases with l. 9, the lines which follow on each tablet containing the personal petitions of the suppliant (cf. Appendix II).

V. Another Version of the Creation of the World by Marduk.[1]

OBV.

1. EN[2] E AZAG-GA E DINGIR-E-NE KI MIN NU MU-UN-RU
   bītu el-lim bīt ilāni[pl] *ina aš-ri el-lim ul e-pu-uš*

2. GI NU E GIŠ NU DIM
   ḳa - nu - u ul a - ṣi i - ṣi ul ba - ni

3. MUR NU ŠUB GIŠ - U - RU NU DIM
   li-bit-ti ul na - da - at na - al - ban - ti ul ba - na - at

4. E NU RU URU NU DIM
   bītu ul e - pu - uš alu ul ba - ni

5. URU NU DIM A - DAM NU MU-UN-[GAR]
   alu ul e - pu - uš nam - maš - šu - u ul ša - kin

6. EN - LIL(KI) NU RU E-KUR-RA NU DIM
   Ni - ip - pu - ru ul e - pu - uš E - kur ul ba - ni

7. UNUG(KI) NU RU E-AN-NA NU DIM
   U - ruk ul e - pu - uš E - MIN *ul ba - ni*

8. ABZU NU RU NUN(KI) NU DIM
   ap - su - u ul e - pu - [uš] [alu]*Eridu ul ba - ni*

---

[1] For the text, see *Cuneiform Texts*, part xiii, pls. 35 ff. (82–5–22, 1,048); and for previous translations, see Pinches, *J.R.A.S.*, vol. xxiii (new series), pp. 393 ff.; Zimmern in Gunkel's *Schöpfung und Chaos*, p. 419 f.; and Jensen in Schrader's *Keilins. Bibl.*, vi, pp. 38 ff. The variant legend of the creation is contained on the portion of the obverse of the tablet which has been preserved, but it does not form the principal subject of the composition; it

V. Another Version of the Creation of the World by Marduk.

OBV.

1. The holy house, the house of the gods, in the holy place had not yet been made;
2. No reed had sprung up, no tree had been created.

3. No brick had been laid, no building had been set up;
4. No house had been erected, no city had been built;
5. No city had been made, no creature had been created.
6. Nippur had not been made, E-kur had not been built;
7. Erech had not been created, E-ana had not been built;
8. The Deep had not been created, Eridu had not been built;

is merely an elaborate introduction to an incantation which was intended to be recited in honour of E-zida, the great temple of Nabû at Borsippa. The reverse of the tablet contains the concluding lines of the incantation. For a further discussion of the legend on the obverse, see the Introduction.

[2] EN, i.e. *šiptu*, "incantation," the word placed at the beginning of most religious and magical compositions intended for recitation.

9. E AZAG DINGIR-RI-E-NE KI-DUR-BI NU DIM
*bītu el-lum bīt ilāni*pl *šu-bat-su ul ip-še-it*

10. [NIGIN] KUR-KUR-RA-GE A-AB-BA-A-BA
nap-ḫar ma-ta-a-tu tam-tum-ma

11. [U] ŠAG A-AB-BA-GE RAD-NA-NAM
i-nu ša ki-rib tam-tim ra-ṭu-um-ma

12. [U-BI-A NUN(KI)] BA-RU E-SAG-IL-LA BA-DIM
ina u-mi-šu alu*Eridu e-pu-uš E*-MIN *ba-ni*

13. [E-SAG-IL]A ŠAG ABZU E-E-NE (DINGIR) LUGAL-DUL-AZAG-GA MU-NI-IN-RI-A
E-MIN *ša ina ki-rib ap-si-i* ilu*Lugal-dul-azag-ga ir-mu-u*

14. [KA-DINGIR-RA](KI) BA-RU E-SAG-IL-LA ŠU-UL
*Bābilu*KI *e-pu-[uš] E-sag-ila šuk-lul*

15. [(DINGIR) A]-NUN-NA-GE-E-NE URU-BI BA-AN-RU
*ilāni*pl ilu*A-nun-na-ki mit-ḫa-riš e-pu-uš*

16. [URU] AZAG-GA KI-DUR ŠAG-DUG-GA GE-E-NE-MU-MAḪ-A MI-NI-IN-SA-A
alu el-lum šu-bat ṭu-ub lib-bi-šu-nu ṣi-riš im-bu-u

17. [(DINGIR)] GI-ŠI-MA GI-DIR I-NE-NA A NAM-MI-NI-IN-KEŠDA
ilu*Marduk a-ma-am ina pa-an me-e ir-ku-us*

18. SAḪAR-RA NI-SAR A-KI A-DIR NAM-MI-IN-DUB
e-pi-ri ib-ni-ma it-ti a-mi iš-pu-uk

19. DINGIR-RI-E-NE KI-DUR ŠAG-DUG-GA NE-IN-DUR-RU-NE-EŠ-A-MA
ilāni ina šu-bat ṭu-ub lib-bi ana šu-šu-bi

9. Of the holy house, the house of the gods, the habitation had not been made.

10. All lands were sea.

11. At that time there was a movement in the sea;

12. Then was Eridu made, and E-sagil was built,

13. E-sagil, where in the midst of the Deep the god Lugal-dul-azaga[1] dwelleth;

14. The city of Babylon was built, and E-sagil was finished.

15. The gods, the Anunnaki, he[2] created at one time;

16. The holy city, the dwelling of their hearts' desire, they proclaimed supreme.

17. Marduk laid a reed upon the face of the waters,

18. He formed dust and poured it out beside the reed.

19. That he might cause the gods to dwell in the habitation of their hearts' desire,

---

[1] Or, Lugal-du-azaga. [2] I.e., Marduk.

20. NAM - LU - GIŠGAL - LU BA - RU
a - me - lu - ti ib - ta - ni

21. (DINGIR) A - RU - RU KUL *do.* DINGIR - TA[1] NE - IN - SAR
ilu MIN *zi - ir a - me - lu - ti it - ti - šu ib - la - nu*

22. BIR - ANŠU GAR - ZI - IG EDIN - NA BA - RU
bu-ul ṣēri ši - kin na-piš-ti ina ṣi - e - ri ib - ta - ni

23. (ID) IDIGNA (ID) BURANUNU ME-DIM KI GAR-RA-DIM
MIN *u* MIN *ib - ni - ma ina aš - ri iš - ku - un*

24. MU - NE - NE - A NAM - DUG MI - NI - IN - SA - A
šum - ši - na ṭa - biš im - bi

25. GI-BE GI-ŠE-RU ŠUG GIŠ-GI GIŠ-TER-GID-GE BA-DIM
uš-šu di-it-ta ap-pa-ri ḳa-na-a u ki - šu ib - ta - ni

26. U - RIG EDIN - NA BA - RU
ur - ki - it ṣi - rim ib - ta - ni

27. [KUR - KU]R - RA ŠUG GIŠ - GI - NA - NAM
ma - ta - a - tum ap - pa - ri a - pu - um - ma

28. [. . . .] GUD-LID-BA GE ŠURIM . . . LU AMAŠ-A
lit-tu pu-ur-ša me-ru la-aḫ-ru pu-ḫad-sa im-mir su-pu-ri

29. [. . . .] - TER GIŠ - TER - BI - NA - NAM
ki - ra - tu u ki - ša - tu - ma

30 [. . . . .] MI - NI - IN - LU - UG
a - tu - du šap - pa - ri iz - za - az - ru - šu

31. [. . . . .] ZAG A-AB-BA-GE [. . . .]
be-lum ilu Marduk ina pa-aṭ tam-tim tam-la-a u-mal-li

32. [. . . . .] GIŠ - GI PA - RIM NE - [IN - GAR]
[. . . . - *n*]*a a - pa na - ma - la iš - ku - un*

20. He formed mankind.

21. The goddess Aruru together with him[1] created the seed of mankind.

22. The beasts of the field and living creatures in the field he formed.

23. He created the Tigris and the Euphrates, and he set them in their place;

24. Their names he declared in goodly fashion.

25. The grass, the rush of the marsh, the reed, and the forest he created,

26. The green herb of the field he created,

27. The lands, the marshes, and the swamps;

28. The wild cow and her young, the wild calf; the ewe and her young, the lamb of the fold;

29. Plantations and forests;

30. The he-goat and the mountain-goat . . . . him.

31. The lord Marduk laid in a dam by the side of the sea,

32. [He . . . .] a swamp, he made a marsh,

[1] The Sumerian version reads "together with the god."

33. [. . . . . .] MU - UN - TUK
[. . . . . .] *uš - ta - ši*

34. [GI BA - RU] GIŠ BA - DIM
[*ḳa - na - a ib - t*]*a - ni i - ṣa ib - ta - ni*

35. [. . . . .] KI - A BA - DIM
[. . . . .] *ina aš - ri ib - ta - ni*

36. [MUR BA - AN - ŠUB] GIŠ - U - RU BA - AN - RU
[*li - bit - tu id - di na - a*]*l - ban - tu ib - ta - ni*

37. [E BA - RU] URU MU - UN - DIM
[*bītu e - pu - uš alu ib - ta - n*]*i*

38. [URU MU - UN - DIM] A - DAM KI MU-UN-GAR-[RA]
[*alu e - pu - uš nam - maš - šu - u iš - t*]*a - kan*

39 [EN - LIL(KI) BA - RU] E - KUR - RA - GE BA - DIM
[*Ni - ip - pu - ru e - pu - uš E - kur ib - ta - ni*]

40. [UNUG(KI) BA - RU E - AN - N]A BA - D[IM]
[*U - ruk e - pu - uš E* - MIN *ib - ta - ni*]

[The rest of the Obverse and the beginning of the Reverse of the tablet are wanting.]

REV.

1. [. . . . .]
[. . . . . .] *- mat par - ṣi* [. . . . . .]

2. [. . . . .]
[. . . . . . *i*]*k - ki - lim - mu - u* [. . . . .]

3. [. . . . GAL]-AN-ZU KI-GAL DINGIR-RI-[E-NI-GE]
4. *suk-kal-la-ka ṣi-i-ru* *ilu* *Pap-sukal ir-šu ma-lik ilāni*

5. (DINGIR) NIN-A-ḪA-KUD-DU DU (DINGIR) EN-KI-GA-GE
ilu MIN *mar - ti* *ilu* *E - a*

33. [. . . . . . .] he brought into existence.

34. [Reeds he form]ed, trees he created;

35. [. . . . .] he made in their place.

36. [Bricks he laid], buildings he set up;

37. [Houses he made], cities he built;

38. [Cities he made], creatures he created.

39. [Nippur he made], E-kur he built;

40. [Erech he made, E-an]a he built.

[The rest of the Obverse and the beginning of the Reverse of the tablet are wanting.]

Rev.

1. [. . . . . .] the decree [. . . . . .]

2. [. . . . .] . . [. . . . . .]

3 f. Thy exalted minister is Papsukal, the wise counsellor of the gods.

5. May Nin-aḫa-kudu, the daughter of Ea,

6. NIG - NA - [. . . .] ḪU - MU - RA - AB - EL - LA
ina nik - na - ki el - lu ul - lil - ka

7. GI - BIL - LA EL - [LA] ḪU - MU - RA - AB - LAḪ - LAḪ - GA
ina MIN *ib - bi ub - bi - ib - ka*

8. DUK-A-GUB-BA [EL-LA ABZU] KI NER-DU-NA-ZU U-MU-UN-NA-AZAG

9. *ina* MIN-*e el-la ša ap-si-i a-šar tal-lak-ti-ka ul-lu*

10. MU - DUG - GA (DINGIR) ASAR - LU - ŠAR LUGAL AN - KI - ŠAR - RA - GE
ina MIN-*e* [ilu]*Marduk šar kiš-šat šamē(e) u irṣitim(tim)*

11. ḪE-GAL KUR-RA-GE ŠAG-ZU ḪA-BA-RA-AN-TU-TU
nu - ḫuš ma - a - ti ana lib - bi - ka li - ru - ub

12. ME - ZU U - UL - DU - A - ŠU ŠU - ḪA - RA - AN - DU - DU
par - ṣu - ka ana u - mu [ṣa] - a - ti liš - tak - li - lu

13. E - ZI - DA KI - DUR MAḪ AN - NA (DINGIR) NINNI KI - DUR ME - EN

14. *E* - MIN *šub - tum ṣir - tum na - ram lib - bi* [ilu]*A - nu u* [ilu]*Iš - tar at - ta*

15. AN - GIM ḪE - EN - AZAG - GA [KI - GIM ḪE] - EN - EL - LA ŠAG - AN - GIM ḪE[1]

16. [. . . . .] . . . ḪE - IM - TA - GUB[2]

---

[1] The scribe has not written out the rest of the verb; it is probable that he intended it to be read as *ḫe*-[*en-laḫ-laḫ-ga*], as indicated in the translation. In Assyrian the line would read *kīma šamē lilil kīma irṣiti libib kīma kirib šamē limmir.*

6. Purify thee with the pure censer,

7. And may she cleanse thee with cleansing fire!

8 f. With a cup of pure water from the Deep shalt thou purify thy way!

10. By the incantation of Marduk, the king of the hosts of heaven and earth,

11. May the abundance of the land enter into thee,

12. And may thy decree be accomplished for ever!

13 f. O E-zida, thou glorious dwelling, thou art dear unto the hearts of Anu and Ishtar!

15. May (Ezida) shine like the heavens, may it be bright like the earth, may it [be glorious][1] like the heart of heaven,

16. [And may . . . .] be firmly established![2]

---

[2] In Assyrian *lizziz*. Line 17 gives the title of the prayer as INIM-INIM-MA [. . . .] GA-GA-NE-GE; and l. 18 gives the catch-line to the next tablet, which may perhaps be restored as *šiptu* *kakkabu* [*Mar-gid-da*] *ṣumbu ša-ma-mi*, "O [Margida], thou waggon of the heavens!"

VI. The "Cuthaean Legend of the Creation."[1]

COLUMN I.

[The upper half of the column is wanting.]

1. [*a-* . . . . . .][2] 2. *bēl* ME-GAN [. . . . .]

3. *di - en - šu purussū* [. . . . .]

4. *utukku pir'u - šu ekimmu pir'u - š*[*u* . . . . . .]

5. *bēl elāti*^{pl} *u šaplāti*^{pl} *bēl* ^{ilu}*A-nun-n*[*a-ki* . . .]

6. *ša mē*^{pl} *dal-ḫu-te išatū*(*u*) *mē*^{pl} *za-ku-te l*[*ā išatū*(*u*)]

7. *ša ši-ik-la-šu šab - šu ummānu šu - a - tu ik - mu - u ik - šu - du i - na - ru*

8. *ina narī*[3] *ul šaṭir ul ezib-am-ma*[4] *pag-ri u pu-u-ti*[5]

---

[1] The text is taken from the tablet K. 5,418*a* and its duplicate K. 5,460 (see *Cuneiform Texts*, part xiii, pls. 39–41). The legend was for some years known as "the Cuthaean legend of the Creation." It was thought that the text was put in the mouth of the god Nergal, who was supposed to be waging war against the brood of Tiamat; and it was assumed that Nergal took the place of Marduk in accordance with local tradition at Cuthah. It is clear, however, that the speaker is not the god Nergal, but an old Babylonian king, who recounts how the gods delivered him and his land from hordes of monsters. In the description of the monsters in col. i, Tiamat is said to have suckled them, but this reference does not justify their identification with the monster brood of the Creation Series; it is more probable that Tiamat is called their foster-mother in order to indicate their terrible nature. In *The Chaldean Account of Genesis*, pp. 102 ff., George Smith gave

VI. The "Cuthaean Legend of the Creation."[1]

COLUMN I.

[The upper half of the column is wanting.]

1. [. . . . .][2] 2. He was lord of . . [. . . .];
3. His judgment was the decision [of . . . .].
4. The fiend was his offspring, the spectre was his offspring [. . . .];
5. He was lord of the height and of the depths, he was lord of the Anunnaki [. . . .].
6. A people who drink turbid water, and drink not pure water,
7. Whose sense is perverted, had taken (men) captive, had triumphed over them, and had committed slaughter.
8. On a tablet nought was written, nought was left (to write).[4] In mine own person[5]

---

a translation of the legend, and, though he describes it as a "Legend of Creation," he correctly recognized the general character of its contents. For later translations see Sayce, *Records of the Past*, vol. xi, pp. 109 ff., and vol. i (new series), pp. 149 ff.; Zimmern, *Zeits. für Assyr.*, xii, pp. 319 ff.; and Jensen, *Keilins. Bibl.*, vi, pp. 290 ff. For earlier publications of the text of K. 5,640, see S. A. Smith, *Miscellaneous Texts*, pl. 6 f., and of the text of K. 5,418, see Winckler, *Sammlung von Keilschrifttexten*, ii, pl. 70 f.

[2] The first six lines which are preserved are taken from K. 5,640.

[3] K. 5,640, *abnu narī*.

[4] I.e., the land was in confusion, so that no business was transacted and no records were kept.

[5] Cf. Zimmern, *Z.A.*, xii, p. 323.

9. *ina māti*[1] *ul u-še-ṣi-ma ul aḳ-ta-rab-šu*

10. *ummān*^{pl} *pag-ri iṣ-ṣur*[2] *ḫur-ri a-me-lu-ti*[3]
a-ri-bu pa-nu-šu-un
11. *ib-šu-nu-ti-ma ilāni*^{pl} *rabūti*^{pl}
12. *ina ḳaḳ-ḳar ib-nu-u ilāni*^{pl} *a-lu-šu*

13. *Ti-a-ma-tu u-še-niḳ-šu-nu-ti*
14. *ša-sur-šu-nu* ^{ilu}*Be-lit-i-li u-ban-ni*
15. *ina ki-rib šadī(i) ir-ti-bu-ma*[5] *i-te-it-lu-ma*
ir-ta-šu-u mi-na-ti

16. *VII šarrāni*^{pl}*(ni)*[6] *at-ḫu-u šu-pu-u ba-nu-tu*
17. *CCCLX . M*[7] $^{A\text{-}AN}$ *um-ma-na-tu-šu-nu*

18. *An-ba-ni-ni abu-šu-nu šarru ummu-šu-nu*
[šar]-ra-tu ^{f}*Me-li-li*
19. *aḫu-šu-nu rabū(u) a-lik pa-ni-šu-nu* ^{m}*Me-ma-an-gab šum-šu*

20. *šanū(u) aḫu-[šu-nu]*[8] ^{m}*Me-du-du šum-šu*
21. *šalšu(šu) aḫu-[šu-nu* ^{m} . . . *]-lul šum-šu*

---

[1] The reading is not certain; MU is possible, i.e. *šatta*, "for a year." The phrase is omitted by K. 5,640, in which the line begins with *ul*.

[2] K. 5,640, *iṣṣur*.

[3] K. 5,640, *ta*.

[4] Literally, "city."

9. From my land[1] I went not forth, and I did not give them battle.
10. A people who had the bodies of birds of the hollow, men who had the faces of ravens,
11. Had the great gods created,
12. And in the ground the gods created a dwelling-place[4] for them.
13. Tiamat gave them suck,
14. The Lady of gods brought them into the world.
15. In the midst of the mountain (of the world) they became strong, they waxed great, they multiplied exceedingly.
16. Seven kings, brethren, fair and comely,
17. Three hundred and sixty thousand[7] in number were their forces.
18. Anbanini, their father, was king; their mother, Melili, was queen.
19. Their eldest brother, their leader, was named Memangab;
20. [Their][8] second brother was named Medudu;
21. [Their] third brother was named [. . . .]lul;

[5] K. 5,640, *ir-te-[bu]-u-ma*; the scribe has omitted *bu* by mistake.

[6] K. 5,640 omits *ni*.

[7] It is probable that 360,000, and not 6,000, should be read, in view of the large numbers which occur in col. ii, ll. 19 ff.

[8] The restoration of the pronominal suffix in this and the following lines is conjectural.

22. *ribū(u)* *a[ḫu - šu - nu* ^{m} . . . . . *-d]a·-da* *šum - šu*
23. *ḫanšu(šu)* *[aḫu - šu - nu* ^{m} . . . . . *] - daḫ* *šum - šu*
24. *se[ššu(šu)* *aḫu - šu - nu* ^{m} . . . . . *- r]u* [1] *šum - šu*
25 *[sibū(u)* *aḫu - šu - nu* ^{m} . . . . . . *]* *šum - šu* [2]

COLUMN II.

[The upper half of the column [3] is wanting.]

1. [. . . .]
2. [*u-tuk* (?)]-*ki* [*r*]*a*-[*b*]*i-ṣu* *lim-nu-te* [. . . . . .]
3. *ri - du - u* *ṭe - en - šu* *u - t*[*r* - . . .]

4. *ina* [. . . .] *- e* *al - p*[*u* - . . .]
5. [. . . .]-*si* *arrat* *limutti* *mātāti* ^{pl} [4] *it-ta-*[. . .]

6. *a*[*l*] [5] *- si* *mārē* ^{pl} ^{amelu}*barē* ^{pl} *u - ma - ' -* [*ir*]
7. [*VII a - na* *pa - an*] *VII* ^{immeru}*puḫadu* *al - pu - t*[*u*] [6]
8. [*u - kin* *guḫḫē*] ^{pl} [7] *ellūti* ^{pl}
9. *a - šal - m*[*a*] *ilāni* ^{pl} *rabūti* ^{pl}
10. ^{ilu}*Iš-tar* ^{ilu}[. . . .] ^{ilu}*Za-ma-ma* ^{ilu}*A-nu-ni-tum*

11. ^{ilu}[PA [8] . . . .] ^{ilu}*Šamaš* *ku - ra - du*
12. *ik -* [. . . . . . .] *ilāni* ^{pl} *ana* *a - la - ki - ia*
[. . . .] *- e* *ul* *i - di - na - am - ma*

---

[1] Possibly ŠAG.

[2] This is the last line of the column.

[3] The missing portion of the column probably continued the description of the hordes of monsters, who were oppressing the land. The king then enquires of the gods whether he should give the enemy battle (cf. ll. 6 ff.).

[4] This rendering is conjectural.

22. [Their] fourth brother was named [. . . . d]ada ;
23. [Their] fifth [brother] was named [. . . .]daḫ ;
24. [Their] sixth [brother] was named [. . . . r]u ;
25. [Their seventh brother] was named [. . . .].[2]

Column II.

[The upper half of the column[3] is wanting.]

1. [. . . . .]
2. Evil [fiends] and demons that lie in wait [. . .]
3. Pursuing after (a man), turned [him] from his purpose.
4. In [. . . . .] did I [. . . . .]
5. [. . . . .] an evil curse was [cast upon (?)] the lands.[4]
6. [I][5] cried unto the magicians, and I directed them,
7. I set out the lambs for sacrifice [in rows of] seven.
8. [I placed there also] the holy [. . . . .],[7]
9. And I enquired of the great gods,
10. Of Ištar, and [. . . . .], and Zamama, and Anunitum,
11. And [. . . . .], and Šamaš, the warrior.
12. And the gods [commanded me] that I should go, but [. . . . .] they gave not (unto me).

[5] The beginnings of ll. 6–8 are restored from col. iii, ll. 18–20.

[6] The sign is TU, not TÚ (= *ut*).

[7] The ideogram is explained as *gu-uḫ-ḫ*[*u*] in K. 4,174 (see Thompson, *Cun. Texts*, part xi, pl. 47, and Jensen, *K.B.*, vi, p. 294). The traces of the third sign upon the tablet are those of *ḫu*, not *lu*.

[8] Restored from col. iii, l. 23.

13. *ki - a - am ak̦ - bi a - na lib - bi - ia*
um - ma lu - u a - na - ku - ma[1]
14. *ai - u* UR - BAR - [. . . . .] *ib - ri*
15. *ai - u* UR - BAR - [. . . . .] *ša - il - tu*
16. *lul - lik ki - i at*[2] *- kil* [. . .] *- piš lib - bi - ia*

17. *u lu - ud - di*[3] *ša parzilli ia - a - ti lu - uṣ - bat*
18. *šattu maḫ̆ - ri - tu ina ka - ša - di*[4]

---

[1] The exclamatory phrase *lu-u a-na-ku-ma* may perhaps be best rendered in this way.

[2] The sign is AT, not TUR; in other signs the scribe tends to carry through his horizontal wedges.

[3] The word *lu-ud-di* evidently refers to a weapon of some kind.

[4] It was pointed out by Zimmern (*Z.A.*, p. 317 f.) that another version of this portion of the legend is preserved on a fragment of an Old-Babylonian tablet, the text of which is published in Neo-Assyrian characters by Scheil, *Recueil de travaux*, XX, p. 65 f. According to Scheil, the fragment in question forms the third or fourth column of a tablet, and in l. 8 he read the name of the king Tukulti-bēl-niši; but its parallelism with l. 22 f. of col. ii of the "Cuthaean Legend," as Zimmern pointed out, disproved the reading, and in place of Scheil's IZ-KU-*ti* [i.e. *tukulti*(*ti*)], *a-ka-ṣi* [or *ad*], and *a-na-aṣ* in l. 8 f. we may probably read *is-si-ḫ̆u*, *a-ka-la*, and *a-na-ḫ̆i* (cf. also Jensen's transliteration and translation of the text in *K.B.*, vi, pp. 298 ff.). The column of text preserved by the fragment reads as follows: (1) *im-ta-ḫ̆a-aṣ ta-ap-da-a u-ul i-zi-*[. . . . .] (2) *i-na ša-ni-i II š*[*u*]*-š*[*i*] *li-mu um-ma-ni u-še-ṣi-am-ma* (3) *im-ta-ḫ̆a-aṣ ta-ap-da-a u-ma-al-li ṣi-ra* (4) *i-na ša-al-ši šu-ši li-mi um-ma-na u-še-ṣi-am-ma* (5) *e-li ša pa-na u-wa* (i.e. PI)*-at-te-ir šu-a-ti* (6) *iš-tu VI šu-ši li-mi um-ma-ni i-ni-ru* (7) *im-ta-ḫ̆a-aṣ ta-ap-da-a ra-bi-a* (8) *a-na-ku is-si-ḫ̆u en-ni-ši* (9) *a-ka-la a-na-ḫ̆i a-šu-uš am-ṭi-ma* (10) *um-ma a-na-ku* ŠU(?)-AN *a-na pali-ia mi-nam ub-lam* (11) *a-na-ku šar-rum la mu-ša-lim* [*ma*]*-ti-šu* (12) [*u*] *rē'ū la mu-ša-lim ni-ši-šu* (13) *ia-a-ši palē*(*e*) *mi-nam ub-lam* (14) *ki-i lu-uš-ta-ag-*[?]*-ma* (15) *pa-ag-ri u um-ma-ni lu-še-ṣi*

13. Then spake I unto my heart,
Saying: "By my life![1]
14. Who is . . [. . . .] my friend?
15. Who is . . [. . . .] a sorcerer?
16. But I will go, since I have put my trust in the
[. . . .] of my heart,
17. And my weapon[3] of iron will I take!"
18. As the first year drew nigh,[4]

(16) *a-na ḫu-ul-lu-uḳ ṣi-ri Ak-ka-di-i* (17) *amêlu nakra da-an-na id-ki-am-ma* (18) [. . . . .]-*e ta*(?)-*am-ḫa-ri-a ti*-[?]-*gi-a* (19) [. . . . .] *gu-uk-ka-ni-e* (20) [. . . . .] *Ak-ka-di-i sa-pa-nu* [. . . . .], "(1) He fought, and conquered (lit. "he fought a defeat"), and left not [one remaining]. (2) The second time, one hundred and twenty thousand warriors I sent forth, and (3) he fought, and conquered, and filled the plain (with their bodies). (4) The third time, sixty thousand warriors I sent forth, and (5) I caused them to be mightier than before. (6) After he had slain the three hundred and sixty thousand warriors, (7) and had fought, and had achieved a mighty victory, (8) I was desperate, powerless, (9) and afflicted, I was cast down and full of woe, and I lamented, (10) saying: 'As for me . . . what have I brought upon my realm? (11) I am a king who hath brought no prosperity unto his country, (12) and a shepherd who hath brought no prosperity unto his people. (13) As for me and my realm, what have I brought upon (upon us) (14) by . . . . and (15) causing myself and my warriors to go forth? (16) To destroy the plain of Akkad (17) he hath summoned a mighty foe, and (18) [. . . .] my battle . . . . (19) [. . . .] . . . . (20) [. . . . .] to overwhelm Akkad [. . . .].'" From the summary in l. 6, the last line of the preceding column may probably be restored, as "The first time, one hundred and eighty thousand warriors I sent forth." Jensen also connects the fragment K. 8,582 (see Haupt, *Nimrodepos*, p. 78) with the "Cuthaean legend," since it describes in the first person the putting to flight and capture of twelve warriors, and contains the formula [*k*]*i-ạ-am aḳ-bi ana lib-bi-i*[*a*]; cf. *K.B.*, vi, p. 300 f.

19. *II šuši.M ummānu u-še-ṣi-ma ina libbi-šu-nu*
išten(en) balṭu ul itūra(ra)

20. *šanītum(tum) šattu ina kašādi(di) XC.M do.*

21. *šalultum(tum) šattu ina kašādi(di) LX.M + VII.C do.*

22. *is-si-ḫu en-ni-šu a-ka-la*
a-šu-uš uš-ta-ni-iḫ

23. *ki-a-am ak-bi a-na lib-bi-ia um-ma lu-u a-na-ku-ma*

24. *a-na pa-li-e mi-na-a e-ṣip*[1]

25. *a-na-ku šarru la mu-šal-li-mu māti-šu*

COLUMN III.

1. *u ri-e-um la mu-šal-li-mu um-ma-ni-šu*

2. *ki lu-uš-tak-kan-ma pag-ri u pu-ti lu-še-ṣi*

3. *ša-lum-mat ni-ši mu-ši mu-u-tu namṣaru a-ru-ur-tu*

4. *na-mur-ra-tu ḫar-ba-šu ni-pil-su-u ni-ib-ri-tu*

5. *[ḫu-sa-aḫ]-ḫu di-lib-tu ma-la ba-šu-u*

6. [. . . . .] *-šu-nu iṭ-ṭar-da*

7. [. . . . . *li-iš*] *-ša-kin a-bu-bu*

8. [. . . . . *a*] *-bu-ba pāni*[2]

---

[1] Lit., "added to."

19. One hundred and twenty thousand warriors I sent out, but not one returned alive.
20. As the second year drew nigh, ninety thousand warriors I sent out, but not one returned alive.
21. As the third year drew nigh, sixty thousand seven hundred warriors I sent out, but not one returned alive.
22. Despairing, powerless, and afflicted, I was full of woe, and I groaned aloud,
23. And I spake unto my heart, saying: "By my life!
24. "What have I brought upon[1] my realm?
25. "I am a king who hath brought no prosperity unto his country,

COLUMN III.

1. "And a shepherd who hath brought no prosperity unto his people.
2. "But (this thing) will I do. In mine own person will I go forth!
3. "The pride of men, and night, and death, and disease, and trembling,
4. "And fear, and terror, and . . . , and hunger,
5. "And [famine], and misery of every kind
6. "Pursue after their [. . . . .].
7. "[But . . . . let] there be a deluge,
8. "[. . . . . . the] deluge of old time!"

[1] The reading of ŠI as *pāni* is not certain.

9. [1] *ilu*[. . . . . *i*] - *ḳab* - *bi* [2]
10. *i* - *zak* - [*ka* - *ru* . . . .] - *e* - *šu*
11. *ilāni* *pl* [. . . . .] - *ša*
12. *taḳ* - *ba* - *nim* - *ma* [3] [. . . . .] - *ki*
13. *u* *šub* - *šu* - *u* [. . . . .] - *pa*
ta - *ṣur* - [. . . . .] - *a*
14. *zag* - *muk* *ša* *rıbūti*(*ti*) *ša*[*tti* . . . .] - *pa*
15. *ina* *te* - *me* - *ki* *ša* *ilu* *E* - *a* [. . . . . . .] - *a*
ša *ilāni* *pl* [*rabūti*] *pl* [4]
16. *niḳē* *zag* - *muk* *ellūti* *pl* [. . . . .]

17. *te* - *ri* - *e* - *te* *ellūti* *pl* [. . . . .]
18. *al* - *si* *mārē* *pl* *amēlu* *barē* *pl* *u* - [*ma* - ' - *i*]*r*
19. *VII* *a* - *na* *pa* - *an* *VII* *immeru* *puḫadu* *al* - *p*[*u* - *t*]*u*
20. *u* - *kin* *guḫhē* *pl* [5] *ell*[*ūti*] *pl* [4]
21. *a* - *šal* - *ma* *ilāni* *pl* *ra*[*būti*] *pl* [4]
22. *ilu* *Iš-tar* [*ilu* . . . . *ilu* *Za-ma-ma* *ilu* *A-nu-ni-t*]*um*

23. *ilu* PA[. . . . . *ilu* *Šamaš* *ḳu* - *ra* - *d*]*u*
24. *mār* [. . . . .] 25. *i*[*š* - . . . .]

[The lower half of the column is wanting,[6] except for traces of what is probably the last line of the column, preserved by K. 5,640.]

at - [. . . . .]

[1] The fragments of the tablet K. 5,418*a* are not quite correctly put together, the beginnings of ll. 9 ff. being one line higher on the tablet than the ends of the lines to which they correspond.

[2] It would seem that one of the gods urged the king to make offerings and supplication at the Feast of the New Year, before undertaking his fourth expedition. From ll. 14 ff. it is clear that the king followed the god's advice; and, from the conclusion of col. iv, it may be inferred that he at last met with success against his enemies.

9. [1] Then the god [. . . . .] spake,[2]
10. And said [. . . . .]:
11. "The gods [. . . . .]
12. "Thou didst speak unto me[3] and [. . . . . .]
13. "And to make [. . . . .]
thou . . . [. . . . .]."
14. The New Year's Feast in the fourth y[ear . . .],
15. With supplication unto Ea, [the . . . . .] of the great gods,
16. Pure offerings for the Feast of the New Year [. . . .],
17. Pure omens [. . . . . . .].
18. I cried unto the magicians, and I [directed them],
19. I set [out] the lambs for sacrifice in rows of seven.
20. I placed there also the holy . . . ,[5]
21. And I enquired of the great gods,
22. Of Ištar, [and . . . . . , and Zamama, and Anunit]um,
23. And [. . . . . , and Šamaš, the warr]ior.
24. The son [. . . .] 25. [. . . . .]

[The lower half of the column is wanting,[6] except for traces of what is probably the last line of the column, preserved by K. 5,640.]

[. . . . .]

[3] Possibly the 2nd pers. plur., "ye commanded and"; but as the god appears to be addressing the king, the rendering in the translation is preferable.

[4] The end of the sign MEŠ is preserved.

[5] See above, p. 145, n. 7.

[6] It is clear that in the missing portion of the column the king describes the defeat of his foes, since in col. iv he refers to the record of his history as an encouragement to future princes who may succeed him on the throne.

COLUMN IV.

1. *it - t*[*i* . . . . .] 2. *nišē*^{pl} *la* [. . . .]

3. *al nak* - [*ri* . . . .] 4. *alu ša-a-*[*šu* . . .]

5. *a - na* [. . . . .] *i - š*[*u - u*]

6. *šarru dan* - [*nu* . . . .] *ul - lu* - [. . . .]
7. *ilāni*^{pl} [. . . . . - *n*]*e - ti u* - [. . . . .]
8. *ḳa - t*[*i* . . . .] - *ki ul* [. . . -*p*]*il-šu-nu-ti*
9. *at - ta šarru iššakku rubū lu mamma ša - na - ma*

10. *ša ilu i - nam - bu - šu šarru - ta ippuš*(*uš*).
11. *duppa* - [*ši - n*]*a*[1] *e - pu - uš - ka narā aš - ṭur - ka*

12. *i - na Kutū*^{KI} *ina E - šid - lam*
13. *i - na pa - paḫ* ^{ilu}*Nergal e - zi - bak - ka*

14. ^{abnu}*narā an - na - a a - mur - ma*
15. *ša pi - i* ^{abnu}*narā an - na - a ši - me - ma*
16. *la te - si - iḫ - ḫu*[2] *la te - en - niš - šu*
17. *la ta - pal - laḫ*[3] *la ta - tar - ru - ur*
18. *iš - da - a*[4] *- ka lu - u ki - na*
19. *at-ta ina su-un sinništi-ka ši-pir lu tippuš*(*uš*)
20. *dūrāni*^{pl} *- ka tuk - kil*
21. *ḫi - ra - ti - ka mē*^{pl} *mul - li*

---

[1] K. 5,640, *šin*.
[2] K. 5,640, *la te-iš-si-iḫ-ḫu*.

COLUMN IV.

1. Together with [. . . . .] 2. The people did not [. . . . .]
3. The city of the [foe . . . . .] 4. That city [. . . . . .]
5. Unto [. . . . .] there was [. . . . .]
6. A mighty king [. . . . .] . . [. . . . .]
7. The gods [. . . . .] . . . . [. . . . .]
8. My hand [. . . . .] did not conquer them.
9. Thou, O king, or ruler, or prince, or anyone whatsoever,
10. Whom the god shall call to rule over the kingdom,
11. A tablet concerning these matters have I made for thee, and a record have I written for thee.
12. In the city of Cuthah, in the temple E-shidlam,
13. In the shrine of Nergal, have I deposited it for thee.
14. Behold this memorial tablet,
15. And hearken unto the words thereof,
16. And thou shalt not despair, nor be feeble,
17. And thou shalt not fear, nor be affrighted.
18. Stablish thyself firmly,
19. Sleep in peace beside thy wife,
20. Strengthen thy walls,
21. Fill thy trenches with water,

[3] K. 5,640, *la-aḫ*.
[4] K. 5,640 omits *a*.

22\. *pi - sa - an - na - ti - ka* *še - im - ka* *kaspa - ka*
bušā - ka *makkura - ka*
23\. [. . .][1] - *k[a u] - nu - ti - ka* *šu - rib*
24\. [. . . . *ru - k]u - us - ma* *tub - ḳa - a - ti* *e - mid*

25\. [*pa - gar - ka*] *u - ṣur* *pu - ut - ka* *šul - lim*
26\. [. . . . .] *e* *tu - ṣi - šu*
27\. [. . . . .] - *ma* *e* *ta - as - niḳ - šu*
28\. [. . . . .] - *ka*[2]

[The lower half of the column is wanting.]

[1] One sign is wanting at the beginning of the line; the traces suggest GUD, i.e. *alpu-ka*, "thy cattle." The reading of the second sign as *ka* is not certain.

[2] In this address to future rulers, the general moral which the king would draw from his own history appears to be, that safety is to be found in following the commands of the gods. Furthermore, he recommends his successors upon the throne, not to take

22. Bring in thy treasure-chests, and thy corn, and thy silver, and thy goods, and thy possessions,
23. And thy [. . .],[1] and thy household stuff.
24. Fix firmly [the . . .], and build surrounding walls.
25. Guard [thy body] and take heed for thy person.
26. [. . . . .], thou shalt not go out unto him,
27. [. . . . .], thou shalt not draw nigh unto him.
28. [. . . . .] thy [. . . . .].[2]

[The lower half of the column is wanting.]

---

the field against an invading foe, but to shelter themselves behind the walls of the city of Cuthah. It will be seen from the above translation that the text does not contain a legend of creation (cf. p. 140 f., note 1). The reference to Tiamat in col. i, however, is of considerable interest from the evidence which it furnishes with regard to the early date of the dragon-myth; see further, the Introduction.

Appendices.

I.

Assyrian Commentaries and Parallel Texts to the Seventh Tablet of the Creation Series.

THE Seventh Tablet of the Creation Series was a composition which received much attention from the Babylonian and Assyrian scribes, and specimens of three classes of commentaries have come down to us, which were compiled to explain the whole, or portions, of its contents. The first and most important class consists of a commentary to each line of the text; and of this class we have a single version inscribed upon fragments of two large tablets, duplicates of one another. A second class seems to have contained a kind of running commentary to passages selected not only from the Seventh Tablet, but also from the other tablets of the Creation Series; the fragment S. 747 belongs to this class of explanatory text. A third class, represented by K. 2,107 + K. 6,086, gives explanations of a number of titles of the god Marduk, several of which occur in those portions of the text of the Seventh Tablet which have been recovered. The greater part of this Appendix deals with these commentaries, and with the information which they supply concerning the contents and interpretation of the Seventh Tablet. At the end of the Appendix some fragments of texts are discussed, which bear a striking resemblance to the Seventh Tablet, and prove that the religious literature of Babylonia included parallel texts composed on very similar lines. The evidence which the commentaries and the fragments of parallel texts furnish, with regard to the form and literary development of the Creation Series, is also of considerable value.

To the commentary of the first class, which refers to every line of the Seventh Tablet, the following fragments belong:

S. 11 + S. 980 + S. 1,416, K. 4,406, 82–3–23, 151, R. 366 + 80–7–19, 288 + 293, K. 2,053, and K. 8,299. These six fragments are separate portions of two large tablets, which were inscribed with duplicate texts. I think there is little doubt that S. 11 + S. 980 + S. 1,416 (vol. ii, pls. li ff. and lv) and K. 4,406 (pl. liv f.) are parts of the same tablet, a large one inscribed with five or six double columns of writing on each side; 82–3–23, 151 (pl. liv) is a smaller fragment of the same tablet. The remaining three fragments R. 366 + 80–7–19, 288 + 293 (pls. lvi ff.), K. 2,053 (pl. lix f.), and K. 8,299 (pl. lx) are parts of a duplicate commentary to the Seventh Tablet. The commentary is in the form of a bilingual list, and presupposes the existence of a Sumerian version of the Seventh Tablet of the Creation Series; it gives a list of the Sumerian words, or ideograms, and opposite each word is added its Assyrian equivalent, generally in the order in which the words occur in the Assyrian text. The compartments, or sections, into which the columns of the commentary are divided, refer to the separate couplets, and frequently to the separate lines of the Seventh Tablet; and it will be seen that it is often possible to restore the text of the Seventh Tablet from the information which they furnish.[1] The following paragraphs deal with the sections of the commentary which have been preserved :—

S. 11 + S. 980, Obv., col. i (pl. li), ll. 1–10, the commentary to ll. 1 and 2 of the text, read : (1) [*ilu*] ASAR-RI *ša-riḳ* (2) RU : *ša-ra-ku* (3) SAR : *mi-riš-tu* (4) A : *iz-ra-tu* (5) SI-DU : *ka-a-nu* (6) RU : *ba-nu-u* (7) SAR : *še-im* (8) SAR : *ḳu-u* (9) MA : *a-ṣu-u* (10) SAR : *ar-ḳu*. From this we may restore ll. 1 and 2 of the Seventh Tablet (see the text of K. 2,854 in the block on p. 159) as *ilu Asar-ri ša-riḳ mi-riš-t[i mu-kin*

[1] For references to previous publications of various portions of the commentary, see the Introduction. The text of five additional fragments of the Seventh Tablet, which I came across after the lithographed texts in vol. ii had been printed off (see Appendix II), are published in this Appendix near the paragraphs dealing with the portions of the commentary which refer to them.

iz-ra-ti], and *ba-nu-u še-am u ki e mu-š*[*e-ṣi ur-ki-ti*]. As the verb *ša-ra-ku* occurs in l. 2 of the commentary, it would be possible to take the signs GAR and RIG in l. 1 as part of the title, and transliterate the line as [*ilu*] ASAR-RI-GAR-RIG; and this would agree with the explanations of the title given in the Seventh Tablet, as GAR = *kānu* (cf. Brünnow, No. 11,962) and RIG = *urḳītu* (cf. Br., No. 5,165). But in l. 1 of the Seventh Tablet the signs GAR-RIG are clearly to be rendered

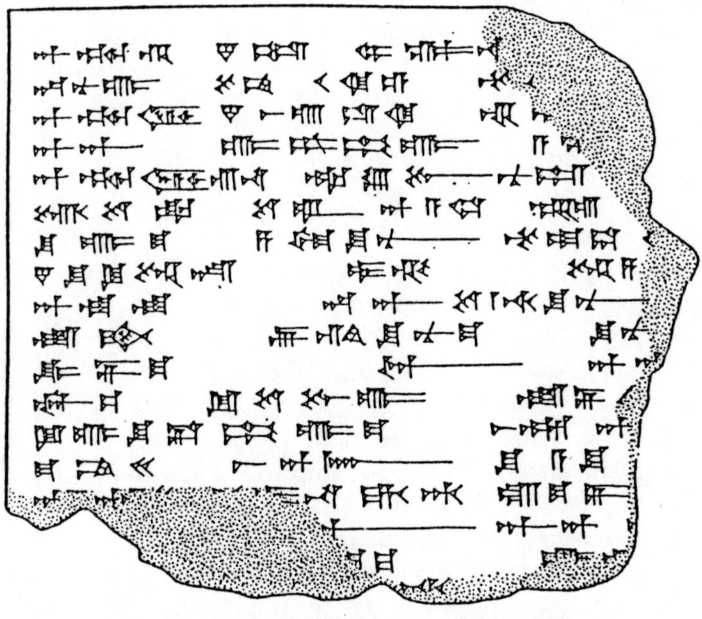

Creation Series, Tablet VII, ll. 1-18 (K. 2,854).

ša-riḳ, and it is preferable to render them in this way also in the commentary. The title *ilu* ASAR-RI is therefore explained as *ša-riḳ* (as in R. 366, etc., Obv., col. i, l. 1, *ilu* TU-TU is explained as *ba-a-nu*); or, which is perhaps preferable, the scribe wrote the two opening words of the Semitic version of the text as a heading to the commentary.

S. 11, etc., Obv., col. i, ll. 11-16, the commentary to l. 3 of the text, read: (11) *ilu* ASARU-ALIM (12) SA: *bi-i-tu* (13) SA: *mil-ku* (14) ALIM: *kab-tu* (15) SA: *at-ru* (16) SA: *mil-ku*.

The text reads ^{ilu}*Asaru-alim ša ina bīt mil-ki kab-t*[*u* . . . .]; the end of the line may therefore be restored as *a-tar mil-ki*, or possibly as *at-ru mil-ki-šu*. Lines 17–20, the commentary to l. 4 of the text, read (17) DINGIR : *i-lum* (18) SA : *u-ḳu-u* (19) [DI]R-DIR : *a-da-ru* (20) [DIR]-DIR : *a-ḫa-zu*. The text reads *ilāni u-taḳ-ḳu-u a-d*[*ir* . . . .]; the end of the line may perhaps be restored as *a-d*[*ir i-ḫu-us-su-nu-ti*]. Lines 21–22, the beginning of the commentary to l. 5 of the text, give the title [^{ilu}]AS[ARU]-ALIM-NUN-NA, and the explanation [. .]-*ru-bu*, which may be restored from the text as [*ka*]-*ru-bu*. The text reads ^{ilu}*Asaru-alim-nun-na ka-ru-bu nu-ur* [. . . .]; see further, p. 93, n. 6.

R. 366 + 80–7–19, 288 + 293, Obv., col. i (pl. lvi), ll. 1–4, corresponding to l. 9 of the text, read: (1) ^{ilu}TU-TU : *ba-a-nu* (2) TU : *ba-nu-u* (3) TU : *e-de-šu* (4) DA : *šu-u*. From this l. 9 may be restored as ^{ilu}*Tu-tu ba-an te-diš-ti-šu-nu* [*šu-u*], see above, p. 93, n. 10. Lines 5–9 (cf. also S. 1,416, col. i, pl. lv), corresponding to l. 10 of the text, read: (5) [ ] KU : *el-lum* (6) [D]U : *sa-gu-u* (7) [D]A : *šu-u* (8) [Š]A : *lu-u* (9) [. .]: *pa-ša-ḫu*. The text of the line reads *li-lil sa-gi-šu-nu-ma šu-nu lu-u* [. . . .]; the end of the line may be conjecturally restored as *lu-u* [*pa-aš-ḫu-ni*], see above, p. 94 f. Lines 10–13, corresponding to l. 11 of the text, read: (10) TU : [*ba-nu*]-*u* (11) MU : *šip-tum* (12) DINGIR : *i-l*[*um*] (13) TI : *na-a-ḫu*; l. 11 may therefore be conjecturally restored as *lib-ni-ma šip-ti ilāni li-*[*nu-ḫu*], see above, p. 94 f. Lines 14–18, corresponding to l. 12 of the text, read: (14) IB : *a-ga-gu* (15) ŠA : *lu-u* (16) IB : *te-bu-u* (17) TU : *ni-'-u* (18) GABA : *ir-tum*, from which l. 12 may be restored as *ag-giš lu te-bu-u li-ni-'-u* [*i-rat-su-nu*], see above, p. 94 f. Lines 19–24, which form two sections upon the tablet, read: (19) DA : *lu-u* (20) DA : *ša-ḳu-u* (21) TA : *i-n*[*a*] (22) MU : *p*[*u-* . . . .] (23) DINGIR : [*i-lum*] (24) [. . . .]: [. . . .]. It will be seen that these two sections correspond to a single line (l. 13) of the text, which reads: *lu-u šu-uš-ḳu-u-ma ina puḫur ilāni* [. . . .]; from l. 22 of the commentary we therefore obtain the new value MU = *p*[*u-uḫ-ru*].

K. 2,053, Obv. (pl. lix), ll. 1–4 (cf. pl. li, S. 11 + S. 980, Obv., col. ii, l. 1), the commentary to l. 17 of the text, read: (1) ZI : [. . . .] (2) ZI : [. . . . .] (3) ZU : [. . . . .] (4) NA : [. . . . .]. The text reads *al-kat-su-un iṣ-ba-tu-ma u-ad-du-u* [. . . . .]; l. 2 of the commentary may therefore be restored as ZI : [*ṣa-ba-tu*], cf. Br., No. 2,330; ZU in l. 4 is the equivalent of *u-ad-du-u*, and the equivalent of NA in l. 4 may possibly be restored as *šu-nu*, the 3 m. pl. pron. suffix (but cf. p. 95, n. 15). S. 11 + S. 980, Obv., col. ii, ll. 2–7 (cf. also K. 2,053, Obv., ll. 5–10), which form two sections upon the tablet, correspond to l. 18 of the text and read: (2) TA : *a*[. . .] (3) KU : *ba*[. . .] (4) TA : *i*-[*na*] (5) UKKIN : *a-p*[*a-ti*] (6) IB : *ip-še*-[*ti*] (7) GAB : *ku-u*[*l*- . . .]. The text reads *ai im-ma-ši i-na a-pa-ti ip-še-ta*-[. . . . .]; it is clear therefore from l. 3 that the commentary gives a slightly variant text, or at any rate a variant reading for the second word in the line. Lines 8–13 (cf. also K. 2,053, Obv., l. 11), corresponding to l. 19 of the text, read: (8) [ilu]do. [ilu]NA-ZI-AZAG-G[A] (9) RU : *ba-nu*-[*u*] (10) RU : *ni-bu*-[*u*] (11) ZI : *ka-a-nu* (12) AZAG : *el-lum* (13) AZAG : *te-lil-tum*. The text reads [ilu]*Tu-tu* [ilu]*Zi-azag šal-šiš im-bu-u mu-kil te-lil-ti*; the commentary thus gives a variant form of the title, and presupposes a longer (or an alternate) form of the line, for no equivalents occur in the text to ll. (9) and (12); while for *mu-kil* the text of the commentary read *mu-kin* (as in l. 21 of the text, cf. l. 23 of the commentary). Lines 14–19, corresponding to l. 20 of the text, read: (14) DINGIR : *i-lum* (15) TU (so glossed) : *ša-a-ri* (16) DU (so glossed) : *ṭa-a-bi* (17) DINGIR : *be-lum* (18) ZI : *še-mu-u* (19) ZI : *ma-ga-ru*. The text reads *il ša-a-ri ṭa-a-bi be-el taš-me-e u ma-ga-ri*. Lines 20–24, corresponding to l. 21 of the text, read: (20) ZI : *ba-šu-u* (21) AZAG : *ṣi-im-ru* (22) ḪA : *ku-bu-ut-te-e* (23) ZI : *ka-a-n*[*u*] (24) [. .] : *ḫeg*[*allu*]. The text reads *mu-šab-ši ṣi-im-ri u ku-bu-ut-te-e mu-kin ḫegalli*.

S. 1,416, col. ii (see pl. lv), joining S. 11, etc., gives traces of two sections of the commentary which should correspond to about l. 25 of the text. S. 11 + S. 980, Obv., col. iii (pl. li) gives traces of three sections of the commentary. The third section (l. 9) begins with a title of Marduk; this may possibly refer to l. 33 or l. 35 of the text, but the traces of the preceding section do not appear to correspond to l. 32 or l. 34. According to its position in the commentary, however, this fragment should refer to about that portion of the text. The fragment 82-3-23, 151 (pl. liv) includes traces of the right half of three sections of the commentary; the second section consists of the following words: *um-mu*, *ir-pi-e-tu*, *ma-lu-u*, *ka-ṣi-pu*, *ni-ši*, *ti-'-u-tu*, and *na-da-nu*. The signs *um-mu*, taken in conjunction with *ir-pi-e-tu*, may perhaps be compared with the phrase *Mu-um-mu ir-pi-e-tu ut-taḳ-ṣi-ba-am-ma*, which occurs in the explanatory text S. 747, Rev., l. 10 (see below, p. 170), where it is followed by the comment *Mu-um-mu* = *rig-mu*. We might perhaps restore the first line of the section as *ilu Mu-um-mu*, running across the column; but Mummu, explained as *rigmu*, is certainly not the title of Marduk, but the name of Apsû's minister; it is therefore possible *um-mu* in the commentary refers to Tiamat, and may perhaps be regarded as a title (cf. Ummu-Ḫubur). The sense of the second half of the line appears to be that Marduk is the guardian of mankind and gives them nourishment.

K. 8,299, Obverse (pl. lx) gives traces of the right half of three sections of the commentary. The Reverse, ll. 3–14 give the right half of the commentary to the first two lines preserved by the fragment K. 12,830 (see the block on p. 163). Lines 3–6 read: (3) [. . .]: *ni*(?)-*bu*-[*u*] (4) [. . .]: *kib-ra-a-te* (5) [. . .]: *ṣal-mat ḳaḳḳadi* (6) [. . .]: *ba-nu-u*. The first line preserved by K. 12,830 reads [. . . . . .] *ṣal-mat* [. . . . . .]; this may conjecturally be restored as [*ib-bi kib-ra-a-te*] *ṣal-mat* [*ḳaḳḳadi ib-ni-ma*]. The first sign in l. 3 of K. 8,299 is broken and its reading as *ni* is not certain; *ir* is possible, as suggested in the copy on pl. lx. Lines 7–14, from the right half of the commentary to the second line preserved by K. 12,830, read: (7) [. . .]: *e-li* (8) [. . .]:

ša-a-šu (9) [. . . .]: *ṭe-e-mu* (10) [. . . .]: [. . .]-*mu* (11) [. . . .]: [*l*]*a-a* (12) [. . . .]: [*i*]-*du-u* (13) [. . .]: [. . .]-*lum* (14) [. . .]: [. . .]-*an*. The text reads [. . . . . .]-*a-šu ṭe*-[. . . . . .]; the first part of the line may therefore be restored as [*e-li ša*]-*a-šu ṭe*-[*e-mu* . . . . .], but the restoration of the second half of the line is not certain.

K. 4,406, Reverse,[1] col. i (pls. liv f.), corresponding to the fourth line preserved by the fragment K. 13,761 (see the

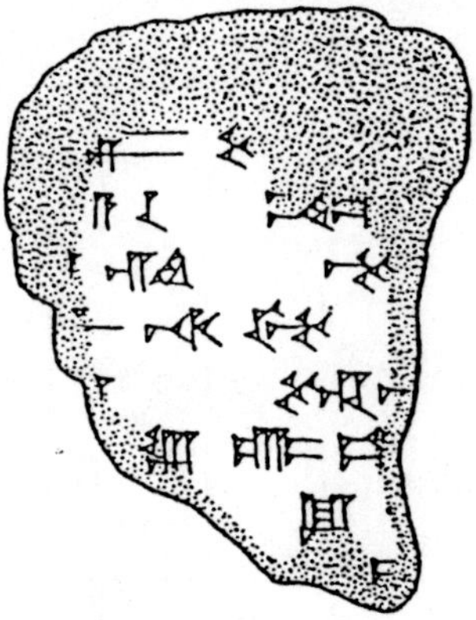

Fragment of the Seventh Tablet of the Creation Series (K. 12,830).

block on p. 164), read: (1) ^ilu^GIL: *ma*-[. .] (2) IL: *ša-ḳu*-[*u*] (3) MA: *na-sa*-[*ḳu*(?)] (4) GIL: *a-gu*-[*u*] (5) GIL: *a-ša*-[*ru*] (6) GIL: *šal-t*[*um*(?)] (7) *šar a-gi-e*: *šar-ra*-[. .]. Of the text only the beginning of the title is preserved, ^ilu^*A-gi*[*l* . . . . .]; in l. 1 of the commentary the sign A is omitted before GIL, and it is possible that *ma*-[. .] in the right half of the line is not to be taken as an explanation of the title, but as part of the title itself. Lines 8–13, corresponding to the next line of the text, read:

[1] It is possible that the text of K. 4,406 is from the obverse and not from the reverse of the tablet; see above, p. 104, n. 2.

(8) MA : *ba-nu-u* (9) IM : *ir-ṣ[i-tu]* (10) AN : *e-[lu-u]* (11) GIŠ : *mu-[. . .]* (12) GIN : *k[a-a-nu(?)]* (13) DINGIR : *[i-lum(?)]*. Of the text only the first word, *ba-nu-u*, has been preserved. Lines 14–25 correspond to the next two lines of the text, and the title in l. 14 may be restored from the text as *ilu* ZU-[LUM-MU]. The next line of the text reads *ilu Mu-um-mu ba-a[n . . . . . .]*; the commentary, ll. 26–29, evidently presupposes a variant reading for this line, for it does not begin with the title *ilu* MU-UM-MU, although MU-UM-M[U], without the determinative, occurs in ll. 27 and 29.

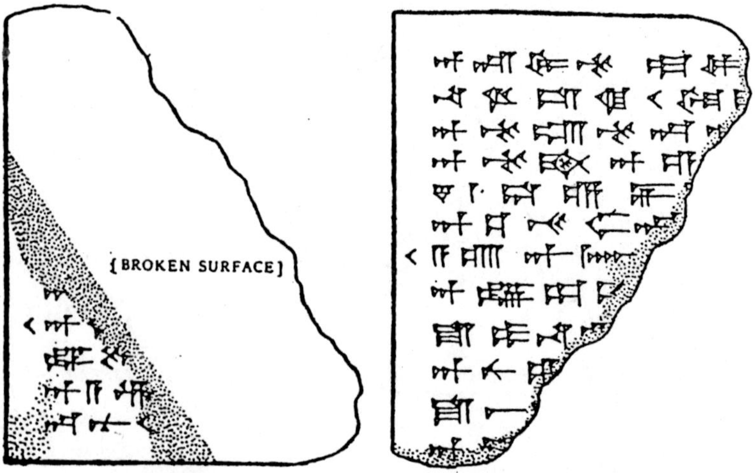

OBVERSE. REVERSE.

Fragment of the Seventh Tablet of the Creation Series (K. 13,761).

K. 4,406, Rev., col. ii, ll. 1–7 give the following words in the explanatory half of the column : *i-na*, *i-lum*, *a-ḫu*, *šu-ru-bu-u*, *ra-bu-u*, *e-til-lum*, and *nap-ḫar-rum*. They should correspond to the fourth line preserved by the fragment K. 8,519 (see the blocks on p. 165), which reads [. . . . *ša-ka*]-*a e-mu-ka-šu*. It is clear therefore that they presuppose a variant reading for the line, which may perhaps be conjecturally restored as *i-na ilāni a-ḫi-e-šu šur-bu-u ra-bu-u e-til nap-ḫa-ri*, " He is mighty among the gods his brethren, great is the lord of all!" With *e-til-lum* and *nap-ḫar-ru* may be compared [*n*]*ap-ḫar be-lim*, which occurs at the end of the preceding line preserved by K. 8,519. Lines 8–13,

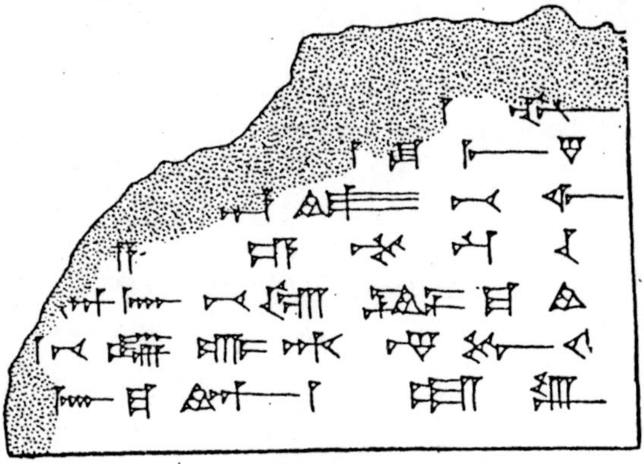

OBVERSE.

Fragment of the Seventh Tablet of the Creation Series (K. 8,519).

the commentary to the following line on K. 8,519, read: (8) [^{ilu}] LUGAL-DUR-MAḪ (9) LUGAL: *šar-ru* (10) DUR: *nar-ka-su* (11) DINGIR: *i-lum* (12) LUGAL: *be-lum* (13) DUR-

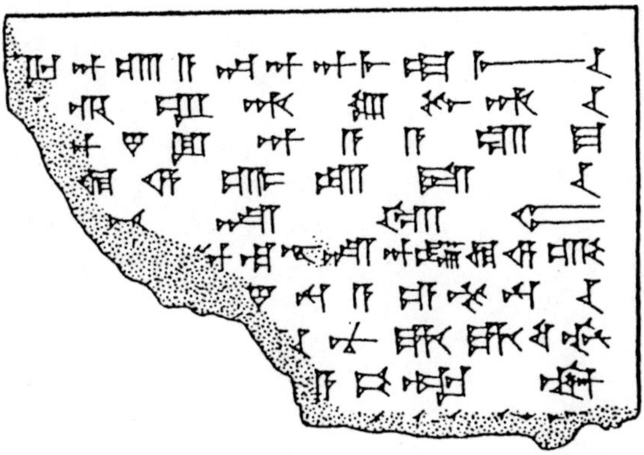

REVERSE.

Fragment of the Seventh Tablet of the Creation Series (K. 8,519).

MAḪ: *dur-ma-ḫu*. The text of K. 8,519 and its duplicate K. 13,337 (see the block on p. 166) may be restored as ^{ilu}*Lugal-dur-maḫ šar m*]*ar-*[*k*]*as ilāni*^{pl} *be-el dur-ma-ḫi.* Lines

14–22, the commentary to the following couplet on K. 8,519, read: (14) LU : *ša-a* (15) KU (DUR ?) : *i-na* (16) DUR : *šub-tum* (17) LUGAL : *šar-ru* (18) MAḪ : *ru-bu-u* (19) KU (DUR ?) : *a-na* (20) DINGIR : *i-lum* (21) MAḪ : *ma-'-du* (22) MAḪ : *ṣi-i-ru*. The text of the two lines reads *ša ina šu-bat šarru-u-ti šur-bu-u* and [*ša*] *ina ilāni*^{pl} *ma-'-diš ṣi-ru*. Lines 23–28, the commentary to the following line on K. 8,519, read: (23) ^{ilu} A-DU-NUN-NA (24) A-DU : *mil-ku* (25) NUN : ^{ilu}*E-a* (26) RU (so glossed) : *ba-nu-u* (27) DINGIR : *i-lum* (28) A : *a-bu*. The text may therefore be restored as [^{ilu}*A-du-nun-na*] *ma-lik* ^{ilu}*E-a ba-an ilāni*^{pl} *abē*^{pl}*-šu*. Lines 29–35, the

Fragment of the Seventh Tablet of the Creation Series (K. 13,337). Duplicate of K. 8,519.

commentary to the following couplet on K. 8,519, read: (29) RA : *ša-a* (30) RA : *a-na* (31) A-[D]U : *a-lak-tu* (32) [. .] : [*ru*][1]*-bu-u* (33) NU : *la-a* (34) RU (?) : [*ma-ša-lu* (?)] (35) DIN[GIR] : [*i-lum*]. The text of the two lines may therefore be restored as *ša a-*[*na*] *tal-lak-ti ru-bu-ti-šu* and *l*[*a-a u*]*-maš-ša-lu ilu ai-um-ma*.

K. 4,406, Rev., col. iii (pls. liv and lv) gives traces of four sections of the commentary. Of the first section only the ends of words in the right half of the column remain. The second section reads: (9) [. . .] - SIGIŠŠE - SIGIŠŠE

[1] The sign is much defaced (cf. the traces given on pl. lv), but is probably *ru*.

(10) UD-DU: *ša-ḳu-u* (11) RA: *i-na* (12) E: *bi-i-tu* (13) SIGIŠŠE-SIGIŠŠE: *ik-ri-bu* (14) RA: *ra-mu-u* (15) RA: *a-ša-bu*. Line 9 appears to give the end of a title of Marduk, which is perhaps explained as *ša-ḳu-u ina bītāti*[pl], "Who is exalted in the temples"; the second half of the line probably contained a second explanatory phrase. Lines 16–19 read: (16) DINGIR: *i-lum* (17) IGI: *maḫ-ru* (18) [T]U: *e-ri-bu* (19) [. . .]: *ḳat-ru-u*; from this it is possible to build up the line as *ilāni ma-ḫar-šu li-še-ri-bu ḳat-ra-šu-un*, "Let the gods bring their gifts into his presence"; a reference to this line is possibly contained in the explanatory text, S. 747, Rev., l. 6, which begins [. . . . . *l*]*i-še-ri-bu ḳat-ra-šu-un* (see below, p. 170); the fourth section gives the first word of the next line as *a-di*.

S. 11 + S. 980, Rev., col. i (pls. lii f.), and its duplicates, K. 2,053, Rev., col. i (pls. lix f.), and R. 366 + 80-7-19, 293, Rev., col. i (pl. lvii), give traces of seven sections of the commentary, which appear to correspond to a portion of the text between ll. 90 and 100. S. 11 + S. 980, Rev., col. ii (pl. lii), ll. 1–6, corresponding to l. 106 of the text, read: (1) [. . . .]: [. . .]-*ru* (2) [. . . .]: [*ka*]*k*-[*k*]*a-b*[*u*] (3) [R]A: *ša*-[*a*] (4) RA: *i-na* (5) AN: *ša-me-e* (6) DU-DU: *šu-pu-u*. The text reads [. . . . -*r*]*u kakkaba š*[*a* . . . .], so that the end of the line may be conjecturally restored as *š*[*a i-na ša-me-e šu-pu-u*]. Ll. 7–12, corresponding to l. 107 of the text, read: (7) RA: *lu-u* (8) RA: *ṣa-ba-tu* (9) KUN-SAG-GE: *ri-e-šu ar-kat* (10) AN: *ri-e-šu* (11) RU: *ar-kat* (12) [. .]-ŠA-A-RU: *pa-la-su*. The text reads *lu-u ṣa-bit rēšu-arkāt šu-nu ša-a-šu lu-u pal-su* [. .], see above, p. 106 f. Lines 13–21 (cf. pl. lix for the duplicate commentary, K. 2,053, Rev., col. ii, ll. 1–5), corresponding to l. 108 of the text, read: (13) [ ] MA: *ma-a* (14) [ ] MA: *ma-ru* (15) RA: *ša-a* (16) RA: *i-na* (17) IR (so glossed on S. 11, etc., cf. l. 26): *kir-bu* (18) NE-RU (possibly ERIM, cf. Brünnow, No. 4,603): *tam-tim* (19) GID: *e-bi-ru* (20) RA: *la-a* (21) NE: *na-a-ḫu*. The text reads *ma-a ša kir-biš Ti-amat i-tib-bi*-[. . . . .], and from the commentary the end of the line may conjecturally be restored as *i-tib-bi-[ru la a-ni-ḫu]*. Lines 22–26 (K. 2,053, ll. 6–10), corresponding to l. 109 of the text, read: (22) NE: *šu-uš-šu* (23) RA: *lu-u* (24) NI-BI-RU: *Ni-bi-ru* (25) RA: *a-ḫa-zu* (26) IR (so glossed): *kir-bu*. The text reads *šum-šu lu* ilu *Ni-bi-ru a-ḫi-zu kir-bi-šu*. Lines 27–31 (K. 2,053, ll. 11–14), corresponding to l. 110 of the text, read: (27) RA: *ša-a* (28) AN: *kak-ka-bu* (29) AN: *šamē(e)* (duplicate *ša-me-e*) (30) RA (so glossed): *a-la-ku* (31) RA (so glossed): *ka-a-nu*. The text reads *ša kakkabāni*pl *ša-ma-me al-kat-su-nu li-ki-il-lu*; for *li-ki-il-lu* the commentaries thus give the variant reading *likīn*, "he ordained." Lines 32–38 (K. 2,053, ll. 15–21), corresponding to l. 111 of the text, read: (32) ḪAR: *ki-ma* (33) RI: *ṣi-e-nu* (34) RI: *ri-'-u* (35) DINGIR: *i-lum* (36) ḪAR: *lib-bi* (37) ŠAG: *lib-bi* (38) ŠAG: *pu-uḫ-ru*. The text reads *kīma ṣi-e-ni li-ir-ta-a ilāni gim-ra-šu-un*; thus for *gim-ra-šu-un* the text of the commentaries evidently gave a variant reading. Lines 39–44, corresponding to l. 112 of the text, read: (39) IR: *ka-mu-u* (40) NE-RU (see above): *tam-tim* (41) IR: *ši-*[. .] (42) ŠI: *na-p[iš-tu]* (43) KIR: *sa-[a-ku]* (44) KIR: [. . .]. The text reads: *lik-me Ti-amat ni-ṣir-ta-ša* (var. *na-piš-ta-šu*) *li-si-iḳ u lik-ri*; the commentary thus supports the variant reading to the text.

R. 366 + 80–7–19, 293, Rev., col. ii (pl. lvii), l. 1, which reads [. . .]: [*ṣa*]*-a-t*[*i*], corresponds to the last word of l. 114 of the text. Lines 2–8, corresponding to l. 115 of the text, read: (2) IR: *šu-u* (3) AN: *aš-ru* (4) *aš-ru*: *ša-mu-u* (5) RU (so glossed): *ba-nu-u* (6) RU: *pa-ta-ḳu* (7) RU: *dan-ni-ni* (8) *dan-ni-nu*: *irṣitim(tim)*. The text reads *aš-šu aš-ri ib-na-a ip-ti-ḳa dan-ni-na*; ll. 4 and 8 of the commentary explain *ašru* as referring to heaven, and *danninu* as referring to the earth; a reference to this line also possibly occurs in the explanatory text, S. 747, Rev., l. 10 (see below, p. 170). Lines 9–13, corresponding to l. 116 of the text, read: (9) EN KUR-KUR (i.e. *bēl mātāti*): *šum-šu* (10) MA: *šu-mu* (11) MA: *na-bu-u* (12) A: *a-bu* (13) EN KUR-KUR: ilu EN-LIL (i.e. ilu *Bēl*); l. 9 thus explains *bēl mātāti* as "his name," i.e. Marduk's name, and l. 13 gives it as the title of Enlil, or the elder Bēl, who in the text transfers it to Marduk. The text of the line reads *be-el mātāti šum-šu it-ta-bi a-bi* ^{ilu}*Bēl.* Lines 14–17, corresponding to l. 117 of the text, read: (14) MA : *zik-ri* (15) AN : ^{ilu}*Igigi* (16) MA : *ni-bu* (17) UZU : *nag-bu.* The text reads *zik-ri* (var. *ina zik-ri*) ^{ilu}*Igigi im-bu-u na-gab-šu-un.* Lines 18–23, corresponding to l. 118 of the text, read: (18) [. . .]: *še-mu-u* (19) [. . .]: ^{ilu}[*E-a*] (20) [. . .]: *k*[*a-bit-tu*] (21) [ ] LI : *ra*-[. . .] (22) [ ] LI : *na-g*[*u-u*] (23) [ ] LI : *ḫi*-[. . .]. The text of the line reads *iš-me-ma* ^{ilu}*E-a ka-bit-ta-šu i-te-en-gu*; the text of the commentary therefore gave a fuller form for the second half of the line. Lines 24–27, corresponding to l. 119 of the text, read: (24) A : *ma*-[*a*] (25) A : *a*-[*bu*] (26) A : *šur-r*[*u-ḫu*] (27) MA : *zik*-[*ri*]. The text of the line reads *ma-a ša abē*^{pl}*-šu u-šar-ri-ḫu zik-ru-u-šu.*

At this point the scribe of R. 366, etc., ceases to give the commentary in the form of a bilingual list, and in ll. 28–34 he writes out the text of the Assyrian version of ll. 120–124 of the composition. Then follows a colophon of three lines which read: (35) *an-nu-u-tu* (?) *ul kalū u* [. . . . .] (36) *ša* LI *šumē*^{pl} *ša* [. . . . .] (37) *ša ina libbi* ^{ilu}*Asar-ri* [. . . . .], "These are not all (?) and [. . . . .] of the fifty-one names of [. . . . .] which are in (the composition entitled) 'Asari [. . . . .].'" The reading of l. 35 is not certain, but the colophon seems to imply that the commentary was not complete, or else that the fifty (or fifty-one) names of Marduk were not all given in the composition itself. Two important facts may be deduced from the colophon. The first is that the Seventh Tablet of the Creation Series is here treated as an independent composition which takes its title from its opening line. The second is that in this independent form the composition ended with l. 124 of the tablet. It is clear, therefore, that ll. 125–142 of the Seventh Tablet are in the nature of an epilogue, which was added to the composition at the time it was incorporated as the concluding tablet in the series *Enuma eliš.*

The supposition that the text of the Seventh Tablet ended originally at l. 124 receives additional support from the explanatory text S. 747 (see *Cuneiform Texts*, pt. xiii, pl. 32).[1] When complete it is probable that the tablet, of which S. 747 formed a part, contained a kind of running commentary to the whole of the Creation Series; only fragments of the beginning and of the end of the commentary are preserved by S. 747, and these refer to the First Tablet and to the Seventh Tablet of the Series respectively. Thus, S. 747, Obv., l. 1, which reads [. . . . . .] *riš-tu-u za-ru-šu-un*, followed by the comment *za-ru-u* = [. . . . . .], refers to Tablet I, l. 3; l. 3, which reads [. . . . . . . -*t*]*i ṣu-ṣu-u nap-pa*-[. . .], refers to Tablet I, l. 6; and the mention of *Ea* in l. 5 is in accordance with the prominent part which the god plays in Tablet I, in detecting and defeating the plot of Apsū and Tiamat. On the other hand, the reverse of S. 747 appears to deal with the Seventh Tablet of the Series; thus, l. 3 may perhaps be compared with the equation NUN = *ilu E-a*, given by K. 4,406, Rev., col. ii, l. 25, in the commentary to a line of the Seventh Tablet (see above, p. 166); l. 6 possibly contains a reference to the line of the Seventh Tablet to which the commentary K. 4,406, Rev., col. iii, ll. 16–19, corresponds (see above, p. 167); the words in l. 10, [. . .] *dan-ni-na* (or [. . . *u*]-*dan-ni-na*) *ir-ṣi-tum*, possibly refer to l. 115 of the Seventh Tablet, while the second half of the same line perhaps contains a reference to the line of the Seventh Tablet, to which the commentary 82–3–23, 151, section 2, corresponds (see above, p. 162, and for the verb *ut-taḳ-ṣi-ba-am-ma*, cf. Tablet V, l. 20); and the words *ri-e-šu ar-ka-tu* in l. 11 clearly refer to l. 107 of the Seventh Tablet. Line 12 of S. 747 quotes l. 124 of the Seventh Tablet, followed by the explanatory equations L (i.e. "Fifty") = *Ḫa-an-ša-a* (i.e. Marduk's last title) and L = *ilu Bēl*. Now, as l. 12 is the last line of S. 747, it is not unreasonable to suppose that the

[1] See above, p. 157.

portion of text it explains came at the end of the composition to which the commentary refers.

The tablet K. 2,107 + K. 6,086 (pls. lxi f.), which has already been referred to,[1] is not strictly a commentary to the Seventh Tablet of the Creation Series, but is of value for explaining some of the titles of Marduk which occur therein. The second column is subdivided by a perpendicular line; in the left half of the column are inscribed the titles of Marduk, and in the right half the explanations are set opposite them. Lines 9–18 form a single section, and probably give a number of alternative explanations referring to a single title which was written in the left half of l. 9. In the following transliteration of the text a translation of each Assyrian rendering in the right half of the column is added beneath it:—

TITLE.		EXPLANATION.
1. [Wanting.]	:	[. . . . . .]-*ni ma-tim ali u ni-ši* "[The . . .] of land, city, and people."
2. [Wanting.]	:	[. . . *ma - ti*]*m ali u ni - ši* "[The . of la]nd, city, and people."
3. [Wanting.]	:	[. . . . . .] *maš-ki-ti ana ali u ni-ši* "[The . . . .] of drink unto city and people."
4. [Wanting.]	:	[. . . . . .] *a-li-id* *ilu* *Sin u* *ilu* *Šamaš* "[The . . .] Begetter of the Moon and the Sun."
5. [Wanting.]	:	[. . .] *nap-ḫar be-li a-ša-rid nap-ḫar be-li* "[The . . .] of all lords, the Chief of all lords."
6. [Wanting.]	:	[. . . . . . . -*n*]*i ka-la ti-me-a-ti* "[The Creator(?)] of all words(?)."

[1] See above, p. 157.

TITLE.	EXPLANATION.
7.	[. . . . . -*n*]*i* *nap-ḫar* *ti-me-a-ti*[1] "[The Creator(?)] of all words(?)."
8. [Wanting.] :	[. . .]*pl* *šar* *ka-la* *ili* *u* *šarri* "[The . . .] of the [. . .], the King of all gods and kings."
9. [Wanting.] :	[. . .] *ilāni*[p] "[The . . .] of the gods."
10.	[. . . *šam*]*ē*(*e*) *u* *irṣitim*(*tim*) "[The . . . of hea]ven and earth."
11.	[. . . *šamē*](*e*) *u* *irṣitim*(*tim*) "[The . . . of heaven] and earth."
12.	[. . . . .] *ilu* *Bēl* "[The . . . . . .] of Bēl."
13.	*be-lum* [. . . *šam*]*ē*(*e*) *u* *irṣitim*(*tim*) "The Lord [. . .] of heaven and earth."
14.	*be - lum* *a - ši - ir* *ilāni*[pl] "The Lord, the Blesser of the gods."
15.	*be - lum* *ga - me - il* *ilāni*[pl] "The Lord, the Benefactor of the gods."
16.	*be - lum* *ša* *e - mu - ḳa - a - šu* *ša - ḳa - a* "The Lord, whose might is supreme."
17.	*be - el* *Bābili* KI "The Lord of Babylon."
18.	*mud - diš* *Bābili* KI "The Renewer of Babylon."

[1] This line gives a slightly variant explanation of the title in l. 6.

TITLE.		EXPLANATION.
19. *ilu* LUGAL-EN-AN-KI-A	:	*be-el ilāni pl ša šamē u irṣiti šar ilāni pl ša šamē u irṣiti* "The Lord of the gods of heaven and earth, the King of the gods of heaven and earth."
20. *ilu* A-DU-NUN-NA	:	*ma-lik ilu Bēl u ilu E-a* "The Counsellor of Bēl and Ea."
21. *ilu* TU-TU	:	*mu-al-lid ilāni pl mu-ud-di-iš ilāni pl* "The Begetter of the gods, the Renewer of the gods."
22. *ilu* GU-GU	:	*mu-tak-kil ilāni pl* "The Strengthener of the gods."
23. *ilu* MU-MU	:	*mu-uš-pi-iš ilāni pl* "The . . . of the gods."
24. *ilu* DU-ṬU	:	*ba-ni ka-la ilāni pl* "The Creator of all the gods."
25. *ilu* DU-DU	:	*mu-ut-tar-ru-u ilāni pl* "The Leader of the gods."
26. *ilu* MU-AZAG	:	*ša ši-pat-su el-lit* "Whose Incantation is pure."
27. *ilu* MU-AZAG	:	*ša tu-u-šu el-lit* "Whose Spell is pure."
28. *ilu* ŠAG (-SUD)-ZU	:	*mu-di-e libbi ilāni pl lib-bu ru-u-ḳu (ḫi-bi eš-šu)*[1] "Who knoweth the heart of the gods, the wide heart (recent break)."

[1] The note *ḫi-bi eš-šu*, which is written in smaller characters, signifies that the end of the line was broken in the original tablet from which the scribe was copying.

	Title.	Explanation.
29.	Zi (- *do.*) - UKKIN	: *nap - šat nap - ḫar ilāni*^{pl} "The Life of all the gods."
30.	^{ilu}Zi (- *do.*) - SI	: *na - si - iḫ ša - bu - ti* "The Remover[1] of the mighty."
31.	^{ilu}SUḪ (- *do.*) - KUR	: *mu - bal - lu - u ai - bi* "The Destroyer of the foe."
32.	^{ilu}[. . .](-*do.*)-KUR	: *mu-bal-lu-u nap-ḫar ai-bi na-si-iḫ rag-gi* "The Destroyer of all foes, the Remover of the wicked."
33.	[Wanting.]	: *na - si - iḫ nap - ḫar rag - gi* "The Remover of all the wicked."
34.	[Wanting.]	: [. . . *ra*]*g-gi e-šu-u rag-gi* "[The . . . of the] wicked; the Annihilator of the wicked."
35.	[Wanting.]	: [. . . *rag*]-*gi e-šu-u nap-ḫar rag-gi* "[The . . . of the wick]ed; the Annihilator of all the wicked."
36.	[Wanting.]	: [. . . . .] - *ti* "[. . . . .]."

In the earlier part of the text the titles which were given on the left side of the column in ll. 1–6 and 8 and 9 are wanting, but the explanations on the right side recall many phrases of the Seventh Tablet, from among which we may compare those given in l. 5 with the end of the 3rd line preserved by the fragment K. 8,519 (see above, p. 104 f.), and that in l. 16 with the 4th and 14th lines of the same fragment. Of the

[1] I.e., "Destroyer."

titles given in ll. 19 ff., compare l. 20 with *ilu* *A-du-nun-na* and its explanation in the 8th line preserved by K. 8,519; l. 21 with *ilu* *Tu-tu* in l. 9 of the Seventh Tablet (see above, p. 92 f.); l. 27 with *ilu* *Mu-azag* in l. 33 (see above, p. 98 f.); l. 28 with *ilu* *Šag-zu* in l. 35 (see above, p. 98 f.); l. 29 with *ilu* *Zi-ukkin-na* in l. 15 (see above, p. 94 f.); l. 30 with *ilu* *Zi-si* in l. 41 (see above, p. 100 f.); and l. 31 with *ilu* *Suḫ-kur* in l. 43 (see above, p. 100 f.). It is possible that col. i of the Obverse of K. 2,107 + K. 6,086 (see pl. lxi) also contained explanations of the Seventh Tablet, or at any rate referred to the Creation Series, as l. 4 reads [. . . . .] *Apsû* and l. 15 [. . . . . *Ti* (?)]-*amat*.

It was stated on p. 157 that fragments exist of compositions very similar in character to the Seventh Tablet of the Creation Series. Remains of one such composition are preserved by the fragment of a Neo-Babylonian tablet, No. 54,228, the text of which is published in vol. ii, pl. lxiii, and by its two Assyrian duplicates, R. 395 (see vol. ii, pl. lxii) and R. 2, 538 (see the block on p. 176). R. 2, 538 is a duplicate of No. 54,228, Obv., ll. 6–15; R. 395, Rev., ll. 3–5 correspond to No. 54,228, ll. 8, 10, and 12. The Obverse of R. 395, which does not correspond to any portion of the text preserved by the other two fragments, reads as follows:—

1. [. . . . . .] 2. [ ] *ilu* [. . . . . .]
3. *ai ib - ba - ši - [m]a* *ilu* [. . . . . .]
4. *ip-te-ma ina inâ*[II] *ša nârâti*[*pl* . . . . . .]
5. *e - piš zib - bat - sa tur - ma* [. . . . . .]
6. *ri - eš ta - mar - ti it - b[a -* . . . . . .]
7. *iš - mi - ma* *ilu* *Bêl pâ - šu* [. . . . . .]
8. *iš - ši - ma miṭ - ṭa i[m -* . . . . . .]
9. *iš - tu* [. . . . . .] 10. *ilu* [. . . . . .]

If this fragment is in the form of narrative, it follows that ll. 1–6 are the concluding lines of a speech, since l. 7 reads

"Bēl hearkened and his mouth [. . . . .]." Bēl did not answer, however, for l. 8 reads "He raised the club [. . . .]." Now the phrase *iš-ši-ma miṭ-ṭa* occurs in Tablet IV of the Creation Series, l. 37, but the context on this fragment does not suggest a variant account either of the arming of Marduk for battle or of the actual fight with Tiamat. Moreover, the Reverse of the fragment, which is in part a duplicate of No. 54,228 and R. 2, 538 (see above), is inscribed with addresses in honour of Marduk under some of the titles

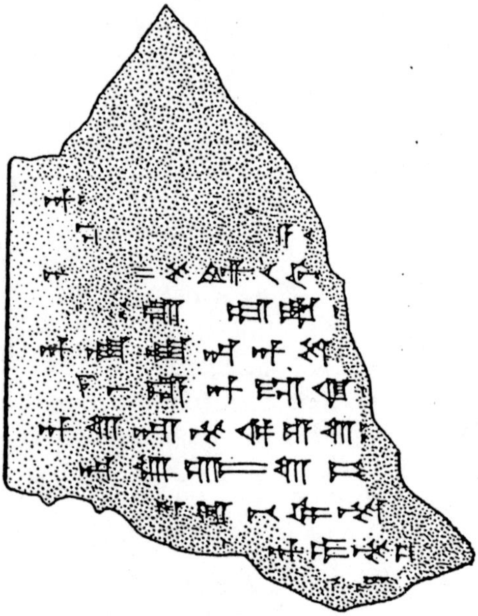

Fragment of a parallel text to the Seventh Tablet of the Creation Series (R. 2, 538). Duplicate of No. 54,228.

which occur on the Seventh Tablet of the Creation Series. It is therefore probable that the Obverse of R. 398 contains a part of the same composition. Line 4, which reads "He opened [. . . .] at the sources of the rivers [. . . .]," would in that case refer to some act of creation on the part of Marduk, and the lines which follow would celebrate incidents in the battle with Tiamat.

Only a few traces of characters are preserved on the Reverse of R. 395, but enough is left to prove that ll. 3, 4, and 5 are duplicates of No. 54,228, Obv., ll. 8, 10, and 12. The following is the text of No. 54,228 with restorations and variants from R. 395 and R. 2, 538 :—

OBV.

1. [. . . .] *ḫa* [. . . .] 2. [. . . .] ^{ilu}*Ea ib-*[. . . .],
3. *li - pu - uš iz - ri -* [. . . . .]
4. *iṣu a - rik iš - kur*(?) *nu*[1] - [. . . . . .]
5. GIŠ - GID - DA *a - rik* [. . . . .][2]
6. ^{ilu}*Asar - ri ša - riḳ me -* [*riš - ti*[3] . . . .]
7. *iz - ra - tum a -* [. . . . .]
8. *ba - nu - u še - im u gu - e* [. . . . . .]
9. *g*[*u*] *- u*[4] *ṣi - ḫir - t*[*u* . . . .]
10. ^{ilu}*Tu - tu ba - an*[5] *te - diš -* [*ti - šu - nu* . . . .]
11. *šum ilāni*^{pl} *ša ma - ḫa - zi*[6] [. . . .]
12. ^{ilu}*Šag - zu mu - di - e lib - bi il*[*āni*^{pl}[7] . . . .]
13. ^{ilu}*Šag - gar*(?)[8] *ba - ru - u lib - bi* [. . . .]

---

[1] Possibly *ḫ*[*a-* . . .].

[2] It will be noticed that ll. 4–17 are written in couplets, the second half of each couplet being set back a little from the edge of the tablet. It is just possible that these second lines give explanations of phrases in the lines which precede them. It appears on the whole more probable, however, that they form part of the actual text; in that case the couplets in ll. 8 f., 10 f., and 12 f. are written as single lines on the fragment R. 395.

[3] Restored from Tablet VII, l. 1, see above, p. 92.

[4] So the traces upon No. 54,228 appear to read; R. 2, 538 [*g*]*u-um*.

[5] R. 395, *ni*.

[6] For l. 11, R. 2, 538 reads *ša ina Bābili*^{KI}[. . . . . .].

[7] The traces of the following lines upon R. 395 do not correspond to the portions of the text preserved by No. 54,228.

[8] R. 2, 538 omits the title at the beginning of the line.

14. *ilu En-bi-lu-lu be-lum mu-diš māti - šu* [. . . .]
15. *na - mad šu - ' - u*[1] *mu - šab - šu* [. . . .]
16. *ilu Tutu*[2] *ša pi - ti - iḳ māti i* - [. . . . . .]
17. *ilu Tutu ilu Marduk tam - tum b*[*a* (?) . . . .]
18. *Ti - amat iddu*(*du*) *šu - lu* - [. . . . .]
19. *ša ina ri - e - ši u ar - ka* - [*ti*[3] . . . .]
20. *ilu Nabū ina* BAR - NAM[pl 4] *ūmu VI* KAN [. . . .]
21. *ilu A - du - nun - na ma - lik ilu*[. . . . . .]
22. *ilu Ninib ilu Ḫanšā ib* - [. . . . .]
23. [. . .] *a - lak - ti ru* - [. . . . .]
24. [. . .] *ṣilli* [. . .] 25. [. . . . . .]

Rev.

1. [. . . . .] 2. *mu* - [. . . . . .]
3. *gi - pa - ri* [. . .] 4. *mi* - [. .] - *ri* (?) - [. . . .]
5. *ir - ṣi - tum* [. . .] 6. [. . . .]-*ma* [. . . .]

Fragmentary as the text of No. 54,228 is, a glance at the above transliteration will suffice to show that it preserves part of a composition which is very similar in character to the Seventh Tablet. That it does not form a missing portion of the text of that composition, is clear from the occurrence of certain phrases and titles of Marduk found in parts of the text of the Seventh Tablet which have already been identified; moreover, they are here arranged in a different order and with a different context. Thus, l. 6 f. correspond to the

---

[1] R. 2, 538, *i*.

[2] In this and the following line TU + TU is written as a conflate sign.

[3] Conjectural restoration.

[4] Possibly *ina parakki šīmāti*[pl].

opening line of Tablet VII; l. 8 corresponds to Tab. VII, l. 2[1]; l. 10 corresponds to Tab. VII, l. 9; l. 12 corresponds to Tab. VII, l. 35,[2] and l. 13 may be compared with the second half of the same line; l. 19 is clearly parallel to Tab. VII, l. 107; l. 21 corresponds to the line of Tab. VII preserved by K. 8,519, l. 8 (see above, p. 104); with ^ilu^*Ḫanšā* in l. 22, cf. Tab. VII, l. 123; and with l. 23, cf. K. 8,519, l. 8, and the commentary to this line, K. 4,406, Rev., col. ii, l. 31 (see above, p. 166, and vol. ii, pl. lv), which gives the reading *a-lak-tu*. It may also be noted that in ll. 4 and 5 we have a reference to *iṣu arik*, "Long-bow," the first name given by Anu to Marduk's bow upon K. 3,449*a*, which probably forms part of the Fifth Tablet (see above, p. 82 f.); GIŠ-GID-DA in l. 5 is evidently the Sumerian form of the name. The title of Marduk, En-bilulu, which occurs in l. 14, and is there explained as "the Lord who hath renewed his land," is found also upon the fragment K. 5,233, which is described in the following paragraph.

---

[1] It may here be noted that on the fragment S. 298 occur the phrases [. . . . .] *ba-nu-u še-im u ki-e mu-diš-šu* [. . . . .], "[. . . .], Creator of grain and plants, Renewer of [. . . .]"; as two other lines of the same fragment read [. . . . .] *muš-te-ši-ru a-d*[*i-* . . . . .], "[. . . .] Director of the decrees of [. . . .]," and [. . . . . *ba*]*-nu-u te-ni-šil* [. . . . .], "[. . . . .] Creator of mankind [. . . . .]," it is clear that the fragment is part of a composition containing addresses to Marduk as lord of Creation. Too little is preserved to show whether in this text, as in the Seventh Tablet, he was addressed under his Sumerian titles.

[2] On an Assyrian fragment of a hymn, K. 12,582, occurs the following couplet:—

^ilu^*Šag-zu mu-di-e lib-b*[*i* . . . .]
a-pir a-gi-e bēlu-u-tu [. . . . .]
"Šag-zu, who knoweth the heart [of the gods . . . . .]
"Who weareth the crown of dominion [. . . . . . .]."

It is possible that this fragment also belonged to a composition, similar in character to the Seventh Tablet of the Creation Series.

It has already been remarked that the commentaries to the Seventh Tablet presuppose the existence of a Sumerian version of the text, and in the fragment K. 5,233, the text of which is given in the accompanying block, we may see a confirmation of this supposition. The fragment is part of an Assyrian tablet inscribed with a bilingual composition, and in each line of the Sumerian text which is preserved Marduk is addressed under a new title. In the following

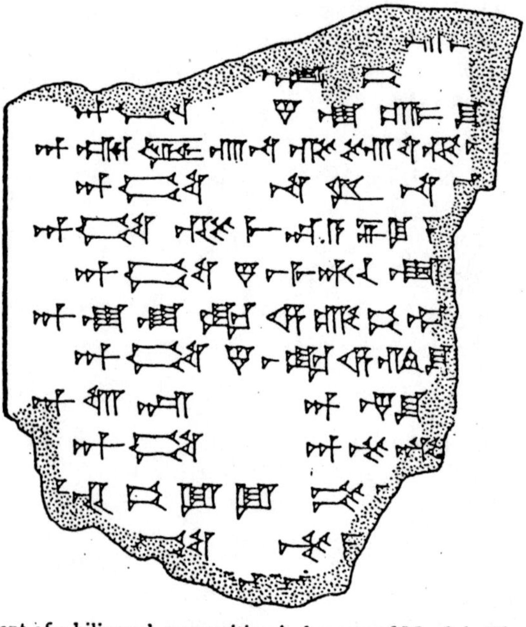

Fragment of a bilingual composition in honour of Marduk (K. 5,233).

transliteration and translation of the fragment the first couplet preserved is numbered "1," but it should be noted that it does not mark the beginning of the text :—

1. [DINGIR . . . . . .] MU - BI [. . . . .]

ilu *Marduk ša tu - u - šu* [. . . . .]

Marduk, whose spell [. . . . .] !

2. [DINGIR] ASARU-ALIM-NUN-NA ZI SU-UD-GAL-[. . . .]
   [ilu] *Marduk* *na - din* *na - p[iš - ti* (?) . . . .]
   Marduk, the giver of [life . . . .]!

3. [DINGIR] . . . NAM-IŠIB-BA-A-NI-KU GA[R- . . . .]
   [ilu] *Marduk* *ša* *ina* *šip - ti - šu* *li* - [. . . .]
   Marduk, who by his incantation [. . . .]!

4. [DINGIR] TU - TU SAR - AZAG - GA - BI [. . . . . .]
   [ilu] *Marduk* *ša* *ina* SAR-AZAG-*gi-šu* [. . . .]
   Marduk, who by his . . . [. . . . . .]!

5. [DINGIR] ŠAG - ZU [DINGIR] SUḪ - [KUR . . . .]
   [ilu] *Marduk* [ilu] *Mu - bal* - [*lu - u* *ai - bi* . . . .]
   Marduk, the Destroyer [of the foe . . . .]!

6. [DINGIR] EN - BI - LU - LU GAB - [. . . . .]
   [ilu] *Marduk* *mu* - [. . . . .]
   Marduk, who [. . . . .]!

It is possible that the title in l. 1 may be restored as [DINGIR] MU-AZAG from Tab. VII, l. 33. Of the other titles under which Marduk is here addressed, ASARU-ALIM-NUNA (l. 2) occurs in Tab. VII, l. 5, TUTU (l. 4) in Tab. VII, l. 9, ŠAG-ZU (l. 5) in Tab. VII, l. 35, and SUḪ-KUR in Tab. VII, l. 43. The restoration of the Assyrian version of l. 5 is taken from K. 2,107 + K. 6,086, Obv., col. ii, l. 31 (see above, p. 174, and vol. ii, pl. lxii). The title EN-BILULU also occurs in the parallel text to the Seventh Tablet preserved by No. 54,228 and R. 2, 538 (see above, p. 178 f.).

II.

On some fragments of the Series "Enuma elish," and on some texts relating to the History of Creation.

In this appendix some unpublished fragments of tablets of the Creation Series are given, which I came across after the lithographed plates of vol. ii had been printed off. At the beginning of the present year, while engaged on making a hand-list of the smaller fragments in the various collections from Kuyunjik, I identified ten such fragments as belonging to copies of the First, Second, Fifth, and Seventh Tablets of the Creation Series. The texts of five of these (KK. 2,854, 12,830, 13,761, 8,519, and 13,337), which belong to copies of the Seventh Tablet, are included in Appendix I under the sections dealing with those portions of the commentary which rendered it possible to identify them.[1] The texts of the remaining five fragments (KK. 7,871, 4,488, 10,008, 13,774, and 11,641), belonging to copies of the First, Second, and Fifth Tablets, are given in the following sections which are marked A, B, and C. In section D two small Assyrian fragments (K. 12,000*b* and 79-7-8, 47) are described, which possibly contain portions of the text of the Creation Series. In section E the text is given of the fragment (S. 2,013), which contains a reference to *Ti-amat e-li-ti* and *Ti-amat šap-li-ti*. Section F deals with the fragments K. 3,445 + R. 396 and K. 14,949, which probably contain an account of the creation of the world by Anšar, in place of Marduk. In section G the text is given of an address to the River of Creation which occurs in the opening lines of incantations upon the fragments S. 1,704 and 82-9-18, 5,311. Finally, in

[1] It may be noted that all of them have been used for the text of the Seventh Tablet as transliterated and translated on pp. 92 ff.

section H the tablet K. 3,364, which has been supposed to contain the instructions given by Marduk to man after his creation, is shown to be part of a long text containing moral precepts.

A. TWO FRAGMENTS OF THE FIRST TABLET OF THE CREATION SERIES.—The fragment K. 7,871, the text of which is given in the accompanying block, is from the right-

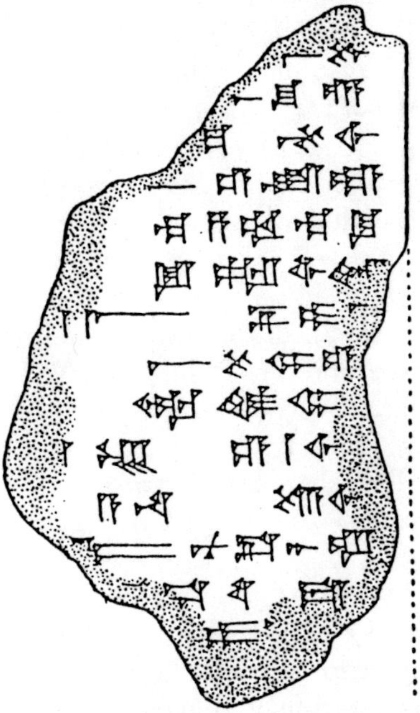

Creation Series, Tablet I, ll. 33–47 (K. 7,871).

hand edge of the obverse of a tablet, and the ends of lines which it preserves correspond to Tablet I, ll. 33–47. As the first sheet of this volume had been printed off at the time I came across it, the information it supplies as to this imperfectly preserved portion of the text of the First Tablet[1] may be briefly noted.

[1] See above, pp. 6–9.

In l. 33 the new fragment supports the reading *sak-pu* at the end of the line; in l. 34 it confirms the suggested restoration [*ma-ri-e-šu-un*], probably reading [*mārē*][pl]-*šu-un*; the couplet, ll. 35 and 36, which may be conjecturally restored as *Ap*[*sū pa*]-*a-šu i-pu*-[*šam-ma i-ḳab-bi*], *a-na* [*T*]*i-am*[*at*] *el-li-tu-ma i-za*[*k-kar a-ma-tum*], it condenses into a single line which may probably be restored as [*Apsū pa-a-šu i-pu-šam*]-*ma izakkar-ši*, "[Apsū opened his mouth] and spake unto her"; the end of l. 37 may now be restored as *al-kat-su-nu e-li-ia*, i.e. "their way [is . . . .] unto me"; the suggested restoration of the end of l. 38 as *mu-ši* [*la ṣal-la-ak*] is confirmed, the fragment reading [. . . . .] *la ṣa-al-la-ku*; the end of l. 39 may now be restored as *lu-šap-pi-iḫ*, i.e. "Their way will I destroy and cast down"; the suggested restoration of the end of l. 40 as [*ni-i-ni*] is confirmed, the fragment reading *ni-i-n*[*i*]; the suggested restoration of the end of l. 41 as *i-na* [*še-mi-ša*] is confirmed, the fragment reading *ina še-mi-e*-[*ša*]. The suggested restoration (from Tab. IV, l. 89 and Tab. III, l. 125) of the phrase *il-ta-si e-li*-[*ta*] in l. 42 is shown to be incorrect, the fragment reading [. . . . .] *eli ḫar-mi*-[. .]; the line should run *i-zu-uz-ma* (var. [*e*]-*ziz-m*[*a*]) *il-ta-si e-li* (var. *eli*) *ḫar-mi*-[*ša*(?)]. For the end of l. 43 K. 7,871 reads [. . . . .]-*gat e-diš-ši*-[. . .], and the verb preserved by No. 45,528 + 46,614 (see vol. ii, pl. iii) may probably be read *ug*-[*g*]*u-ga*[*t*]; the line may thus be partly restored as [. .] *mar-ṣi-iš*[1] *ug*-[*g*]*u-ga*[*t*] *e-diš-ši*-[. . . . .], "[. .] she was grievously angered, alone [she . . . .]"; K. 7,871 probably gave a variant reading for the verb, as the traces it gives of the sign before *gat* (or *kat*) are not those of *gu*.[2] The suggested restoration of the end of l. 44 as *a-na* [*Apsū i-zak-ḳar*] is shown by K. 7,871 to be incorrect, the fragment reading [. . . . .] *a-na kar-ši*-[. .]; the

[1] It may here be noted that the principal traces of this line upon the obverse of 81–7–27, 80 (see *Cun. Txts.*, part xiii, pl. 2) probably represent the word *mar-ṣi-iš*.

[2] The restoration of the line as [. .] *mar-ṣi-iš ug*-[*g*]*u-gat e*-[. . .]-*kat e-diš-ši*-[. .] is also possible.

line may probably be restored as *li-mut-ta* (var. *ti*) *it-ta-di a-na kar-ši-*[*ša* (?)], "She plotted evil in [her] heart (?)." The end of l. 45, according to the fragment, reads [. . . . .]-*u nu-uš-ḫal-laḳ* ; it is possible that we may restore the line as [*mi*]-*na-a ni-i-nu ša ni-i*[*p-pu-uš lu*]-*u nu-uš-ḫal-laḳ*, "What, then, shall we do? Let us destroy!" The end of l. 46, according to the fragment, reads [. . . . .]-*du-tu da-*[. .]; unless this represents a variant reading, the suggested restoration *i ni-*[*iṣ-lal ni-i-ni*] is incorrect. For

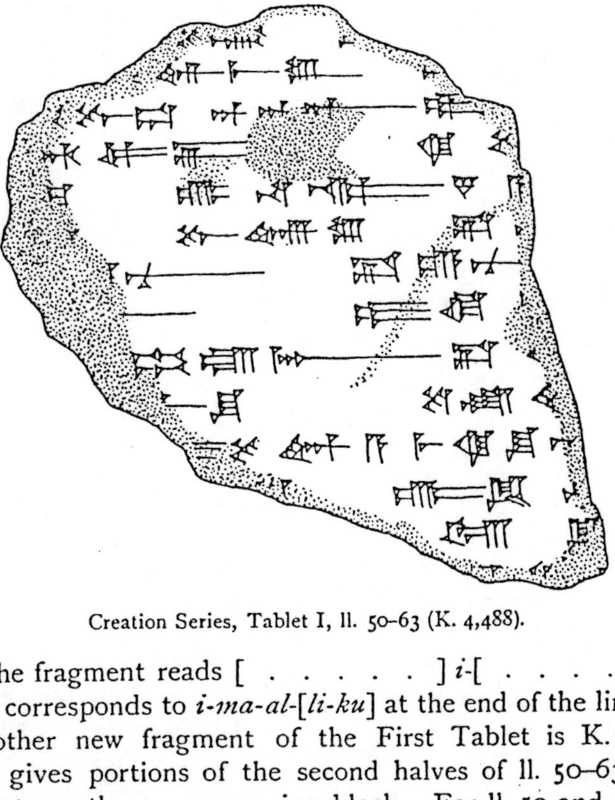

Creation Series, Tablet I, ll. 50–63 (K. 4,488).

l. 47 the fragment reads [. . . . .] *i-*[. . . . .], which corresponds to *i-ma-al-*[*li-ku*] at the end of the line.

Another new fragment of the First Tablet is K. 4,488, which gives portions of the second halves of ll. 50–63 ; for the text see the accompanying block. For ll. 50 and 51 the fragment reads [. . . . . *m*]*u-šiš l*[*u* . . . . .] and [. . . . .] *im-me-ru p*[*a-* . . . . .], and gives no variants to the text as known from other tablets ;

for l. 52 the fragment reads [. . . . . . *i*]*k-pu-du an ilāni mār*[. . .], which gives the variants *an* for *a-na* and *mār*[*ē*^pl^ *-šu*] for *m*[*a*]*-ri-e-šu* ; the fragment reads [. . . . .]*-ti-di-ir ki-šad-*[. .] for l. 53, which may probably be restored as [. . . .] *i-te-dir* (var. [.]*-ti-di-ir*) *ki-šad-*[*su*], "[. . . . his] neck was troubled." For l. 54 the fragment reads [. . . . . . *-š*]*u u-na-šak ša-a-*[. .]; it is clear, therefore, that for the restoration [*i*]*-na-ša-ku* we should read [*u*]*-na-ša-ku*, and that the duplicate 81–7–27, 80 reads *u-na-aš-ša*[*k*], as suggested on p. 11, n. 8. For l. 55 the fragment reads [. . . . .] *pu-uḫ-ru-uš-*[. .]; for the suggested reading (upon 81–7–27, 80 and No. 46,803) *bu-*[*u*]*k-ri-šu-un*, "their first-born," we should read *pu-*[*u*]*ḫ-*[1] *ri-šu-un*, "they all," or "their assembly," and the line may be translated "[Because of the evil] which they had planned together." For l. 56 the fragment reads [. . . . . *-š*]*u-nu uš-tan-nu-*[. .], and gives no variants to the text; the verb at the end of l. 57 may be restored from the fragment as *i-dul-lu*, "they lay in wait."[2] For l. 58 the fragment reads [. . . . .]*-ku-um-meš uš-*[. .], and confirms the

[1] The traces of this sign upon No. 46,803 are those of *uḫ*, rather than *uk* (see vol. ii, pl. ix).

[2] This verb occurs also in Tablet I, l. 89, which reads [. . . .] *i-du-ul-*[*li*], i.e. "[. . . .] he lay in wait," and again in l. 99, which reads [. . . . .]*-ḫi-iš ta-du-ul-l*[*i*], i.e. "[. . . .] thou hast lain in wait." The meaning of the verb *dālu* has been pointed out by Thompson in *Hebraica*, vol. xvii, p. 163, note 3, where he shows that its participle occurs in an Assyrian letter in the sense of "scout"; he also cites IV R, pl. 30*, Obv., l. 16, where *i-du-*[*ul*] (var. *i-dul*) may well have the meaning "to prowl" or "to lie in wait." On p. 13, note 11 and p. 66, note 5 it was suggested that the verb *i-ṭul-lu-šu*, which occurs in Tablet IV, ll. 63 and 64, should be transliterated *i-dul-lu-šu* and connected with the verbs in Tablet I, ll. 89 and 99. The reading *i-ṭul-lu-šu*, suggested by Delitzsch, gives good sense, but is not quite satisfactory from the omission of the doubled dental. Jensen (cf. K.B., vi, pp. 24 f., 334) reads *i-dul-lu-šu*, and also suggests for

suggested restoration of the second half of the line as [*ša-ḳu-um*]-*mi-iš uš-bu*. Of l. 59 the fragment gives the end as [. . . . . .]-*šu te-li*-[’(?)], the traces of the last sign reading HI[.]; in l. 60 it gives the variant *me-ki-šu-n*[*u*] for *me-ki-šu-un* ; of l. 61 it gives the last word as [. . . . .] *u-ḳi-š*[*u*], "[. . . .] he watched him"; in l. 62 it gives the variant *el-lu* for *el-lum*, and of l. 63 it only gives slight traces of two signs.

B. A FRAGMENT OF THE SECOND TABLET OF THE CREATION SERIES.—The fragment K. 10,008 is probably a fragment of the Creation Series, and if this is so the only place to which it is possible to assign it is the gap between ll. (85) and (104) of the Second Tablet (see above, p. 32 f.); this will be clear for the following reasons. It will be seen that the greater part of the fragment is inscribed with part of a speech of Anšar. Lines 10 and 11 read [. . . . . *ilu*]*A-nam ul i-li-’*-[. . . . .] and [. . . . .]-*mud i-dur-ma i-t*[*u-* . . . . .], and may be restored as [*aš-pur-ma ilu*]*A-nam ul i-li-’*-[*a ma-ḫar-ša*], [*ilu Nu-dim*]-*mud i-dur-ma i-t*[*u-ra ar-kiš*], "[I sent] Anu, but he could not [withstand her]; [Nudim]mud was afraid and turned [back]." Now these lines occur in Tablet III, l. 53 f., in the course of Anšar's instructions to Gaga, and again in l. 111 f., in Anšar's message as delivered by Gaga to Laḫmu and Laḫamu. Now, although the phrase *ilu Marduk abkal ilāni* occurs in the following line in each of these passages, the rest of the context upon K. 10,008 shows that it is not a duplicate of the Third Tablet. It therefore follows that the fragment cannot belong to a later tablet than the Second.

Now ll. (72)–(82) of the Second Tablet describe how Anšar sent Anu against Tiamat, and it is probable that in the gap

---

dālu the meaning "to run round," "to prowl round." In view of the use of the participle in the sense of "scout," we may perhaps render the phrase in Tablet IV, ll. 63 f. as "the gods watched him from hiding"; the repetition of the phrase emphasises Marduk's courage in setting out alone to do battle with Tiamat.

after l. 58 occurred the account of how Nudimmud was sent against Tiamat and how he turned back.[1] It therefore follows that the text of K. 10,008 must be put in the gap between ll. (85) and (104). On this assumption the greater part of the fragment (at least down to l. 12) carries on the speech of Anšar, which begins at l. (85). In this speech Anšar refers to the fate of Apsū (K. 10,008, l. 2), and the subsequent appointment of Kingu by Tiamat to lead the rebel forces[2]

[1] In view of the fact that in Tablet III, ll. 53 f. and 111 f. Anšar refers first to Anu's attempt to oppose Tiamat, and then to that of Nudimmud, it might legitimately be urged that this represents the order in which the events took place. And, as Anu's attempt is described in Tablet II, ll. (72)-(82), I was inclined, before I came across K. 10,008, to put Nudimmud's attempt in the gap between ll. (85) and (104). But the order in which Anšar refers to the setting out of Anu and Nudimmud is not necessarily chronological. Moreover, as Nudimmud had already overcome Apsū, and as it was he who brought the news of Tiamat's revolt to Anšar, it would be only natural that he should be the first to be sent against her; in support of this view it may be further noted that Nudimmud's name occurs in l. 58. On the other hand, if it be insisted that Anšar's references in Tablet III must be taken to imply that Nudimmud's setting out against Tiamat followed that of Anu, it is necessary to place the account referring to Nudimmud after the line conjecturally numbered as (85). And, as the earlier lines of K. 10,008 do not appear to refer to this episode, it follows that the gap after l. 58 is less than ten lines and that after l. (85) is greater than twenty lines; or else that K. 10,008 does not belong to the series *Enuma eliš*, but contains a variant account of the story of Creation. On the whole it appears to me preferable to suppose that the order in which the events are referred to in Anšar's speech is not to be taken as chronological, but as leading up to a climax; he says, "Anu I sent, but he could not withstand her; and even Nudimmud was afraid and turned back."

[2] With the phrase *mi-lam-mi eš-rit* in l. 4 may be compared Tablet I, ll. 118 and 126, and the parallel passages. The apparent reference to ten in place of eleven monsters is noteworthy.

and carry on the war against the gods (l. 7 f.); he then describes how he sent Anu and Nudimmud against Tiamat, and how they could not withstand her and turned back (l. 10 f.), and in the following line (l. 12) he either begins his appeal to Marduk, or, as appears to me more probable,

Fragment of the Second Tablet of the Creation Series (K. 10,008).

states his intention of appealing to Marduk to become the champion of the gods. The fragment may be transliterated as follows:—

1. [. . . . . . . *i*]*š* - [*pu*]*r* [. . . . .]
2. [. . . . . . .] *Apsû* *u*-[. . . . .]
3. [. . . . .] *it* - *tar* - *ru* - *šu* [. . . . .]

4. [. . . . .] *mi - lam - mi eš - ri*[*t* . . . . . .]
5. [. . . .]-*ku* (?) -*ma-'-ni ḫum* (?) -*mu-r*[*a-* . . .]
6. [. . . . .]-*bi ap-ša-na la sa-ki-pa* [. . . . .]
7. [. . . . . -*n*]*u* [ilu]*Kin-gu šu-uš-*[*ḳu-u* . . . .]
8. [. . . . . .] - *ma Ti - a - ma - t*[*i* . . . . . .]
9. [. . . . . .] - *ak lib - bi - šu i* - [. . . . . .]
10. [*aš - pur - ma* [ilu]]*A - nam ul i - li - ' -* [*a ma - ḫar - ša*]
11. [[ilu]*Nu - dim*] - *mud i - dur - ma i - t*[*u - ra ar - kiš*]
12. [. . . [ilu]*Mardu*]*k abkal ilāni*[pl] [. . . . . .]
13. [. . . . . .] *ip - ti - ḳu k*[*u* - . . . .]
14. [. . . . . .] *u - sa - an - ni* [. . . . . . .]
15. [. . . . .] *irpitu* [. . . . .]
16. [. . . . .] *bul - li* - [. . . . .]
17. [. . . . .] *ma - lu* - [. . . . .]
18. [. . . . .]

With l. 13 we may compare *lip-ti-ḳu ku-ru-na* in Tablet III, l. 9, and *ip-ti-ḳu* [*ku-ru-na*] in l. 134; and with *u-sa-an-ni* we may compare Tablet III, l. 135. These phrases upon K. 10,008 may be explained by supposing that Anšar's appeal to Marduk was accompanied by the mixing and drinking of wine.

C. Two fragments of the Fifth Tablet of the Creation Series.—The first eleven lines of the fragment K. 13,774 correspond (with some interesting variants) to the text of the Fifth Tablet, ll. 6–16; while the last three lines of the fragment give a variant text to that found in ll. 17–19 upon other copies of the Fifth Tablet. The unimportant variants may be first noted as follows: in l. 6 K. 13,774 gives the variant *ru* as the last syllable of [ilu]*Ni-bi-ri*, and for *ana* reads *a-na*; in l. 10 it reads *u-dan-ni-na* for *ud-dan-ni-na*; in l. 13 it reads *šuk-nat* for *šu-uk-nat*; in l. 14 it reads *ag*[*ī*] for *a-gi-*[*e*]; and in l. 16 it reads *a-na* for *ana.* In l. 8 it gives a more interesting variant, reading [ilu]*A-num* in place of ^{ilu}*E-a*; that is to say, l. 8, according to this version, would read, "He set the station of Bēl and Anu along with him," in place of "He set the station of Bēl and Ea along with him." For a further discussion of this reading, see the Introduction.

In l. 12 occurs a still more interesting variant; according to K. 13,774 the first half of the line runs [. . . *kak*]*kaba-šu uš-te-pa-a*, "[. . . .] his star he caused to shine forth," in place of ^{ilu}*Nannar-ru uš-te-pa-a*, "The Moon-god

Creation Series, Tablet V, ll. 6–19 (K. 13,774).

he caused to shine forth." As the beginning and end of the line are wanting, it would be rash to conjecturally restore them; but it may be regarded as certain that the phrase *šuk-nat mu-ši*, "a being of the night," in l. 13 refers to the Moon-god, and that the lines which follow contain Marduk's charge to him. In the course of Marduk's address to the Moon-god, in ll. 17 and 18, which upon other copies of the Fifth Tablet contain directions with regard to the 7th and 14th days of the month, K. 13,774 gives the variant readings

(17) [. . . . . .] *IV* ^{KAN} *V ūmu* [. . . . . .] and (18) [. . . . . .] ^{KAN} *V ūmu* [. . . . . .]. The traces of l. 19 upon K. 13,774 do not correspond to the text of this line as already known.

K. 11,641 is part of another copy of the Fifth Tablet, and contains on its obverse parts of ll. 14–22, and on its reverse

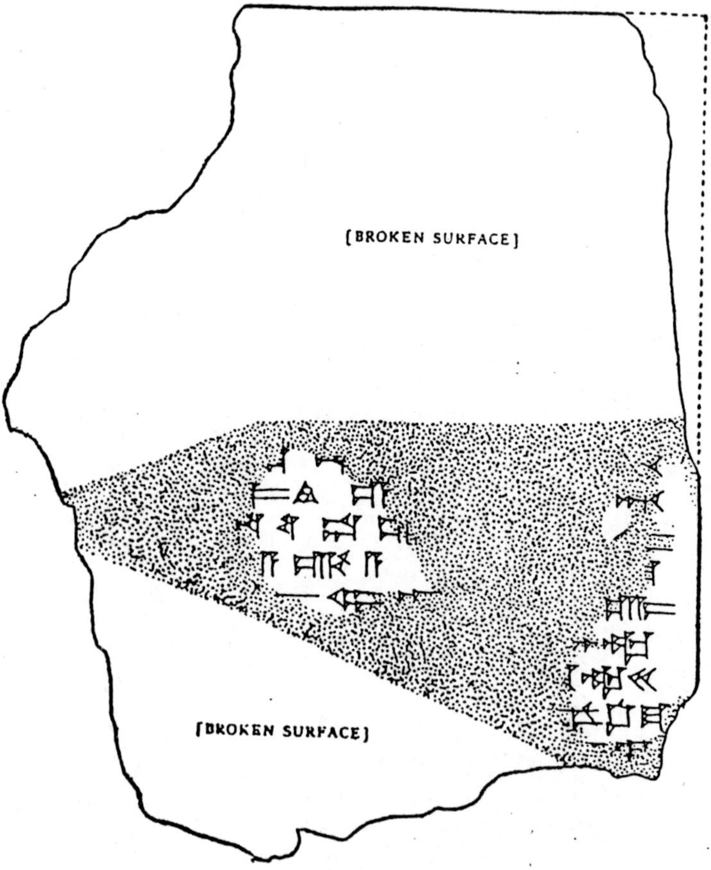

Creation Series, Tablet V, ll. 14-22 (K. 11,641, Obverse).

parts of lines which may be conjecturally numbered as ll. (128)–(140). The information which the obverse of the fragment supplies with regard to the text of the Fifth Tablet is not very great, and may be noted as follows: the traces of ll. 14 and 17 upon K. 11,641 give no variants nor restorations; for l. 15 the fragment reads [. . . . . . -*p*]*a-ḫi e*-[. . . . .]-*ti*, and proves that the suggested restoration

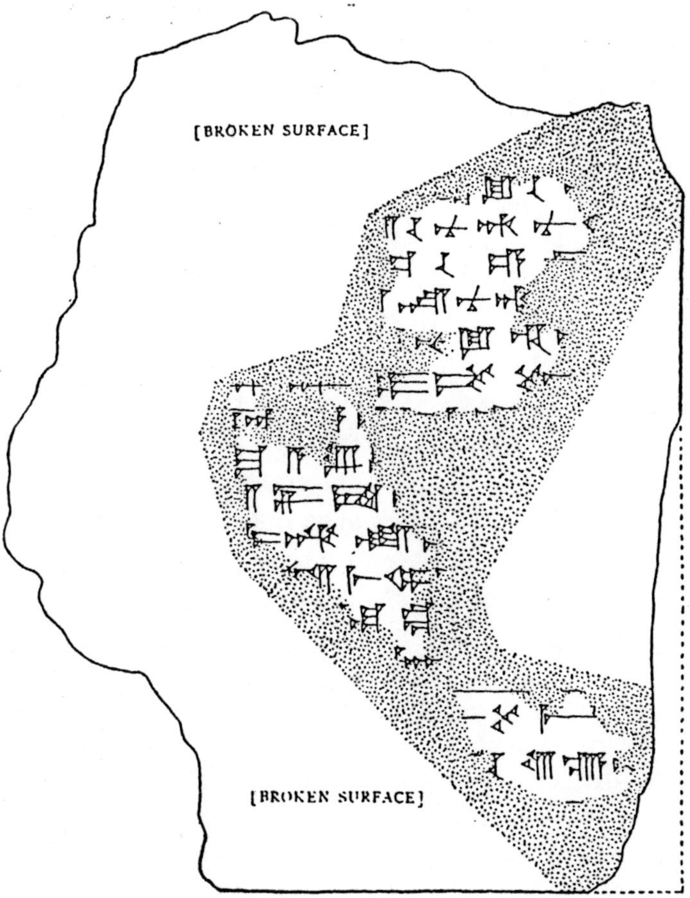

Creation Series, Tablet V, the last thirteen lines (K. 11,641, Reverse).

i-na] is incorrect; the end of this line should read *e*-[*li*] *na-a-ti*, which gives the same sense as before. In l. 16 the fragment gives the variant [*a*]-*na* for *ana*; in l. 18 for *meš-l*[*i*] it gives the variant *mi-i* (?)-[. . . .]; in l. 19 it gives traces of the last character but one in the line, which does not correspond to those given by K. 3,567 + K. 8,588 ; at the end of l. 20 it gives the variant reading [*a*]*r-ka-niš*, and it is possible that K. 3,567, etc., read *ar-k*[*a-nu*]-*uš*; in l. 21 it confirms the suggested restoration of the sign *ma* at the end of the line; and in l. 22 it gives slight traces of the last two characters in the line.

The reverse of K. 11,641 has already been used on p. 84 f., in the transliteration and translation of the end of the Fifth Tablet. On p. 85, note 3, it is pointed out that the last six lines contain the complaint of the gods to Marduk in consequence of which he conceived the plan of creating mankind. It may here be noted that of the last line of the tablet, K. 11,641 seems to give traces of MEŠ, the plural sign ;

A possible fragment of the Creation Series (79-7-8, 47).

this may have been followed by a pronominal suffix, *ka*, or may have immediately preceded the word *ni-i-nu* preserved by the fragment K. 8,526.

D. TWO POSSIBLE FRAGMENTS OF THE CREATION SERIES.—In *Cuneiform Texts*, part xiii, pl. 24, the text is given of a small fragment, K. 12,000 *b*, of which the following is a transliteration : (1) [. . . . . . .] (2) [. . .] *a-n*[*a* . . . . . .] (3) [. . .] *um-ma* [. . . .] (4) [. . . . .] *Ti-amat uš*-[. . . . . .] (5) [. . .] *in-na-at*-[. . . . . .] (6) [*a*]*r-nu-uš-šu lu*[. . . . . .] (7) [*i-p*]*u-lu-šu* [. . . . .] (8) [. . . . .]. From the style of the writing and the mention of Tiamat, it is possible that the fragment belongs to the Creation Series.

Another possible fragment of the Creation Series is 79-7-8,

47, the text of which is given in the block on p. 194. In the character of the clay and the style of writing it closely resembles K. 11,641, which is a fragment of a copy of the Fifth Tablet (see above, pp. 192 ff.); while the mention of the gods ^{ilu}*La-ḫa-mu* in l. 2, *An-šar* in l. 3, and [^{ilu}*B*]*ēl* in l. 4 is in favour of its being a fragment of a tablet of the series.[1]

[1] Reference may also be made to the fragment R. 982 + 80–7–18, 178, of which the first few lines of the obverse are given in transliteration by Delitzsch, *Weltschöpfungsepos*, p. 110 f., note 1; for the text, see *Cuneiform Texts*, part xiii, pl. 31. In the character of its clay and in its style of writing this fragment resembles tablets of the Creation Series; cf. also l. 2 f. of the reverse, *ina ki-rib apsī ib-n*[*a* . . . . .], *ib-ni-šu-ma* ^{ilu}*E-a* [. . . . .]. The fragments of legends, K. 7,067 and K. 8,572 have been catalogued by Bezold as possibly belonging to tablets of the series *E-nu-ma e-liš*, and their texts are therefore given in *Cun. Txts.*, part xiii, pl. 31; the first line preserved by K. 7,067 probably reads ^{ilu}*E-a ina* [*ap*]*sī* [. . . . .], followed by the line *ilāni*^{pl} *rabūti*^{pl} *im-tal-ku-ma* [. . . . .], while the first line of K. 8,572 reads [. . . . .]-*da a-me-lu šum-šu i*-[. . . . .], but the grounds are slender for assigning them to the Creation Series. To this series the minute fragment K. 11,048 (see *Cun. Txts.*, part xiii, pl. 31) is assigned (with a query) by Bezold in the *Catalogue*, vol. v, p. 2,078, presumably from the character of the writing, unless K. 11,048 is a misprint. The fragment K. 12,000*c* (*Cun. Txts.*, part xiii, pl. 31) is also assigned by Bezold to the series (see *Catalogue*, vol. v, p. 2,078). Its colophon states that it is the First Tablet of a series styled *E-n*[*u-ma* . . . . .], but as the traces of the last four lines of the text do not correspond to the last four lines of the First Tablet of the series *Enuma eliš*, and as the catch-line does not correspond to the first line of the Second Tablet, it is clear that K. 12,000*c* is a fragment of the First Tablet of some other series. K. 10,791 (*Cun. Txts.*, part xiii, pl. 31) is another fragment which Bezold suggests may belong to the series *Enuma eliš*, presumably from the occurrence of the verbs *ib-ba-ni* in ll. 2 and 3 and *ib-ba-nu-u* in l. 4. As, however, it belongs to a text which is arranged in columns and divided into sections, it is clear that it does not belong to the Creation Series.

E. A REFERENCE TO "THE WATERS THAT WERE ABOVE" AND "THE WATERS THAT WERE BENEATH" THE FIRMAMENT.—The text may here be given of an interesting fragment, S. 2,013, which has been copied by Bezold (cf. Jensen in Schrader's *Keilins. Bibl.*, vi, p. 307) and by Delitzsch (cf. *Handwörterbuch*, p. xii), but has, I believe, not yet been published. If it is part (as is hardly probable) of the Creation Series, the reference to the upper and the lower Tiamat in l. 10 f. shows that it cannot belong to an earlier tablet than the Fifth; while in general style it appears to resemble the addresses found on the Seventh Tablet, rather

Fragment referring to the Upper Tiamat and the Lower Tiamat (S. 2,013).

than to be in narrative form. It will be seen, however, from the accompanying block that the lines are divided in writing into halves; this is characteristic of several neo-Babylonian copies of tablets of the Creation Series, but does not occur upon any of the Assyrian copies that have yet been identified. The text of the fragment may be transliterated as follows:—

1. [. . . . .] [. . . . .] *rabîti*[(*ti*?) . . . . .]
2. [. . . . .] [. . . . .] *tu u* [. . . . .]
3. [. . . . .] [. . . *a*]*g ne šu* [. . . . .]
4. [. . . . .] [. . . .] *ḳabli u ta-ḫa-*[*zi* . . .]
5. [. . . . .] [. . . .]*-tu iz-zi-tu* [. . . . .]
6. [. . . . .] [*ma*]*ḫar bît ziḳḳurrati*[1] *ib-ba-*[. . .]
7. [. . . . .] *nam - ru šal - ba - bu* [. . . . .]
8. [. . . . .] *ša šamê*(*e*) *ru-ḳu-u-ti* [. . . . .]
9. [. . . . .] *ša Ḫu - bur pal-ka-ti* [. . . . .]
10. [. . . . .] *ša ina Ti-amat e-li-ti* [. . . .]
11. [. . . . .] *ša ina Ti-amat šap-li-ti* [. . . .]
12. [. . . . .] [. . . .] *u-ri-kis ka-l*[*a-mu* (?) . .]
13. [. . . . .] [. . . . .] *s*[*a* (?)]*-k*[*ip* . . . . .]

For a discussion of the title *Ḫubur* and of the phrases *Ti-amat e-li-ti* and *Ti-amat šap-li-ti*, see the Introduction.

F. ANŠAR AND THE HISTORY OF CREATION.—A fragment, which it has been thought may perhaps belong to one of the later tablets of the Creation Series,[2] is K. 3,445 + R. 396 (cf. *Cun. Texts*, part xiii, pl. 24 f.)[3]; the smaller fragment K. 14,949 (op. cit., pl. 24) is a duplicate. Lines 1–26 of the obverse contain only traces of the beginnings of lines, among

[1] Possibly read [*ma*]*ḫar E-igi-e-nir*.

[2] Cf. George Smith, *Chaldean Account of Genesis*, pp. 67 ff., Bezold, *Catalogue*, vol. ii, p. 534, and Delitzsch, *Weltschöpfungsepos*, pp. 19, 51 ff., 87 f., 109 f. The text of the reverse of K. 3,445 was given by S. A. Smith in *Miscellaneous Texts*, pl. 10.

[3] In shape and writing the fragment resembles some of the tablets of the Creation Series. It may be noted that each tenth line of the text is indicated in the margin of the tablet by the figure "10." Thus, on the Obv., ll. 2, 12, 22, and 32 are so marked, and on the Rev., ll. 7, 16, 25, and 35; on the Rev. sometimes two lines of the text are written in one line of the tablet.

which it may be noted that l. 11 possibly begins with the name of Marduk. From l. 27 onwards the obverse reads: (27) *ul-tu u-me u*-[. . . . .] (28) *ma-aṣ-rat mu-ši u im*-[*mi* . . . . .] (29) *ru-pu-uš-tu ša Ti-a*[*mat* . . . . .] (30) *Anšar ip-ta*-[1][. . . . .] (31) *ik-ṣur-ma ana* [. . . . .] (32) *te-bi ša-a-ri* [. . . . .] (33) *šu-uk-tur im*-[. . . . .] (34) *u-ad-di-ma r*[*a*- . . . . .] (35) *iš-kun ḳaḳḳada* [. . . . .] (36) *naḳ-bu up-te-it*-[. . . . .] (37) *ip-te-e-ma n*[*a*- . . . . .] (38) *na-ḫi-ri ša up*-[. . . . .] (39) *iš-pu-uk n*[*a*- . . . . .] (40) *nam-ba-'*-[. . . . .]. The occurrence of the names of Anšar (l. 30) and possibly of Marduk (l. 11), the reference to "the slayer," or "the breadth," of Tiamat (l. 29) and possibly to her head (l. 35), and the mention of "springs" (l. 36f.), "deeps" (l. 40), and monsters of the deep ("dolphins?") in l. 38, would not be inconsistent with the fragment forming part of the Fifth Tablet of the Creation Series.

The reverse of the fragment reads as follows:—(1) [. . . . .] (2) *ḫa-šur-ru* [. . . . .] (3) [. . . . .]-*ki-ik-ma* [. . . . .] (4) [. . . . .]-*me šar*-[. . . . .] (5) [. . . . .] *ilu Adad* [. . . . .] (6) *iš-kun eli* [. . . . .] (7) *uš-bar šul-me* [. . . . .] (8) *ul-tu me-lam-me* [. . . . .] (9) *a-za-mil-šu apsū ra-šub*-[*bu* . . . . .] (10) [2] *ina e-ma-ši aš-ša*[*k*- . . . . .] (11) *ina si-ma-ak-ki-šu* [. . . . .] (12) *ilāni pl ma-la ba-šu*-[*u* . . . . .] (13) *ilu Laḫ-mu u* [3] *ilu* [[4] . . . . .] (14) *i-pu-šu-ma pa* (?)-[. . . . .] (15) *pa-na-a-ma An-šar* [. . . . .] (16) *i ilu Sin ša*[*r*- . . . . .] (17) *ša-nu-u iz-zak-ru* [. . . . .] (18) *ilu* [. . . . .] (19) *e-nu-ma a-na*

[1] The sign following *ta* is not *ni*, so that the reading *ib-ta-ni* is impossible.

[2] The duplicate K. 14,949 gives a variant reading for this line: *šu*-[. . . . .].

[3] Omitted by K. 14,949.

[4] The traces of the first sign of the name upon K. 14,949 suggest *La*, i.e. *ilu L*[*a-ḫa-mu*].

[. . . . . .] (20) *pī(?)-ka ma-ak-tum ki-*[. . . . . .] (21) *ul-tu u-me at-ta* [. . . . . .] (22) *mim-mu-u at-ta ta-ḳab-bu* [. . . . . .] (23) *An-šar pa-a-šu epuš(uš)-ma i-ḳab-bi : a-na* [ilu][. . . . . .] (24) *e-li-nu ap-si-i šu-bat* [. . . . . .] (25) *mi-iḫ-rit E-šar-ra ša ab-nu-u a-na-ku :* [. . . . . .] (26) *šap-liš aš-ra-ta-u-dan-ni-n*[*a* . . . .] (27) *lu-pu uš-ma bīta lu šu-bat* [. . . . . .] (28) *kir-bu-uš-šu ma-ḫa-za-šu lu-šar-šid-ma :* [. . . . .] (29) *e-nu-ma ul-tu apsī i-be-*[. . . . . .] (30) *aš-ru* [. . . . . .] *nu-bat-ta* [. . . . . .] (31) *e-*[. . . . . .]*-pat ṣilli* [. . . . . .] (32) *aš-r*[*u* . . . . . . *n*]*u-bat-ta kun-* [. . . . . .]*-ku-nu* [. . . . . .] (33) *ḳ*[*i-* . . . . .]*-ki bītāti ilāni*[pl] *rabūti*[pl] [. . . . . .] *ni-ip-pu-*[. . . . . .] (34) [. . . . . .] *abu-šu an-na-a* [. . . . . .]*-a-šu* [. . . . . .] (35) [ilu][. . . . . .]*-lu-ka-ma : eli mimma ša ib-na-a ḳa-ta-a-ka* [. . . . . .] (36) *man-*[*nu* . . .]*-ka i-ši: eli ḳaḳ-ḳa-ru ša ib-na-a ḳa-ta-a-*[*ka* . . . .] (37) *man-*[*nu* . . . . . .]*-ka i-ši :* [alu]*Aššur*[KI] *ša taz-ku-ra mu(?)-*[. . . . . .] (38) *aš-*[. . . . . .]*-ta-ni i-di da-ri-šam* [. . . . . .] (39) [. . . . . .]*-tuk-ka-ni li-bil-lu-ni* [. . . . . .] (40) *ṣ*[*i-* . . . . . .]*-ni : ma-na-ma šip-ri-ni ša-ni* (41) *aš-ru* [. . . . . .]*-na-aḫ ur-* [. . . . . .] (42) *iḫ-du-*[. . . . . .] (43) *ilāni*[pl] *šu-*[. . . . . .] (44) *ša i-du* [. . . . . .] (45) *ip-te-e-* [. . . . . .].

The mention of Laḫmu in l. 13 of the reverse may also be cited in favour of the fragment belonging to the Creation Series, while the references to Adad (l. 5) and to the city of Aššur (l. 37) are not necessarily inconsistent with this view. Lines 23 ff., however, can scarcely be reconciled with the end of the Fourth Tablet of the Creation Series. These lines read: "(23) Anšar opened his mouth and spake, and unto the god [. . . . he addressed the word]: (24) 'Above the Deep, the dwelling of [. . . .], (25) opposite E-šara which I have created, [. . . .] (26) I have strengthened the regions in the depth [. . . .] (27) I will build a house that it may be a dwelling for [. . . .] (28) In the midst thereof will I found his district (lit. city, cf. Tabl. IV, l. 145) and [. . . .].'" In this speech Anšar, and not Marduk, appears as the god of creation, which is scarcely in harmony with the general tenour of the Creation Series. Moreover, in l. 25 Anšar definitely states that he created E-šara, whereas in Tablet IV, ll. 144-146, it is related that Marduk, and not Anšar, created E-šara. Until more of the text of the Fifth and Sixth Tablets is recovered, it would be rash to assert that the fragment cannot belong to the Creation Series; meanwhile, in view of the inconsistencies noted, it is preferable to assume that it does not form part of that work, but is a fragment of a closely parallel version of the story in which Anšar plays a more prominent part.

G. THE RIVER OF CREATION.—On p. 128 f. a transliteration and translation are given of an address to a mystical

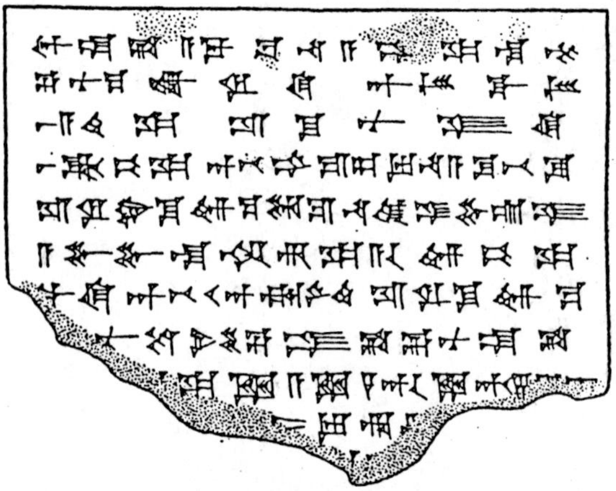

Fragment of an incantation-tablet containing an address to the River of Creation (82-9-18, 5,311, Obverse).

river of creation, which forms the opening lines of incantations upon the reverse of S. 1,704 and the obverse of 82-9-18, 5,311. As the text of these fragments has not been previously published, the obverse of the one and the reverse of the other are given in the accompanying blocks. It will be noted that ll. 1–8 of 82-9-18, 5,311 correspond to ll. 1–7 of

S. 1,704. The eighth line of S. 1,704, which concludes the direct address, or invocation, to the river, is omitted by 82-9-18, 5,311, and from this point onward it would seem that the tablets cease to be duplicates. The insertion of the common formula, given in the ninth line of 82-9-18, 5,311, would not by itself prove this, but what remains of the tenth line of 82-9-18, 5,311 does not correspond to the ninth line

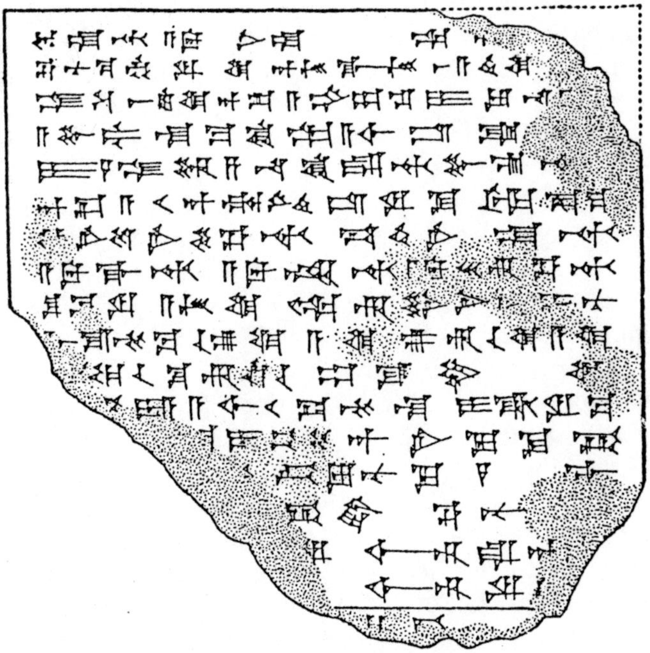

Fragment of an incantation-tablet containing an address to the River of Creation (S. 1,704, Reverse).

of S. 1,704. We are justified, therefore, in treating the address to the river as an independent fragment, which has been employed as the introduction to two different incantations.

H. THE SUPPOSED INSTRUCTIONS TO MAN AFTER HIS CREATION.—The tablet K. 3,364 (*Cun. Txts.*, pt. xiii, pl. 29 f.) was thought by George Smith to contain the instructions given to the first man and woman after their creation. In

The Chaldean Account of Genesis, p. 80, he says, "The obverse[1] of this tablet is a fragment of the address from the deity to the newly created man on his duties to his god"; and a little later on he adds, "The reverse of the tablet appears, so far as the sense can be ascertained, to be addressed to the woman, the companion of the man, informing her of her duties towards her partner." In his *Babylonische Weltschöpfungsepos*, pp. 19 f., 54 f., 88 f., and 111 f., Delitzsch also treats the tablet as forming part of the Creation Series.[2] The recovered portion of the Sixth Tablet of the Creation Series, however, and the Neo-Babylonian duplicate of K. 3,364, the text of which is published in vol. ii, pls. lxiv–lxvi (No. 33,851), together disprove the suggested connection of K. 3,364 with the Creation Series. The reasons on which this conclusion is based may be briefly stated as follows:—(1) The recovered portion of the Sixth Tablet indicates that the description of the creation of man there given was very similar to the account furnished by Berossus; and it follows that the greater part of the text must have been in the form of narrative. If Marduk gave man any instructions after his creation, these can have occupied only a small part of the tablet. But both the obverse and reverse of K. 3,364 contain moral precepts, and the same is the case with columns ii and iii of the new duplicate No. 33,851.[3] For such a long series of moral instructions there is no room upon the Sixth Tablet of the Creation Series. (2) Col. ii of No. 33,851 refers to certain acts which are good, and to others which are not good,

[1] The side of the tablet which George Smith refers to as the obverse is really the reverse; this is rendered certain by the duplicate No. 33,851.

[2] In my *Babylonian Religion and Mythology*, p. 82 f., I also provisionally adopted this view.

[3] In col. i of this tablet only the ends of lines are preserved, and in col. iv a part of the colophon.

in the eyes of Šamaš.[1] This is quite consistent with the character of Šamaš as the judge of heaven and earth, but he does not appear in this character in the Creation Series, where he is referred to merely as the sun which Marduk created and set upon his course. (3) In the duplicate, No. 33,851, the text is arranged in columns, two on each side of the tablet. This fact in itself is sufficient to prove that the composition has nothing to do with the series *Enuma eliš*. The text upon tablets of the Creation Series is never arranged in columns, but each line is written across the tablet from edge to edge. This characteristic applies not only to the copies of the Creation Series from Kuyunjik, but also to the Babylonian copies of all periods, and even to the rough "practice-tablets" on which students wrote out extracts from the poem.

The text inscribed upon K. 3,364 and No. 33,851 is, in fact, a long didactic composition containing a number of moral precepts, and has nothing to do with the Creation Series.[2] The composition in itself is of considerable interest, however, for enough of it remains to show that it indicates a high standard of morality.

---

[1] Cf. l. 9, *ul ṭa-a-bi eli* [ilu] *Šamaš i-*[. . . . . .]; and l. 13, *ṭa-a-bi eli* [ilu] *Šamaš i-*[. . . . . .]. The signs AN-UD in these passages are clearly to be rendered [ilu] *Šamaš*, and not *ilu-tu*, "godhead," in the sense in which *ilu-u-ti* occurs in K. 3,364, Rev., l. 14.

[2] It may be noted that the phrase *a-kil kar-ṣi* (K. 3,364, Rev., l. 5, and No. 33,851, col. iii, l. 4), which has been thought by some to be the title of a power of evil termed "the Calumniator" (cf. Bezold, *Catalogue*, vol. ii, p. 526), is not a proper name or title, but should be rendered simply as "a slanderer."

III.

On some traces of the History of Creation in Religious and Astrological Literature.

THERE is abundant evidence to prove that under the late Assyrian kings, and during the Neo-Babylonian and Persian periods, the history of the Creation as told upon the Seven Tablets of the series *Enuma eliš* was widely read and studied, and there can be no doubt that it exercised a considerable influence on the religious literature which continued to gather around Marduk's name. In the fragmentary hymns and prayers which have come down to us, however, it is difficult to determine how far the priestly and popular conceptions of Marduk were influenced by the actual story of the Creation as we know it, and to what extent they were moulded by earlier legends and beliefs, and by Marduk's own position as the native god of Babylon. That actual phrases from the Seventh Tablet of the Creation Series were made use of in other similar compositions is sufficiently proved by the fragments published at the end of Appendix I; and in view of this fact we may perhaps hear echoes from the earlier tablets of the series in some of the phrases and attributes applied to Marduk in the contemporary religious texts. It would be impossible within the limits of the present work to attempt an exhaustive treatment of this subject, but, as a striking instance of such allusions to the Creation story, reference may here be made to the fragment K. 3,351, which, I believe, has not hitherto been translated.[1]

[1] A rather rough copy of this tablet is included in Craig's *Religious Texts*, pl. 43. As several signs, including l. 4, are there omitted, and others are incorrectly copied, the text of the obverse is given in the block on p. 205.

The upper part of the tablet is broken and rubbed, but the greater part of the text is well preserved and clearly written, and may be transliterated as follows :—

1. [. . . . *e*]-*til-lum mār* ^{ilu} *E-a* [. . . .] *mut-tal-lum*

2. [. . .] *k*[*iš-šat*] *šamē*(*e*) *u irṣiti*(*ti*) *m*[*u*]-*šim ši-ma-a-ti*

3. [. . . . .] *bi-nu-tu*

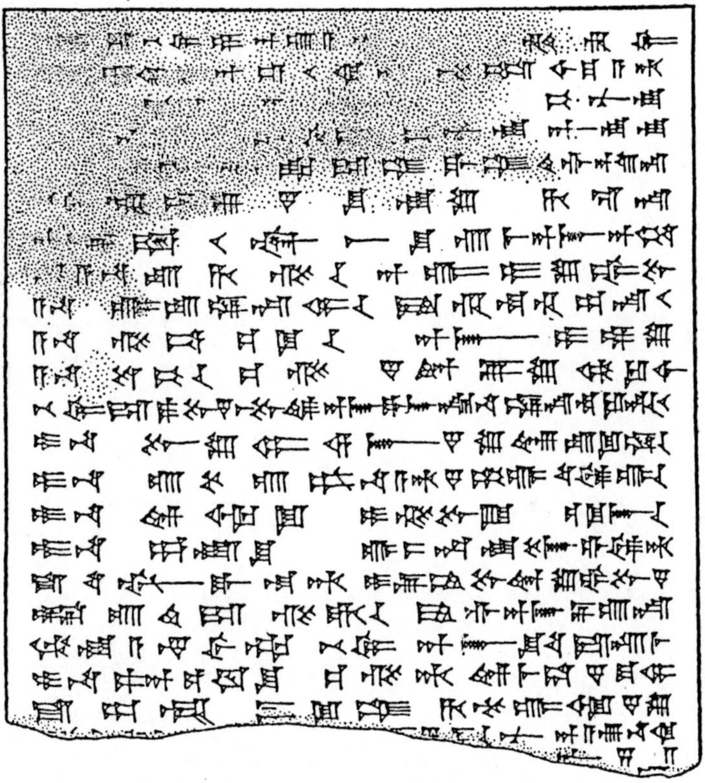

Part of a Hymn to Marduk (K. 3,351).

4. [. . . . .] *b*[*i*] - *n*[*u*] - *tu* ^{ilu} *Tu - tu*

5. [. . . . .] *šar-ra-tum rabītum*(*tum*) *ḫi-rat* ^{ilu} *Šag-zu*

6. [*b*]*e* - *l*[*um*] ^{ilu} *B*[*ēl ru*]*bū ša šu - tu - ru ḫa - si - su*

7. [. . .] *ḳabli u taḫāzi ina ḳāt abkalli ilāni*^{pl} ^{ilu} *Marduk*

8. [*š*]*a a-na ta-ḫa-zi-šu šamū(u) i-ru-ub-bu*
9. *a-na u-ta-az-zu-mi-šu id-dal-la-ḫu ap-su-u*
10. *a-na zi-ḳip kakki-šu ilāni*^pl^ *i-tur-ru*
11. *a-na te-bi-šu iz-zi ša-'-ir-ru ul ib-ši*
12. *be-lum ra-aš-bu ša ina pu-ḫur ilāni*^pl^ *rabūti*^pl^ *šin-na-as-su la ib-ba-šu-u*
13. *i-na bu-ru-mi ellūti*^pl^ *ša-ru-uḫ ta-lu-uk-šu*
14. *i-na E-kur bīt tak-na-a-ti ša-ḳu-u par-ṣu u-šu*
15. *i-na im-ḫul-lu i-nam-bu-ṭu kakkē*^pl^*-šu*
16. *i-na nab-li-šu u-tab-ba-tu šadāni*^pl^ *mar-ṣu-ti*
17. *ša tam-tim gal-la-ti i-sa-am-bu-' ru-up-pu-ša*
18. *apil E-šar-ra zi-kir-šu ḳar-rad ilāni*^pl^ *ni-bit-su*
19. *ul-tu a-sur-rak-ka be-lum ilāni*^pl^ *šu-ut da-ad-me*
20. *i-na pa-an* ^iṣu^*ḳašti-šu iz-zi-ti im-me-du ša-ma-mi*
21. *ša* AB-MAḪ *ṣal-lu-tum ḫa-mu-u u ša-ru*
22. [. . . . .] *š*[*a*] *ka*[*li*]*-šu-nu* ^ilu^*A-nun-na-ki*
23. [. . . . .] ^ilu^*Igigi*
24. [. . . .]

The fragment contains the opening lines of a hymn to Marduk,[1] of which the following is a translation :—

1. O lord [. . . .], son of Ea, the exalted [. . . .],
2. [Who . . . .] the [hosts] of heaven and earth, who ordaineth destinies !

[1] The composition is addressed to Marduk, who is named in l. 7 and is referred to in the three preceding lines under his titles Tutu, Šagzu, and Bēl; moreover, in l. 1 he is termed the "son of Ea." The Reverse of the tablet contains the last five lines of Ašur-bani-pal's common colophon.

3. [. . . . . the . . . .] offspring,
4. [. . . . . the . . . . off]spring is Tutu!
5. [. . . . .], the great queen, the consort of Sagzu!
6. O lord Bēl, thou prince, who art mighty in understanding!
7. [The . . . .] of war and battle is in the hand of Marduk, the director of the gods,
8. At whose battle heaven quaked,
9. At whose wrath the Deep is troubled!
10. At the point of his weapon the gods turned back!
11. To his furious attack there was no opponent!
12. O mighty lord, to whom there is no rival in the assembly of the great gods!
13. In the bright firmament of heaven his course is supreme!
14. In E-kur, the temple of true worship, exalted is his decree!
15. With the evil wind his weapons blaze forth,
16. With his flame steep mountains are destroyed!
17. He overwhelmeth the expanse of the billowing ocean!
18. The Son of E-šara is his name, the Hero of the gods is his title!
19. From the depth[1] is he lord of the gods of human habitations!
20. Before his terrible bow the heavens stand fast!
21. . . . plague and destruction, and tempest,
22. [. . . . .] of all the Aunnaki,
23. [. . . . .] the Igigi!
24. [. . . . .]

[1] In this phrase we may probably see an antithesis to "the heavens" in the following line; for other passages in which the word *asurrakku* occurs, cf. Delitzsch, *Handwörterbuch*, p. 111, and Muss-Arnolt, *Concise Dict.*, p. 121.

It will be noticed that in ll. 8–11 the hymn describes the quaking of the heavens at Marduk's battle, the trouble of the Deep at his wrath, and the flight of the gods from the point of his weapon. We have here an unmistakable reference to the battle of Marduk with Tiamat, and the subsequent flight of the gods, her helpers. The reference in l. 12 to Marduk's supremacy in the assembly of the gods does not necessarily refer to the Seventh Tablet of the Creation Series, but the *imḫullu*, or "evil wind," in l. 15, and Marduk's "flame" in l. 16 are clearly reminiscences of the Fourth Tablet, ll. 45 and 96, and l. 40; and in "the billowing ocean (*tam-tim*)" in l. 17 we may possibly see a reference to Tiamat. Finally, the mention of Marduk's bow in l. 20 may be compared with the Fourth Tablet, l. 35, and with the fragment of the Fifth Tablet which describes the translation of the bow to heaven as the Bow-star (see above, p. 82 f.).

Such references to the Creation story are of considerable interest, but they do not add anything to the facts concerning Marduk's character which may be gathered from the Creation Series itself. An additional interest, however, attaches to some astrological fragments which I have come across, inasmuch as they show that at a late period of Babylonian history the story of the fight between Marduk and Tiamat had received a very definite astrological interpretation. One of the fragments exhibits Tiamat as a star or constellation in the neighbourhood of the ecliptic, and, moreover, furnishes an additional proof of a fact which has long been generally recognized, viz., the identification of the monster-brood of Tiamat with at any rate some of the signs of the Zodiak.

The most important of the astrological fragments above referred to is made up of three pieces, Nos. 55,466, 55,486, and 55,627, which I have rejoined, and its text is published in vol. ii, pls. lxvii–lxxii. It measures 5¼ in. by 3⅞ in., and is part of a large tablet which was inscribed with two, or possibly three, broad columns of writing on each side. The fragment of the tablet recovered gives considerable portions of the first and last columns of the text, as well as traces of the second column on the obverse and of the last column but one on the reverse. The colophon, which possibly contained the date at which the tablet was inscribed, has not been preserved, but from the character of the writing and the shape of the tablet it may be concluded that it does not belong to an earlier period than that of the Arsacidæ; it may possibly be assigned to as late a date as the first century B.C.

From the first section which has been preserved of col. i it is clear that the text is closely connected with the story of the Creation. This will be apparent from the following transliteration and translation of the portions of ll. 1–7 which have been preserved: (1) [. . . . . .]*-nu ša ḳātē*[II]*-šu mul-mul is-si-ma* [. . . . . .] (2) [. . . . . . [ilu]*Kin*]*-gu ḫa-mi-ri-šu ina kakki la ga-ba-al i*[*t*]*-ta-kis-a*[*m*]*-m*[*a*] (3) [. . . . . .] *Ti-amat ik-mu-u il-ḳu-u šarru-us-su* (4) [. . . . . . *dup*]*šīmāti*[pl] *ša* [ilu]*Kin-gu it-mu-ḫu ḳa-tu-uš-šu* (5) [. . . . . .]*-nu ib-ni-ma bāb ap-si-i u-ša-aṣ-bit* (6) [. . . . . .]*-mu ana la ma-ši-e ip-še-e-ti Ti-amat* (7) [. . . . . .] *u-kal-lam ab-bi-e-šu*, "(1) [. . . . . .] whose hands removed the Spear, and [. . . . . .] (2) [. . . . . . Kin]gu, her spouse, with a weapon not of war was cut off, and (3) [. . . . . .] Tiamat he conquered, he took her sovereignty. (4) [. . . . . .] the Tablets of Destiny from Kingu he took in his hand. (5) [. . . . . .] he created, and at the Gate of the Deep he stationed. (6) [. . . . . .] that the deeds of Tiamat should not be forgotten (7) [. . . . . .] he causeth his fathers to behold."

In the first line we may probably see a reference to Marduk's drawing forth of the *mulmullu*, or spear,[1] which we know from

[1] It is possible that *mul-mul* is here, not Marduk's actual weapon, but *Mul-mul*, the Spear-star of Marduk; and the verb *is-si-ma* may have the intransitive meaning, "disappeared." In view of the fact that the following lines refer to episodes in the Creation story, I think the rendering suggested above is preferable.

Tablet IV of the Creation Series, l. 101, he plunged into the belly of Tiamat, after he had filled her with the evil wind. Line 2 may be explained as referring to Marduk's conquest of Kingu after Tiamat's death, without further fighting, though it is possible that it has some connection with the obscure expression in Tablet IV, l. 120. In l. 3 the text returns to Marduk's defeat of Tiamat; and with the capture of the Tablets of Destiny from Kingu, referred to in l. 4, we may compare Tablet IV, l. 121 f. Line 5 possibly refers to an episode in the Creation which may have been recorded in the missing portion of Tablet V of the Creation Series. With it we may compare the fixing of a bolt by Marduk and the stationing of a watchman, in order to keep the waters above the firmament in their place (cf. Tablet IV, ll. 137 ff.); it is possible that a similar guardian was stationed by Marduk in order to restrain the waters of the Deep. Line 6 f. apparently refer to the instructions given by Marduk to the gods, "his fathers," in order "that the deeds of Tiamat (i.e. her revolt and subsequent conquest by himself) should not be forgotten."[1] It is possible that the instructions which Marduk is here represented as giving to the gods refer to their positions in heaven and to the heavenly bodies associated with them. If this interpretation is correct, it follows that the later Babylonians, at any rate, looked upon the astrological aspect of the Creation story as in accordance with definite instructions given by Marduk himself. While they believed that Marduk actually slew Tiamat and subsequently created the universe as narrated in the tablets of the Creation Series, they held that the association of the principal actors in the story with some of the more important stars and constellations was also Marduk's work, his object being to ensure that the history of the creation of the world should always be kept in remembrance.

The first section which is preserved of the text, referring

[1] This rendering appears preferable to the possible reading, *la ba-ši-e*, i.e. "that the deeds of Tiamat should be no more."

as it does to some of the most striking episodes recorded in the Creation Series, appears to be of the nature of an introduction to what follows. The second section reads: (8) [. . . . . . ^{ilu}*Marduk*](?) *u-kal-la-mu par-ṣi-šu-*[*nu*] (9) [. . . . . .]*-tim E-la-mu-u ša* [. . . . . .] *a-šak-*[*ku*] (10) [. . . . .] *Ti-amat itba-am-ma* [. . . . .] *ni*[*m* . . . . . .] (11) [. . *T*]*i-amat ina lib-bi* ^{ilu}*Sin in-n*[*am* (?)- . . . . . .] (12) [. .] ^{ilu}*Marduk ina lib-bi* ^{ilu}*Tam-tim* [. . . . . .] (13) *ki-i ša ru-bu-u* ^{ilu}*Marduk ana ša-kan a-b*[*u-bu* . . . . .] (14) *i-na ri-kis si-pit-ti u me-lul-ti-šu i-kab-*[. . . . . .] (15) *e-liš u šap-liš li-mut-tum u-ša-tar-ma*[1] *i-kap-pu-du sur-ra-*[*a-tum*] (16) *ina u-mu šu-u agū taš-ri-iḫ-tum ša nu-uk-ku-ri šup-pal u-kal-l*[*i-* . . .] (17) *ana muḫ-ḫi paraṣ e-nu-tum ša la si-ma-a-tum i-šak-kan pa-ni*(?)*-*[*šu*] (18) *ilāni*^{pl} *ma-ḫa-zi* ^{mātu}*Akkadī*^{KI} ^{amēlu}*nišē*^{pl}*-šu-nu u-šaḫ-ḫa-su ul ul-la-a-tum*[2] (19) *a-mat su-uš-tum*(?) *i-dib-bu-bu i-kab-bu-u ma-ag-ri-tum* (20) *mi-il-ki la tuš-šir*(?) *im-tal-lik i-te-ip-šu sur-ra-a-tum* (21) *ig-ga-ag-ma* ^{ilu}*Bēl u-ḫal-laḳ eš-ri-e-tum* (22) *E-la-ma-a ṭi-e-mu i-šak-kan-ma i-sap-pan ma-a-tum* (23) *ana ku-um ša-kan a-bu-bu ana šul-mu* IZ-DIM-MU *epuš*(*uš*) NAM-BUL-BI.

In this section Marduk and Tiamat appear in their astrological characters, Marduk probably as Jupiter, and Tiamat as a constellation in the neighbourhood of the ecliptic. The approach of Tiamat and the Moon and of Marduk (i.e. Jupiter) and Tiamat would seem from ll. 13 ff. to portend the sending of an *abubu*, or deluge,[3] upon the earth, followed by rebellion and tumult among gods and men. If unchecked, the wrath of Bēl (i.e. Marduk) would result in the destruction of the temples and in the ruin of the land. To prevent the sending of a deluge and to change the omen to one of prosperity,

[1] The sign is MA, not IZ.

[2] For *ul ul-la-a-tum*, as parallel to *ma-ag-ri-tum* (cf. l. 19), see Jensen, *Kosmologie*, p. 121 f.

[3] Or, possibly, a thunderbolt.

the text enjoins the performance of certain NAM-BUL-BI prayers.[1]

The third and last section of the first column reads: (24) *ina* ^{arḫu} *Dūzu ša ni-pi-šu ša sa-kap* ^{amēlu} *nakiri ina Bābili* ^{KI} *i-pu-uš* (25) *ina lib-bi ša* ^{ilu} *Muštabarrū-mūtanu u* ^{ilu} *Sin bēlē* ^{pl} *ni-ṣir-tum ša* ^{mātu} *Elamtu* ^{KI} (26) NUM-LU ^{pl}[2] ^{ilu} SAG-ME-GAR *u* ^{ilu} *Šamaš bēlē* ^{pl} *ni-ṣir-tum ša* ^{mātu} *Akkadū* ^{KI} (27) ŠU-[. .]-LU ^{pl} *idāti* [^{pl}] *ša nu-uk-ku-ri palī Bābili* ^{KI} *'-u-kal-lim-'* (28) NAM-BUL-BI *ina ali i-te-pu-uš* KI[3] *ni-ṣir-tum ša* ^{ilu} *Sin* (29) TE ŠU-GI *u Mul-mul* TE *ša Elamtu* ^{KI} (30) KI *ni-ṣir-tum ša* ^{ilu} *Šamaš* ^{kakkabu} LU-KU-MAL ^{ilu} [. . . . . .] (31) KI *ni-ṣir-tum ša* ^{ilu} *Muštabarrū-mūtanu* ^{kakkabu} [. . . . . .] (32) KI *ni-ṣir-tum ša* ^{ilu} SAG-ME-GAR ^{kakkabu} [. . . . . .] (33) *ina* ^{arḫu} *Tap-pat-tum ina ḳar-nu-te di-*[. . . . . .] (34) [. . . . . .]*-ba-ba-an paraṣ e-nu-tum* [. . . . . .] (35) [. . . . . .] *muḫ-ḫi šip* (?)*-tum* [. . . . . .]. This section is concerned with the positions of the planets *Muštabarrū-mūtanu* (Mercury) and SAG-ME-GAR (Jupiter) and of the moon and sun, and of the stars ŠU-GI and *Mulmul*; and it would seem that a change in the dynasty ruling at Babylon was portended by the relative positions of Mercury and Jupiter. To that extent this section resembles the one that precedes it, but there is little apparent connection between this portion of the text and the Creation Series. It is possible, however, that this section was continued in col. ii, and that the missing portion had some connection with the legend.[4]

---

[1] This may be the title of a special class of incantations (cf. my *Magic and Sorcery*, p. 129), or the expression may possibly be employed, as in some other passages, to indicate generally a class of incantations, or ceremonies, intended to avert the effects of an evil omen (cf. Thompson, *Reports of Magicians and Astrologers*, p. xlvii f.).

[2] Cf. Epping and Strassmaier, *Z.A.*, vii, p. 221 f.

[3] Possibly *ašar*.

[4] Of col. ii only traces of the beginnings of a few lines are preserved from the lower half of the column; they read: (1) *a-*[. . . . . .] (2) *ku-*[. . . . . .] (3) IT[I . . . . . .]

The greater part of the reverse of the fragment is inscribed with the upper half of the last column, which in some respects is the most interesting portion of the text. The lines that have been preserved read as follows: (1) *ina* ^{arḫu} *Tap-pat-tum ša ni-pi-šu an-nu-tu* [. . . . .] (2) *ana muḫ-ḫi* ^{ilu} *Marduk illiku(ku) ina ḳaḳ-kar* ^{arḫu} [. . . . . .] (3) *u* ^{ilu} *Kin-gu šu-u : ab-bi :* ^{arḫu} AB : *ab-*[. . . . . .] (4) TE BIR[1] *Ti-amat pu-uḫ-ri ana ṣal-tum ki-i* [. . . . .] (5) *epuš(uš) Ti-amat u* ^{ilu} *Kin-gi ana iš-ten itūrū* ^{pl}*-ma* [. . . . .] (6) *a-ḫa-meš in-nam-mar-ru-' aš-šu an-ni-i* TE *Enzu ša* KI TE *Aḳrabu* PAD [. . . . .] (7) *E-zi-da* : TE *Enzu* : ^{kakkabu} *Uḫ-zu šum-šu par-ṣi ša Ti-amat* (8) *kul-lu gi-iz-za-ni-tum u pu-uš-ša-ni-tum ša it-ti lib-bi* TE^{pl} E(*u*) (9) *ana muḫ-ḫi* ^{kakkabu} *Enzu u* TE MULU-BAD[2] *ina lib-bi* TE BIR KA-BI *Ti-amat u* ^{ilu} *Kin-gi* (10) *šu-nu : gi-iz-za-ni-tu : ki-iz-za-ni-tu šum-šu ana muḫ-ḫi* TE BIR *ki-iz-zu* (11) *pu-uš-ša-ni-tum pu-u-za-ni-tum šum-šu ana muḫ-ḫi* TE KA *ḳa-bi* (12) TE KA : TE MULU-BAD *Ti-amat tu-ra-am-tum šum-šu šanū pa-nu-šu zikru u sinništu šu-u* (13) *ina lib-bi ki-i i-kat ša* TE *Aḳrabu it-ti* ^{ilu} *Nin-lil u* ^{ilu} *Nin-ki-gal* (14) *bašū(u) ina muḫ-ḫi par-ṣa ša Ti-amat aš-ba-' Gud u Aḳrabu iš-ten šu-u* (15) GIR : *zu-ḳa-ki-pu* : GIR *lu-u* : *II . . . -pi aš-šu an-ni-i ina* ^{arḫu} *Tap-pat-tum* (16) KI *a-šak-ku* TE *Enzu ina* KI TE MULU-BAD *ina agī taš-ri-iḫ-tum illiku(ku)* (17) [. . . . .]*-da* TE UTU-KA-GAB-A *ina lib-bi te*

---

(4) ^{ilu} [. . . . .] (5) *alu* [. . . . .] (6) *ša* [. . . . .] (7) TE [. . . . . .] (8) ^{kakkabu} [. . . . . .] (9) *saḫ-*[. . . . .] (10) *ul* [. . . . .]. Similarly, only traces remain of the first column preserved upon the reverse of the tablet, which read: (1) [. . . . .] (2) ^{ilu} *Na-na-*[*a* . . . . .] (3) *ša ḫu-la-*[. . . . .] (4) *ki-na-*[*a-* . . . . .] (5, beginning a new section) *ina* ^{arḫu} [. . . . .] (6) *ku-*[. . . . .] (7) *a*[*lu* . . . . .].

[1] I.e. Caper. The sign was read by Strassmaier and Epping as ŠAḪ, *šaḫū* (see *Astron. aus Bab.*, App., p. 7), but Jensen has shown that it is not ŠAḪ, but the sign Br. No. 2,024 (see *Kosmologie*, p. 313), which perhaps has the value BIR. As the tenth sign of the Zodiac it should possibly be read as *Lalū*.

[2] Explained as *pa-gar ašakki* (ID-PA) in VR., pl. 46, No. 1, Obv., l. 28.

BIR KI *ni-ṣir-tum ša* [mâtu] *Elamtu* [[KI]] (18) [. . . . .]*-šu-nu u-tir-ru-nim-ma ana ṣal-tum iz-zi-zu-u* [ilu] *Samaš ina lib-b* [. . . . .] (19) [. . . . .] *ša* [kakkabu] SAG-ME-GAR *ni-me-du* TE KAK-SI-DI *u* TE PAN *ina pa-ni* [kakkabu] [. . . . . (20) [. . . . .] *ta-ḫa-zi ki-ma iz-zi-zu ri-*[. . . . . (21) [. . . . .] *mi ba* [. . . . .] (22) [. . . . . [ilu] *Šamaš* [*bē*]*lu* [ilu] *Nin-ib šum-šu ana* . . . [. . . . . (23) [. . . . .]*-pu-šu* [amelu] TAB *i-sak-ki-pu* IGI MAR [ilu] *Nin-i*[*b* . . . . .] (24) [. . . . .] *kak-ku šu-u kak-ku a-bu-bu* [ilu] *Marduk ina šumi-šu k*[*a-bi* (25) [. . . . . P]AN[1] *a-bu-bu kak-ka-šu rabā*(*a*) *aš-šu ša* [ilu] *Nin-ib a-ṣi aš-šu an-ni-i* [. . . . .] (26) [. . . . . *i-ḳab-bu-u* KI SIR NAM LUL *ša ūmu XVII* [KAN] *ina* ḲI SIG [. . . . .] (27) [. . . . .] [ilu] *Bēl ḳar-ra-du ša ina ag-gu lib-bi-šu a-šak-ku* [. . . . .] (28) [. . . . .]*-ri-šu i-si-ḫu tu-ḳu-un-tum* [ilu] *Nin-*[. . . . .] (29) [. . . . .]*-tum ina idi-šu* [*i*]*-lul*(*-*)*lu* (?) *E-kur* [. . . . .] (30) [. . . . .]*-ma-šu* [. . . . .]*-an-na ki* [. . . . .] (31) [. . . . .]*-ir ina* [. . . . .] *ik* [. . . . .] *u* [. . . . .] (32) [. . . . .] (33) [. . . . .].

It will be noticed that this portion of the text is in the main explanatory. Unlike col. i, these lines of the text do not run on in the form of connected sentences, but are broken up into a number of equations and explanations of terms and titles ; thus, some terms are explained by a play upon words (cf. ll. 3 and 10f.), while in other places the reason is given for certain titles (cf. ll. 6 and 7) or additional names (cf. l. 12). With regard to the connection of passages in this column with the Creation Series, it may be noted that Kingu, in addition to Marduk and Tiamat, is introduced. He is here associated in an astrological sense with Tiamat, and their alliance in opposition to Marduk is clearly referred to in ll. 4–6. Moreover, the fact that Caper and Scorpio are mentioned in close connection with this passage shows that

[1] Either the Bow-star, or, possibly, [IZ-B]AN, i.e. [iṣu] *ḳaštu*, Marduk's bow.

they here occur, not only in their astronomical sense as constellations of the Zodiac, but also in their mythical character as monsters in the host of Tiamat. The reference to Marduk's "mighty weapon" in l. 24 f. is also noteworthy.

After the sheets of vol. ii had been printed off I came across two other fragments of somewhat similar astrological texts, which furnish additional illustrations of the manner in which the legends of the Creation were connected by the later Babylonians with astrological phenomena. The smaller of these fragments, No. 40,959, the text of which is given in

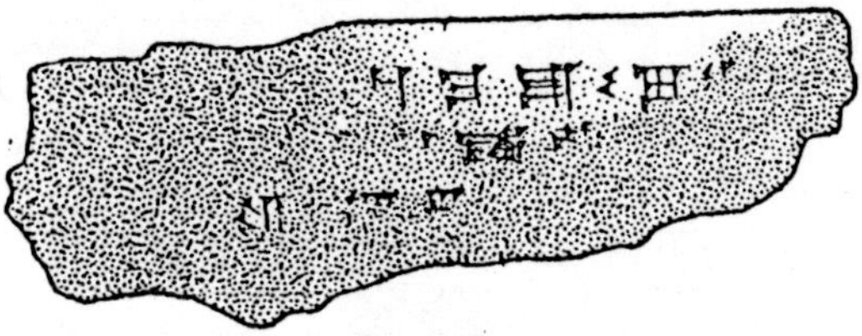

OBVERSE.

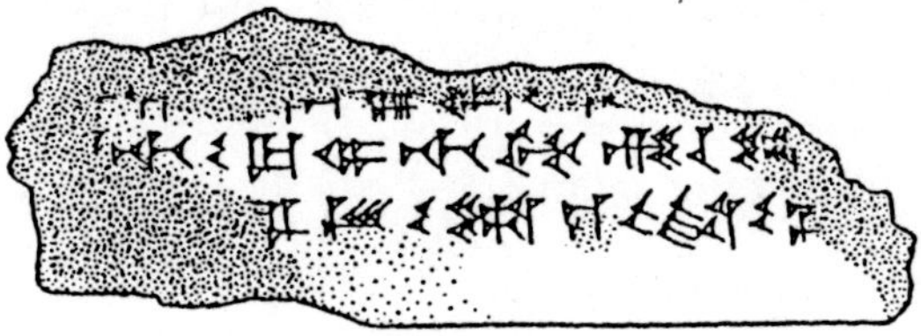

REVERSE.

Fragment of an astrological explanatory text (No. 40,959).

the accompanying block, preserves a few traces of signs from the beginning of the obverse and from the end of the reverse of the tablet. A few complete words occur in l. 2 of the reverse, which reads [. . . . . .]-*ti*: *lik-mi Ti-amat napišta-šu l*[*i-* . . . . . .]; l. 112 of the Seventh Tablet of the Creation Series reads *lik-me* (var. *li-ik-mi*) *Ti-amat ni-ṣir-ta-šu* (var. *na-piš-ta-šu*) *li-si-iḳ u lik-ri* (see above, p. 108 f.), and it is clear that this line is here quoted upon the fragment. Both the obverse and reverse of No. 40,959 resemble the last column of No. 55,466, etc, in being of an explanatory nature, and it is probable that the quotation from the Seventh Tablet is here introduced in an astrological context.

The larger of the two fragments is No. 32,574, and the text of its obverse is published in the accompanying block. This text also is explanatory, and of an astrological character, and, like No. 40,959, it has in some respects a close connection with the Creation Series. Thus l. 2 reads [. . . . . . ALI]M-NUN-NA: *nu-ur ša* [ilu] *Anu* [ilu] *Bēl u* [ilu][*E-a* :] A[SAR]U: [. . . . .]; now [ilu] *Asaru-alim-nun-na* occurs as one of the titles of Marduk in l. 5 of the Seventh Tablet of the

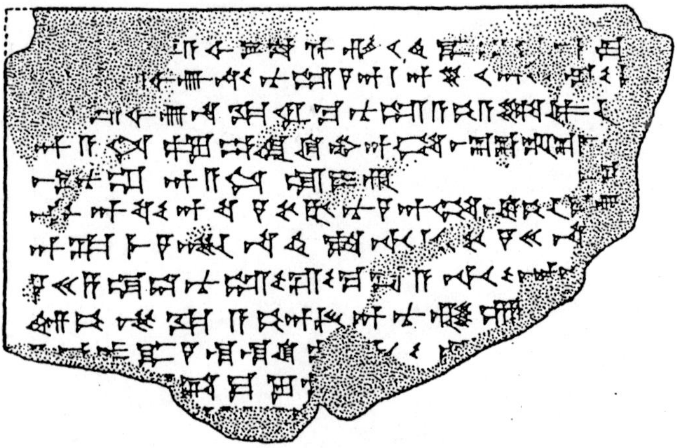

Fragment of an astrological explanatory text (No. 32,574, Obverse).

Creation Series, and with the explanation of the title here given as "the Light of Anu, Bēl, and Ea," we may compare the explanation in l. 6 of the Seventh Tablet, which reads *muš-te-šir te-rit* [ilu] *A-nim* [ilu] *Bēl* [*u* [ilu] *E-a*], "who directeth the decrees of Anu, Bēl, [and Ea]." Moreover, l. 3 of the fragment reads [. . . . . A]LIM-NUN-NA[1] *ka-ru-ba nu-ur a-bi*

[1] At the beginning of the line there is hardly room for the restoration [[ilu] ASARU-A]LIM-NUN NA; it is probable that the line read [[ilu] A]LIM-NUN-NA, which may be regarded as a shorter form of the same title.

a-li-di-šu [. . . . . .]; now l. 5 of the Seventh Tablet reads *ilu Asaru-alim-nun-na ka-ru-bu nu-ur* [. . . . . . .], and the end of the line may probably be restored from the fragment as *nu-ur* [*a-bi a-li-di-šu*].[1] Line 9 of the fragment reads *im-bi šumu-ka a-bi ilāni^pl^* *ilu* NU-NAM-NIR [. . . . .]; this also possibly refers to Marduk, and may be compared with the Seventh Tablet, l. 116 and ll. 118 ff.

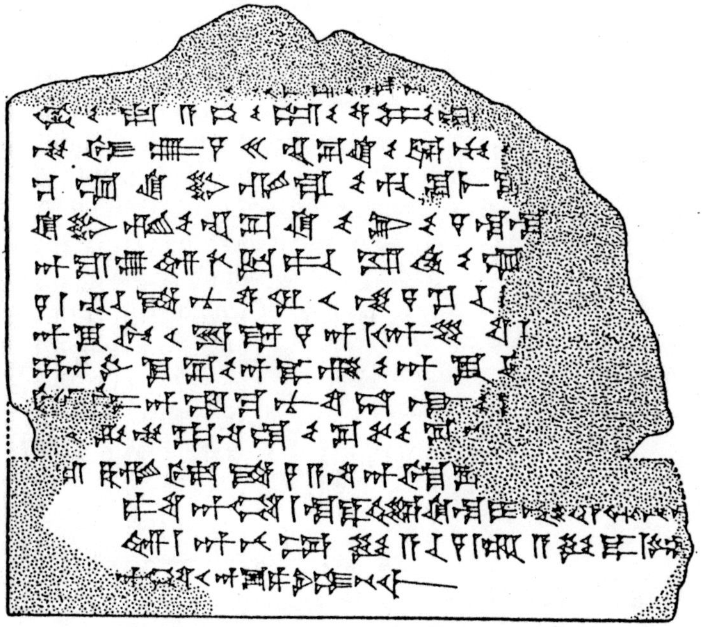

Fragment of an astrological explanatory text (No. 32,574, Reverse and Edge).

The text of the reverse of No. 32,574 (see the accompanying block) is also explanatory, and reads: (1) [. . . . . .] (2) SIGIŠŠE : *ṭa-a-bi* : UR : *zab-lum* : [. . . . . .] (3) *mu-ṣu-u ša šar Nippuri^KI^* : *šul-mu* [. . . . . . .] (4) GIŠ-ŠID KI-IN-GI-RA : *ḫu-la me* [. . . . .] (5) KI-IN-GI : *Nippuru^KI^* :

[1] See above, p. 92 f.

IR : *ša-la-la* [. . . . .] (6) [ilu]*Zu-u im-ḫaṣ kap-pa-šu iš-bir* : ŠID [. . . . .] (7) *ša an-a bēli-šu ḳar-nu ṣab-ru u mu-ša-kil-šu* [. . . . .] (8) [ilu] *Kin-gu u* [arḫu] *Nisannu ša* [ilu] *Anu u* [ilu]*Bēl ūmu I* [. . . . .] (9) [kakkabu] LU - KU - MAL : [ilu]*Dumu-zi* : [ilu]*Kin-g*[*u* . . . . .] (10) [. . . . .] [ilu]*Al-ma-nu* UD-DU AG : [. . . . .] (11) [*ri*]-*ig-mu šak-na-at* : *E-kur* : *E*-[. . . . . .]. In ll. 8 f. Kingu is introduced, but there is no other evidence of a connection between the Creation Series and this portion of the text; in fact, l. 6, beginning, "Zū smote and broke his wing," evidently gives a quotation from a legend of the Storm-god Zū, which has nothing to do with the Creation Series. Indirectly, however, this line proves that other Babylonian legends were, like those of the Creation, connected by the later Babylonians with certain of the heavenly bodies. The four lines inscribed upon the edge of the tablet give a portion of the colophon, from the last line of which we learn that the tablet belonged to a series, the title of which reads [. . . . . [ilu]]*Marduk u* [ilu]*Ṣar-pa-ni-tum* BE-ŠI,[1] and it is possible that the other astrological fragments above described (Nos. 55,466, etc., and 40,959) are parts of tablets belonging to the same series. The occurrence of Marduk's name in the title is in accordance with the suggested connection between these fragments and the Creation Series.

[1] The last two signs are not very carefully written, but they are distinctly BE-ŠI and not EŠ-BAR (i.e. *purussū*). With this title we may compare that which occurs at the beginning or upon the edge of many of the late Babylonian astronomical tablets, viz., *ina a-mat* [ilu] *Bēl u* [ilu] *Bēlti-ia purussū*, "At the word of the Lord and of my Lady, a decision!"; cf., e.g., Epping, *Astronomisches aus Babylon*, p. 153. The *Bēl* and *Bēlti-ia* are probably Marduk and Ṣarpanitum.

IV.

Supposed Assyrian Legends of the Temptation and the Tower of Babel.

In vol. ii, pl. lxxiii f. the text is given of a fragment of a legend (K. 3,657), which was thought at one time, by George Smith and others[1] to contain an Assyrian version of the story of the Tower of Babel (cf. Gen. xi, 1 ff.). The text is very broken, but from what remains of col. i it would appear to be part of a legend concerning a god, or possibly a king, who plotted evil in his heart and conceived a hatred against the father of all the gods. In col. i, ll. 5 ff. the passage occurs on which the supposed parallel with the story of the Tower of Babel was based, for these lines were believed to refer to the building of a tower at Babylon, and to describe how the tower erected by the builders in the day was destroyed in the night by a god, who confounded their speech and confused their counsel. There is, however, no mention of a tower or building of any sort, and Babylon is referred to as suffering through the evil designs of the god or king, described in ll. 2–4. Moreover, the lines supposed to recount the destruction of the tower by night really describe how the complaints of the oppressed people prevented the king, or possibly an avenger of the people, from getting any sleep at night upon his couch. The tablet is too broken to allow of a completely satisfactory explanation of the nature of the legend, but the rendering

---

[1] See *Chaldean Account of Genesis*, pp. 160 ff., German ed. (edited by Delitzsch), p. 122 f.; cf. also Boscawen, *T.S.B.A.*, v, pp. 304 ff., and *Records of the Past*, vol. vii, pp. 129 ff.

of ll. 1–14 given below[1] will suffice to show that the suggested connection between this legend and the story of the Tower of Babel was not justified.

As with the story of the Tower of Babel, so also has it been claimed that an Assyrian legend has been found which presents a close parallel to the story of the temptation of Eve in the garden of Eden, narrated in Gen. iii. That the description of paradise in Gen. ii shows traces of Babylonian influence is certain,[2] and it is not impossible that a Babylonian legend may at some future time be discovered which bears

[1] The first fourteen lines of col. i may be rendered as follows:— (1) [. . . . . . *-s]u(?)-nu ab-*[. . . . .] (2) [. . . . .]-*ti-šu lib-ba-šu il-te-im-na* (3) [. . . . .]*a-bi ka-la ilāni*[pl] *i-zi-ru* (4) [. . . . . *-t*]*i-šu lib-ba-šu il-te-im-na* (5) [. . . . . *Bābilu*[KI]] *ṣa-mi-id a-na il-ki-im* (6) [*ṣi-iḫ-ru u r*]*a-bu-u u-ba-al-lu dul-la* (7) [. . . . . *Bāb*]*ilu*[KI] *ṣa-mi-id a-na il-ki-im* (8) [*ṣi-iḫ-ru*] *u ra-bu-u u-ba-al-lu dul-la* (9) [. . . . . . *-i*]*m-ma-as-si-na ka-la u-mi i-šu-uš* (10) [*i*]*-na ta-az-zi-im-ti-ši-na i-na ma-ai-li* (11) *u-ul u-kat-ta ši-it-ta* (12) [*i-n*]*a ug-ga-ti-šu-ma te-me-ga-am i-sa-pa-aḫ* (13) [*a-na*] *šu-ba-al-ku-ut pa-li-e pa-ni-šu iš-ku-un* (14) [*uš*(?)*-t*]*an-ni ṭe-ma ut-tak-ki-ra mi-lik-šu-un* . . . . "(1) [. . . . .] their [. . . . . .]; (2) [. . . . . .] his heart plotted evil. (3) [. . . . . .] the father of the gods he hated; (4) [. . . . . .] his heart plotted evil. (5) [. . . . . Babylon] was yoked to forced labour; (6) [small and] great rendered(?) service. (7) [. . . . . . Bab]ylon was yoked to forced labour; (8) [small] and great rendered(?) service. (9) [Through] their [. . . .], all day was he afflicted; (10) through their lamentation, upon (his) couch (11) he obtained no sleep. (12) [In] the anger of his heart he put an end to (?) supplication; (13) [to] overthrow the kingdom he set his face. (14) [He chan]ged (their) understanding, their counsel was altered . . . . . ." Too little is preserved of cols. ii and iii to allow of a connected translation, but it may here be noted that col. ii contains references to the gods [ilu] LUGAL-DUL (or DU)-AZAG-GA (l. 1) and [ilu] EN-ḪI (l. 2), and to the goddess [ilu] *Dam-ki-na* (l. 8), and col. iii to the god [ilu] NU-NAM-NIR (l. 5).

[2] For a further discussion of this subject, see the Introduction.

a close resemblance to the story of the temptation of Eve by the serpent.[1] The tablet which has been supposed to contain an Assyrian version of the story[2] is K. 3,473 + 79-7-8, 296 + R. 615, which is one of the principal copies of the Third Tablet of the Creation Series. The closing lines of the Third Tablet recount how the gods gathered to a feast at Anšar's bidding before they decreed the fate for Marduk, their avenger[3]; the passage which recounts how the gods ate bread (l. 134) was believed to contain a reference to man's eating the fruit of the tree of knowledge, and Marduk was supposed to be described in l. 138, not as the avenger of the gods, but as the "Redeemer" of mankind. This suggestion was never widely adopted and has long been given up, but it had meanwhile found its way into some popular works; and, as enquiries are still sometimes made for the Assyrian version of the story of the Temptation, it is perhaps not superfluous to state definitely the fact of its non-existence.

---

[1] The cylinder seal, Brit. Mus., No. 89,326, has been thought to furnish evidence of the existence of such a legend, as it represents a male and a female figure seated near a sacred tree, and behind the female figure is a serpent. George Smith published a woodcut of the scene in *The Chaldean Account of Genesis*, p. 91; for a photographic reproduction of the impression of the seal, see my *Bab. Rel. and Myth.*, p. 113.

[2] The suggestion was first made in the *Bab. and Or. Rec.*, iv (1890), pp. 251 ff.

[3] See above, p. 56 f., ll. 129-138.

V.

A "Prayer of the Raising of the Hand" to Ishtar.

In the following pages a transliteration and a translation are given of a remarkable "Prayer of the Raising of the Hand" to Ištar, No. 26,187, the text of which is published in vol. ii, pls. lxxv ff. An explanation is perhaps necessary of the reasons which have led to the publication of this tablet in a book dealing with legends of Creation and with texts connected therewith. In a previous work, entitled "Babylonian Magic and Sorcery," I had collected all the texts belonging to the series of "Prayers of the Raising of the Hand" which were known to me at the time; when later on I came across the text of No. 26,187 it followed that it must necessarily be published by itself, apart from other tablets of its class. It would, of course, have been possible to delay its publication until it could be included in a work dealing with a number of miscellaneous religious compositions, but, in view of the

Obv.

1. *šiptu u-sal-li-ki be-lit be-li-e-ti i - lat i - la - a - ti*
2. ^{ilu}*Ištar šar-ra-ti kul-lat da-ad-me muš-te-ši-rat te-ni-še-e-ti*
3. ^{ilu}*Ir - ni - ni*[1] *mut - tal - la - a - ti ra - bit* ^{ilu}*Igigi*
4. *gaš - ra - a - ti ma - al - ka - a - ti šu - mu - ki ṣi - ru*
5. *at-ti-ma na-an-na-rat šamē(e) u irṣitim(tim) ma-rat* ^{ilu}*Sin ḳa - rit - ti*

[1] Ištar, to whom the prayer is offered (cf. l. 106), is in this line and in l. 105 addressed by the title Irnini; in l. 12 she is addressed as Gutira. It is well known that in course of time Ištar was identified by the Babylonians and Assyrians with other goddesses,

interesting nature of its contents, it has seemed preferable to make it available without further delay for students of Babylonian religion, by including it as an appendix to the present work. It will be seen that the text, both from the beauty of its language and from its perfect state of preservation, is one of the finest Babylonian religious compositions that has yet been recovered. The tablet measures $6\frac{7}{8}$ in. by $2\frac{7}{8}$ in., and is of the long narrow shape which is one of the characteristics of the larger tablets of the series to which it belongs. From the colophon (cf. Rev., ll. 111 ff.) we gather that it was copied from an original at Borsippa by a certain Nergal-balāṭsu-iḳbi, who deposited it as a votive offering in E-sagila, the temple of Marduk at Babylon, whence it was probably removed before the destruction of the temple. The text is addressed to Ištar in her character as the goddess of battle, and she is here identified with Irnini and with Gutira (see below, note). Lines 1–41 contain addresses to the goddess, descriptive of her power and splendour, and at l. 42 the suppliant begins to make his own personal petitions, describing his state of affliction and praying for deliverance. A rubric occurs at the end of the text (cf. ll. 107 ff), giving directions for the performance of certain ceremonies and for the due recital of the prayer.

1. I pray unto thee, lady of ladies, goddess of goddesses!
2. O Ishtar, queen of all peoples, directress of mankind!
3. O Irnini,[1] thou art raised on high, mistress of the Spirits of heaven;
4. Thou art mighty, thou hast sovereign power, exalted is thy name!
5. Thou art the light of heaven and earth, O valiant daughter of the Moon-god.

e.g., Ninni, Nanā, Anunitum, and Bēlit; and when so identified she absorbed their names, titles, and attributes. In these passages we have two additional instances of her identification with other deities.

Obv.

6. *mut-tab-bi-la-at kakkē*^{pl} *ša-ki-na-at tu - ḳu - un - ti*

7. *ḫa-mi-mat gi-mir par-ṣi a-pi-rat a - gi - e be - lu - ti*

8. ^{ilu}*bēlti*[1] *šu - pu - u nar - bu - ki eli ka-la ilāni*^{pl} *ṣi-ru*

9. *mul-ta-nu-ḳa-a-ti muš-tam-ḫi-ṣa-at aḫē*^{pl} *mit - gu - ru - ti*

10. *mut - ta - ad - di - na - at it - ba - ru*[2]

11. *it - bur - ti be - lit tu - ša - ri mut-tak-ki-pat*[3] *erišti-ia*

12. ^{ilu}*Gu-tir-a*[4] *ša tu-ḳu-un-ta ḫal-pat la - bi - šat ḫar-ba-ša*

13. *gam-ra-a-ti šib-ṭa u purussā liḳ-ti irṣitim(tim) u ša-ma-mi*[5]

14. *suk-ku eš-ri-e-ti ni-me-da u parakkē*^{pl} *u - tuḳ - ḳu ka-a-ši*

15. *e-ki-a-am la šumu-ki e-ki-a-am la par - ṣu - ki*

16. *e-ki-a-am la uṣ-ṣu-ra uṣurâti*^{pl}*-ki e-ki-a-am la innadū*^{pl} *parakkē*^{pl} *- ki*

17. *e-ki-a-am la ra-ba-a-ti e-ki-a-am la ṣi - ra - a - ti*

18. ^{ilu}*A-num* ^{ilu}*Bēl u* ^{ilu}*E-a ul-lu-u-ki ina ilāni*^{pl} *u-šar-bu-u be-lu-ut-ki*

---

[1] As the determinative AN is employed before the ideogram, it is possible that here and in ll. 29 and 104 it should be rendered as the proper name, or title, *Bēlit* (cf. the preceding note). Elsewhere in the prayer, however, the word takes in addition the 1 s. pron. suffix (cf. ll. 43, 56, 59, 72, 73, 79, 93, and 94); it seems more probable, therefore, that the ideogram is employed for the substantive *bēltu*, "lady."

[2] This line probably continues the class of attributes ascribed to the goddess in the preceding line, and does not form a contrast to it; the meaning "strength" rather than "friendship" is

6. Ruler of weapons, arbitress of the battle!
7. Framer of all decrees, wearer of the crown of dominion!
8. O lady,[1] majestic is thy rank, over all the gods is it exalted!
9. Thou art the cause of lamentation, thou sowest hostility among brethren who are at peace;
10. Thou art the bestower of strength![2]
11. Thou art strong, O lady of victory, thou canst violently attain[3] my desire!
12. O Gutira,[4] who art girt with battle, who art clothed with terror
13. Thou wieldest the sceptre and the decision, the control of earth and heaven![5]
14. Holy chambers, shrines, divine dwellings, and temples worship thee!
15. Where is thy name not (heard)? Where is thy decree not (obeyed)?
16. Where are thine images not made? Where are thy temples not founded?
17. Where art thou not great? Where art thou not exalted?
18. Anu, Bēl, and Ea have raised thee on high, among the gods have they made great thy dominion,

---

therefore to be assigned to *il-ba-ru*. In support of this view, cf. the attributes in the following lines, and the occurrence of *il-bur-ti* in l. 11, where any other meaning but "Thou art strong" is out of the question.

[3] It is clear that in this passage we must assign some such active meaning to the Ifteal of *nakāpu*.

[4] See above, p. 222 f., n. 1.

[5] The second half of the line is in apposition to the phrase *šibṭa u purussā*, "the sceptre" representing the control of earth and "the decision" that of heaven.

OBV.

19. *u-ša-aš-ku-ki ina nap-ḫar* ^{ilu}*Igigi u-ša-ti-ru man-za-az-ki*

20. *a-na ḫi-is-sat šu-me-ki šamū(u) u irṣitim(tim) i-ru-ub-bu*[1]

21. *ilāni*^{pl} *i-ru-bu i-nar-ru-ṭu* ^{ilu}*A-nun-na-ki*
22. *šumu-ki ra-aš-bu iš-tam-ma-ra te-ni-še-e-ti*
23. *at-ti-ma ra-ba-a-ti u ṣi-ra-a-ti*
24. *nap-ḫar ṣal-mat ḳaḳ-ḳa-di*[2] *nam-maš-šu-u te-ni-še-e-ti i-dal-la-lu ḳur-di-ki*
25. *di-in ba-ḫu-la-a-ti ina kit-ti u mi-ša-ri ta-din-ni at-ti*

26. *tap-pal-la-si ḫab-lu u šaḳ-šu*[3] *tuš-te-eš-še-ri ud-da-kam*

27. *a-ḫu-lap-ki be-lit šamē(e) u irṣitim(tim) ri-e-a-at nišē*^{pl} *a-pa-a-ti*
28. *a-ḫu-lap-ki be-lit E-an-na*[4] *ḳud-du-šu šu-tum-mu el-lu*

29. *a-ḫu-lap-ki* ^{ilu}*bēlti*[5] *ul a-ni-ḫa šēpā*^{II}*-ki la-si-ma bir-ka-a-ki*

30. *a-ḫu-lap-ki be-lit ta-ḫa-zi ka-li-šu-nu tam-ḫa-ri*

31. *šu-pu-u-tum la-ab-bat* ^{ilu}*Igigi mu-kan-ni-šat ilāni*^{pl} *šab-su-ti*

32. *li-'-a-at ka-li-šu-nu ma-al-ku ṣa-bi-ta-at ṣir-rit šarrāni*^{pl}

33. *pi-ta-a-at pu-su-um-me*[6] *ša ka-li-ši-na ardâti*^{pl}

---

[1] The verb *rābu* is here used of the "quaking" of the heaven and earth (see above, p. 206 f., l. 8), and in the following line of the "trembling" of the gods; for its use in the former sense in the astrological reports, cf. Thompson, *Reports of the Magicians and Astrologers*, vol. ii, p. 129.

[2] Literally "the black-headed," i.e. mankind.

19. They have exalted thee among all the Spirits of heaven, they have made thy rank pre-eminent.
20. At the thought of thy name the heaven and the earth quake,[1]
21. The gods tremble, and the Spirits of the earth falter.
22. Mankind payeth homage unto thy mighty name,
23. For thou art great, and thou art exalted.
24. All mankind,[2] the whole human race, boweth down before thy power.
25. Thou judgest the cause of men with justice and righteousness;
26. Thou lookest with mercy on the violent man, and thou settest right the unruly[3] every morning.
27. How long wilt thou tarry, O lady of heaven and earth, shepherdess of those that dwell in human habitations?
28. How long wilt thou tarry, O lady of the holy E-anna,[4] the pure Storehouse?
29. How long wilt thou tarry, O lady,[5] whose feet are unwearied, whose knees have not lost their vigour?
30. How long wilt thou tarry, O lady of all fights and of the battle?
31. O thou glorious one, that ragest among the Spirits of heaven, that subduest angry gods,
32. That hast power over all princes, that controllest the sceptre of kings,
33. That openest the bonds[6] of all handmaids,

---

[3] The word *šaḳ-šu* is practically synonymous with *ḫab-lu*, and conveys the meaning of "destruction" or "violence," rather than "wrong."

[4] I.e., the temple of Ištar in the city of Erech.

[5] See above, p. 224, n. 1.

[6] The rendering of the word *pusummu* is conjectural.

OBV.

34. *na-an-še-a-at na-an-di-a-at ḳa-rit-ti* [ilu] *Ištar ra-bu-u ḳur-di-ki*

35. *na-mir-tum di-par šamê(e) u irṣitim(tim) ša-ru-ur kal da-ad-me*

36. *iz - zi - it ḳab - lu la ma - ḫar a - li - lat tam-ḫa-ri*

37. *a-ku-ku-u-tum* [1] *ša ana ai-bi nap-ḫat ša-ki-na-at šul-lu-uḳ-ti ik-du-ti*

38. *mu - um - mil - tum* [ilu] *Iš - tar mu-paḫ-ḫi-rat pu-uḫ-ri*

39. *i-lat zikrûti* [pl] [ilu] *Iš-tar sinnišâti* [pl] *ša la i-lam-ma-du mi-lik-šu ma-am-man*

40. *a-šar tap-pal-la-si i-bal-luṭ* [amêlu] *mîtu i - te - ib - bi mar-ṣu*

41. *iš - ši - ir la i - ša - ru a-mi-ru pa-ni-ki*

42. *ana-ku al-si-ki an-ḫu- šu-nu-ḫu šum-ru-ṣu arad-ki*

43. *a-mur-in-ni-ma* [ilu] *bêlti-ia li-ki-e un - ni - ni - ia*

44. *ki-niš nap-li-sin-ni-ma ši-mi-e tas - li - ti*

45. *a-ḫu-lap-ia ki-bi-ma ka-bit-ta-ki lip - pa - aš - ra*

46. *a-ḫu-lap zumri-ia na-as-si ša ma-lu-u e-ša-a-ti u dal-ḫa-a-ti*

47. *a-ḫu-lap lib-bi-ia šum-ru-ṣu ša ma-lu-u dim-ti u ta-ni-ḫi*

48. *a-ḫu-lap te-ri-ti-ia na-as-sa-a-ti e-ša-a-ti u dal-ḫa-a-ti*

49. *a-ḫu-lap bîti-ia šu-ud-lu-bu ša u-na-as-sa-su nissati* [pl]

---

[1] For the meaning of the word *akukûtum*, cf. II R, pl. 39, K. 2,057, Obv., col. ii, l. 5, where *a-ku-ku-t[um]* and *a-šam-šu-tum*

34. That art raised on high, that art firmly established,—
O valiant Ištar, great is thy might!
35. Bright torch of heaven and earth, light of all dwellings,

36. Terrible in the fight, one who cannot be opposed, strong in the battle!
37. O whirlwind,[1] that roarest against the foe and cuttest off the mighty!
38. O furious Ishtar, summoner of armies!
39. O goddess of men, O goddess of women, thou whose counsel none may learn!
40. Where thou lookest in pity, the dead man lives again, the sick is healed;
41. The afflicted is saved from his affliction, when he beholdeth thy face!
42. I, thy servant, sorrowful, sighing, and in distress cry unto thee.
43. Look upon me, O my lady, and accept my supplication,
44. Truly pity me, and hearken unto my prayer!
45. Cry unto me "It is enough!" and let thy spirit be appeased!
46. How long shall my body lament, which is full of restlessness and confusion?
47. How long shall my heart be afflicted, which is full of sorrow and sighing?
48. How long shall my omens be grievous in restlessness and confusion?
49. How long shall my house be troubled, which mourneth bitterly?

occur as equivalents of two ideograms which form a section by themselves; see also Delitzsch, *Handwörterbuch*, p. 53.

OBV.

50. *a-ḫu-lap kab-ta-ti-ia ša uš-ta-bar-ru-u dim-ti u ta-ni-ḫi*

51. ^{ilu}*Ir-ni-ni* [. .][1]*-i-tum la-ab-bu na-ad-ru lib-ba-ki li-nu-ḫa*

52. *ri-i-mu šab-ba-su-u ka-bit-ta-ki lip - pa - aš - ra*

53. *damḳāti*^{pl} *īnā*^{II} *- ki lib - ša - a e - li - ia*

54. *ina bu-ni-ki nam-ru-ti ki-niš nap-li-sin-ni ia-a-ši*

55. *uk-ki-ši u-pi-ša limnēti*^{pl} *ša zumri-ia nūru-ki nam-ru lu-mur*

56. *a-di ma-ti* ^{ilu}*bēlti-ia bēlē*^{pl} *da-ba-bi-ia ni-kil-mu-u-in-ni-ma*

REV.

57. *ina sur-ra-a-ti u la ki-na-a-ti i-kap-pu-du-ni lim-ni-e-ti*

58. *ri - du - u - a ḫa - du - u - a iš - tam - ma - ru eli - ia*

59. *a - di ma - ti* ^{ilu} *bēlti - ia lil - lu*[2] *a-ku-u i-ba-'-an-ni*

60. *ib-na-an-ni muk-ku*[3] *ar-ku-um-ma ana-ku am-mir-ki*[4]

61. *en - šu - ti id - ni - nu - ma ana - ku e - ni - iš*

62. *a - šab - bu - ' ki - ma a - gi - i ša up-pa-ku šāru lim-na*

63. *i - ša - ' it - ta - nap - raš lib - bi ki-ma iṣ-ṣur ša-ma-mi*

64. *a-dam-mu-um ki-ma su-um-ma-tum mu - ši u ur - ra*

65. *na - an - gu - la - ku - ma*[5] *a - bak - ki zar - biš*

---

[1] The scribe has erased the first character of the word and has not rewritten it.

[2] The meaning assigned to *lillu* in the translation is conjectural; among other passages in which the word occurs, cf. especially IV R, pl. 27, No. 4, l. 57, and its context; see also Delitzsch, *Handwörterbuch*, p. 377, and Muss-Arnolt, *Concise Dictionary*, p. 481.

[3] Some such general meaning is probably to be assigned to

50. How long shall my spirit (be troubled), which aboundeth in sorrow and sighing?
51. O [. . .][1] Irnini, fierce lioness, may thy heart have rest!
52. Is anger mercy? Then let thy spirit be appeased!
53. May thine eyes rest with favour upon me;
54. With thy glorious regard truly in mercy look upon me!
55. Put an end to the evil bewitchments of my body; let me behold thy clear light!
56. How long, O my lady, shall mine enemies persecute me?
57. How long shall they devise evil in rebellion and wickedness,
58. And in my pursuits and my pleasures shall they rage against me?
59. How long, O my lady, shall the ravenous demon[2] pursue me?
60. They have caused me continuous affliction,[3] but I have praised[4] thee.
61. The weak have become strong, but I am weak;
62. I am sated like a flood which the evil wind maketh to rage.
63. My heart hath taken wing, and hath flown away like a bird of the heavens;
64. I moan like a dove, night and day.
65. I am made desolate,[5] and I weep bitterly;

---

nukku in this passage; the subject of the verb is probably impersonal, and it may be taken as followed by the double accusative.

[4] It is clear that in this passage an active meaning is to be assigned to *namāru*; cf. *im-mir-šu-ma*, V R, pl. 55, ll. 27 and 37, and *u-mu-ka nam-mar*, 82-3-23, 4,344, etc. (*P.S.B.A.*, xviii, p. 258), cited by Muss-Arnolt, *Concise Dictionary*, p. 684.

[5] iv, 1 from *nagālu*, cf. Syr. *n'gal.*

REV.

66. *ina '-u-a a-a šum-ru-ṣa-at ka-bit-ti*
67. *mi-na-a e-pu-uš ili-ia u* [ilu]*iš-tar-ia a-na-ku*
68. *ki-i la pa-liḫ ili-ia u* [ilu]*ištari-ia ana-ku ip-še-iḳ*

69. *šak-nu-nim-ma mur-ṣu ṭi-'-i ḫu-lu-uḳ-ḳu-u u šul-lu-uḳ-ti*
70. *šak-na-ni ud-da-a-ti suḫ-ḫur pa-ni u ma-li-e lib-ba-a-ti*

71. *uz-zu ug-ga-ti me-nat*[1] *ilāni*[pl] *u a-me-lu-ti*
72. *a-ta-mar* [ilu]*bēlti-ia ūmē*[pl] *uk-ku-lu-ti arḫē*[pl] *na-an-du-ru-ti šanāti*[pl] *ša ni-ziḳ-ti*
73. *a-ta-mar* [ilu]*bēlti-ia šib-ṭa i-ši-ti u saḫ-maš-ti*

74. *u-kal-la-an-ni mu-u-tu u šap-ša-ḳu*
75. *šu-ḫar-ru-ur sa-gi-e-a šu-ḫar-ru-rat a-šir-ti*
76. *eli bīti bābi u ḳar-ba-a-ti-ia ša-ḳu-um-ma-ti tab-kat*

77. *ili-ia ana a-šar ša-nim-ma suḫ-ḫu-ru pa-nu-šu*
78. *sap-ḫat il-la-ti ta-bi-ni pur-ru-ur*
79. *u-pa-ḳa a-na* [ilu]*bēlti-ia ka-a-ši ib-ša-ki uznā*[II]*-ai*

80. *u-sal-li-ki ka-a-ši '-il-ti pu-uṭ-ri*
81. *pu-uṭ-ri ar-ni*[2] *šir-ti ḫab-la-ti. u ḫi-ṭi-ti*

82. *mi-e-ši ḫab-la-ti-ia li-ki-e un-ni-ni-ia*
83. *ru-um-mi-ia ki-rim-ia šu-bar-ra-ai šuk-ni*

84. *šu-te-ši-ri kib-si nam-riš e-til-liš it-ti amēlūti*[pl] *lu-ba-' sūḳi*

85. *ki-bi-ma ina ki-bi-ti-ki ilu zi-nu-u li-is-lim*

---

[1] Literally, "numbers of, the host of."

[2] Under the line, and between the signs *ni* and *šir*, the scribe has written the division mark followed by the word *i-ši-ti*, "my

66 With grief and woe my spirit is distressed.
67. What have I done, O my god and my goddess?
68. Is it because I feared not my god or my goddess that trouble hath befallen me?
69. Sickness, disease, ruin, and destruction are come upon me;
70. Troubles, turning away of the countenance, and fulness of anger are my lot,
71. And the indignation and the wrath of all[1] gods and men.
72. I have beheld, O my lady, days of affliction, months of sorrow, years of misfortune;
73. I have beheld, O my lady, slaughter, turmoil, and rebellion.
74. Death and misery have made an end of me!
75. My need is grievous, grievous is my humiliation;
75. Over my house, my gate, and my fields is affliction poured forth.
77. As for my god, his face is turned elsewhere;
78. My strength is brought to nought, my power is broken!
79. But unto thee, O my lady, do I give heed, I have kept thee in my mind;
80. Unto thee therefore do I pray, dissolve my ban!
81. Dissolve my sin,[2] my iniquity, my transgression, and my offence!
82. Forgive my transgression, accept my supplication!
83. Secure my deliverance, and let me be loved and carefully tended!
84. Guide my footsteps in the light, that among men I may gloriously seek my way!
85. Say the word, that at thy command my angry god may have mercy,

---

confusion"; he probably had omitted the word by mistake and intended it to be inserted after *ar-ni*.

REV.

86. ^{ilu}*ištari ša is - bu - sa li - tu - ra*
87. *e - ṭu - u šu - šub lim-me-ir ki-nu-ni*

88. *bi - li - ti*[1] *li - in - na - pi - iḫ di - pa - ri*
89. *sa - pi - iḫ - tu il - la - ti lip - ḫur*
90. *tarbaṣu li-ir-piš liš-tam-di-lu su - pu - ri*
91. *mug - ri li - bi - en ap - pi - ia ši - me - e su-pi-e-a*

92. *ki - niš nap - li - sin - ni - ma* [erasure by the scribe] [2]
93. *a-di ma-ti* ^{ilu}*bēlti-ia zi-na-ti-ma suḫ-ḫu-ru pa-nu-ki*

94. *a-di ma-ti* ^{ilu}*bēlti-ia ra-'-ba-ti-ma uz-zu-za-at kab-ta-at-ki*

95. *tir-ri ki-šad ki ša ištu ad-di-ia a-mat damiḳtim(tim) pa-ni-ki šuk-ni*
96. *ki-ma mē*^{pl} *pa-šir nāri ka-bit-ta-ki lip - pa - aš - ra*

97. *ik-du-ti-ia ki-ma ḳaḳ-ḳa-ru lu - kab - bi - is*
98. *šab-su-ti-ia kun-nu-šim-ma šu-pal-si-ḫi ina šap-li-ia*

99. *su - pu - u - a u su - lu - u - a lil - li - ku eli - ki*
100. *ta - ai - ra - tu - ki rab - ba - a - ti lib - ša - a eli - ia*
101. *a-mi-ru-u-a ina sūḳi li-šar-bu-u zi - kir - ki*

102. *u ana-ku ana ṣal-mat ḳaḳḳadi ilu-ut-ki u ḳur-di-ki lu-ša-pi*

103. ^{ilu}*Iš - tar - ma ṣi - rat* ^{ilu}*Iš-tar-ma šar-rat*
104. ^{ilu}*bēlti*[3] *- ma ṣi - rat* ^{ilu}*bēlti - ma šar - rat*

---

[1] Probably Perm. Ḳal from *bēlu*; the word, however, is possibly the lengthened form of *bēlti*, its occurrence being due to the necessities of rhythm.

86. And that my goddess, who is wroth, may turn again!
87. The darkness hath settled down, so let my brazier be bright;
88. Thou art the ruler,[1] let then my torch flame forth!
89. May my scattered strength be collected;
90. May the fold be wide, and may my pen be bolted fast!
91. Receive the abasement of my countenance, give ear unto my prayer,
92. Truly pity me, and [accept my supplication]![2]
93. How long, O my lady, wilt thou be angry and thy face be turned away?
94. How long, O my lady, wilt thou rage and thy spirit be full of wrath?
95. Incline thy neck, which (is turned) away from my affairs, and set prosperity before thy face;
96. As by the solving waters of the river may thine anger be dissolved!
97. My mighty foes may I trample like the ground;
98. And those who are wroth with me mayest thou force into submission and crush beneath my feet!
99. Let my prayer and my supplication come unto thee,
100. And let thy great mercy be upon me,
101. That those who behold me in the street may magnify thy name,
102. And that I may glorify thy godhead and thy might before mankind!
103. Ištar is exalted! Ištar is queen!
104. My lady[3] is exalted! My lady is queen!

---

[2] The scribe has erased the second half of the line; we may probably restore some such phrase as *li-ki-e un-ni-ni-ia*, as suggested in the translation.

[3] See above, p. 224, n. 1.

REV.

105. ^{ilu}*Ir-ni-ni ma-rat* ^{ilu}*Sin ḳa-rit-ti ma-ḫi-ra ul isat*

---

106. INIM-INIM-MA ŠU-IL-LA ^{DINGIR}INNANNA(NA)-KAN [1]

---

107. *epuš annā* KI KIŠ TAR AD *gušuru arḳu mū ellu tasallaḫ*
IV *libnāti*^{pl} *libbi ḫalāḳi* (?) [2] *tanaddi(di)*

108. *immeru teliḳe(e)* ^{isu}*ṣarbatu te-ṣi-en išatu tanaddi(di)*
rikkē^{pl} *upuntu burašu*

109. *tattabak(ak) mi-iḫ-ḫa tanakki(ki)-ma lā tuš-kin*
mi-nu-tu an-ni-tu ana pān ^{ilu}*Iš-tar*

110. *šalultu šanitu tamannu(nu)* KI-ZA-ZA-*ma* [3] *ana arki-ka*
lā tabari

---

111. *šiptu ša-ḳu-tum* ^{ilu}*Iš-tar mu-nam-mi-rat kib-ra-a-ti* [4]

112. *gab-ri Bar-sip*^{KI} *kīma labiri-šu* $^{m\ ilu}$*Nergal-balāṭ-su-iḳ-bi*
apil ^{m}*A-ta-rad-kal-me* ^{amēlu}*asipu*

113. *ana balāṭi-šu išṭur ibri-ma ina E-sag-ila u-kin*

---

[1] Line 106 gives the title of the prayer; then follows a rubric of four lines giving directions for the performance of certain ceremonies and for the due recital of the prayer.

[2] In the four bricks, which, if the suggested rendering is correct,

105. Irnini, the valiant daughter of the Moon-god, hath not a rival!

106. Prayer of the Raising of the Hand to Ištar.[1]

107. This shalt thou do . . . . a green bough shalt thou sprinkle with pure water; four bricks from a ruin[2] shalt thou set in place;
108. a lamb shalt thou take; with ṣarbatu-wood shalt thou fill (the censer), and thou shalt set fire (thereto); sweet-scented woods, some upuntu-plant and some cypress-wood
109. shalt thou heap up; a drink offering shalt thou offer, but thou shalt not bow thyself down. This incantation before the goddess Ištar
110. three times shalt thou recite, ... and thou shalt not look behind thee.

111. "O exalted Ištar, that givest light unto the (four) quarters of the world!"[4]
112. (This) copy from Borsippa, (made) like unto its original, hath Nergal-balāṭsu-iḳbi, the son of Atarad-kalme, the magician,
113. written for (the preservation of) his life, and he hath revised it, and hath deposited it within the temple of E-sagila.

·e here directed to be brought from a ruin, we may perhaps see symbolical offering to Ištar in her character of the goddess of attle and destruction.

[3] Possibly *ki za-za-ma*, but cf. Brünnow, No. 9,843.

[4] Line 111 gives the catch-line for the next tablet.

Indices, Glossary, etc.

I.

Index to Texts.

Cuneiform Texts from Babylonian Tablets, etc., in the British Museum, Part XIII (1901), Plates 1–41.

ATE.		
1.	K. 5,419*c*, Obv. :	Cr. Ser., Tabl. I, ll. 1–16.
	,, Rev. :	Traces of catch-line to Tabl. II, and colophon.
	No. 93,015, Obv. :	Cr. Ser., Tabl. I, ll. 1–16.
2.	81–7–27, 80, Obv. :	,, ,, ll. 31–56.
	,, Rev. :	,, ,, ll. 118–142.
3.	K. 3,938, Obv. :	,, ,, ll. 33–42.
	,, Rev. :	,, ,, ll. 128–142.
	No. 93,015, Rev. :	,, ,, ll. 124–142, and colophon.
4.	No. 38,396, Obv. :	,, Tabl. II, ll. 11–29.
	,, Rev. :	,, ,, ll. (105)–(132).
5.	K. 4,832, Obv. :	,, ,, ll. 32–58.
	,, Rev. :	,, ,, ll. (104)–(138).
6.	79–7–8, 178, Obv. :	,, ,, ll. (69)–(75).
	,, Rev. :	,, ,, ll. (76)–(85).
	K. 292, Rev. :	,, ,, ll. (131)–(140), catch-line to Tabl. III, and colophon.
7.	K. 3,473, etc., Obv. :	,, Tabl. III, ll. 1–56.
8.	,, Obv. (cont.) :	,, ,, ll. 57–85.
	,, Rev. :	,, ,, ll. 86–113.
9.	,, Rev. (cont.) :	,, ,, ll. 114–138, and catch-line to Tabl. IV.
	K. 6,650 :	,, ,, ll. 38–55, or 96–113.

PLATE.		
10.	No. 93,017, Obv. :	Cr. Ser., Tabl. III, ll. 47–77.
11.	,, Rev. :	,, ,, ll. 78–105.
12.	K. 8,575, Obv. :	,, ,, ll. 69–76.
	,, Rev. :	,, ,, ll. 77–85.
	K. 8,524 :	,, ,, ll. 75–86.
	83–1–18, 2,116 :	joined to 82–9–18, 5,448 ; see vol. ii, pl. xxxiv.
	83–1–18, 1,868 :	joined to 82–9–18, 6,950 ; see vol. ii, pl. xxix.
13.	82–9–18, 1,403 :	joined to 82–9–18, 6,316 ; see vol. ii, pls. xxv ff.
14.	No. 93,016, Obv. :	Cr. Ser., Tabl. IV, ll. 1–44.
15.	,, Rev. :	,, ,, ll. 116–146, catch-line to Tabl. V, and colophon.
16.	K. 3,437, etc., Obv. :	,, ,, ll. 36–59.
17.	,, Obv. (cont.) :	,, ,, ll. 60–83.
18.	,, Rev. :	,, ,, ll. 84–107.
19.	,, Rev. (cont.) :	,, ,, ll. 108–119.
	R. 2, 83 :	,, ,, ll. 117–129.
20.	No. 93,051, Obv. :	,, ,, ll. 42–54.
	,, Rev. :	,, ,, ll. 85–94.
	79–7–8, 251, Obv. :	,, ,, ll. 35–49.
	,, Rev. :	,, ,, ll. 103–107.
21.	K. 5,420*c*, Obv. :	,, ,, ll. 74–92.
	,, Rev. :	,, ,, ll. 93–119.
22.	K. 3,567, etc., Obv. :	,, Tabl. V, ll. 1–26.
	,, Rev. :	catch-line to Tabl. VI, and colophon.
23.	K. 8,526, Obv. :	Cr. Ser., Tabl. V, ll. 1–18.
	,, Rev. :	,, ,, ll. (138)–(140).
	K. 3,449*a*, Obv. :	,, ,, ll. (66)–(74).
	,, Rev. :	,, ,, ll. (75)–(87).
24.	K. 12,000*b* :	see Appendix II, p. 194.
	K. 14,949 :	see Appendix II, p. 197 f.
	K. 3,445, etc. :	see Appendix II, pp. 197 ff.
25.	,, Rev. (cont.) :	see Appendix II, pp. 198 ff.
26.	K. 8,522, Obv. :	Cr. Ser., Tabl. VII, ll. 15–45.
27.	,, Rev. :	,, ,, ll. 105–137.
28.	K. 9,267, Obv. :	,, ,, ll. 40–47.
	,, Rev. :	,, ,, ll. 109–138.

B. Supplementary Texts, published in Vol. II, Plates I–LXXXIV.

16

PLATE.					
XVII.	No. 40,559,	Obv. (cont.):	Cr. Ser.,	Tabl. II,	ll. 31–40.
XVIII.	,,	Rev.:	,,	,,	ll. (111)–(119).
XIX.	,,	Rev. (cont.):	,,	,,	ll. (120)–(128).
XX.	,,	Rev. (cont.):	,,	,,	ll. (129)–(137).
XXI.	,,	Rev. (cont.):	,,	,,	ll. (138)–(140), catch-line to Tabl. III, and colophon.
XXII.	No. 92,632, etc.,	Obv.:	,,	,,	ll. 14–25.
XXIII.	,,	Obv. (cont.):	,,	,,	ll. 26–29.
	,,	Rev.:	,,	,,	ll. (114)–(119).
XXIV.	,,	Rev. (cont.):	,,	,,	ll. (120)–(131).
XXV.	82–9–18, 1,403, etc.,	Obv.:	,,	Tabl. III,	ll. 5–15.
XXVI.	,,	Obv. (cont.):	,,	,,	ll. 52–61.
XXVII.	,,	Rev.:	,,	,,	ll. 62–71.
XXVIII.	,,	Rev. (cont.):	,,	,,	ll. 72–128.
XXIX.	82–9–18, 6,950, etc.:		,,	,,	ll. 19–26 or 77–84.
XXX.	No. 42,285,	Obv.:	,,	,,	ll. 46–57.
XXXI.	,,	Obv. (cont.):	,,	,,	ll. 58–68.
XXXII.	,,	Rev.:	,,	,,	ll. 69–77.
XXXIII.	,,	Rev. (cont.):	,,	,,	ll. 78–87.
XXXIV.	82–9–18, 5,448, etc.:		,,	,,	ll. 64–72.
XXXV.	No. 92,629,	Obv.:	,,	Tabl. VI,	ll. 1–10.
XXXVI.	,,	Obv. (cont.):	,,	,,	ll. 11–21.
XXXVII.	,,	Rev.:	,,	,,	ll. 138–146, catch-line to Tabl. VII, and colophon.
XXXVIII.	No. 91,139, etc.,	Obv.:	,,	Tabl. VII,	ll. 3–12.
XXXIX.	,,	Obv. (cont.):	,,	,,	ll. 13–21.
XL.	,,	Obv. (cont.):	,,	,,	ll. 22–30.
XLI.	,,	Obv. (cont.):	,,	,,	ll. 31–40.
XLII.	,,	Rev.:	,,	,,	ll. 106–114.
XLIII.	,,	Rev. (cont.):	,,	,,	ll. 115–123.
XLIV.	,,	Rev. (cont.):	,,	,,	ll. 124–132.
XLV.	,,	Rev. (cont.):	,,	,,	ll. 133–141.
XLVI.	No. 35,506,	Obv.:	,,	,,	ll. 14–30.
XLVII.	,,	Obv. (cont.):	,,	,,	ll. 31–36.
	,,	Rev.:	,,	,,	ll. 105–120.

C. Supplementary Texts, published in Appendices I, II, and III.

II.

Index to Registration-Numbers.

REGISTRATION NO.	TEXT.	CONTENTS.
82–9–18, 6,950+ 83–1–18, 1,868.	Vol. II, pl. xxix.	Cr. Ser., Tabl. III, ll. 19–26 or 77–84.
83–1–18, 1,868.	see 82–9–18, 6,950.	
83–1–18, 2,116.	see 82–9–18, 5,448.	
88–4–19, 13.	see No. 93,017.	
No. 26,187.	Vol. II, pls. lxxv–lxxxiv.	see App. V, pp. 222 ff.
No. 32,574.	App. III, p. 216 f.	see pp. 216 ff.
No. 33,851.	Vol. II, pls. lxiv–lxvi.	see App. II, p. 202 f.
No. 35,134.	,, pl. vii.	Cr. Ser., Tabl. I, ll. 11–21.
No. 35,506.	,, pls. xlvi–xlviii.	Cr. Ser., Tabl. VII, ll. 14–36, 105–142.
No. 36,688.	,, pl. vii.	Cr. Ser., Tabl. I, ll. 38–43.
No. 36,726.	,, pl. viii.	Cr. Ser., Tabl. I, ll. 28–33.
No. 38,396.	Cun. Txts., XIII, pl. 4.	Cr. Ser., Tabl. II, ll. 11–29, (105)–(132).
No. 40,559.	Vol. II, pls. xiv–xxi.	Cr. Ser., Tabl. II, ll. 1–40, (111)–(140).
No. 40,959.	App. III, p. 215.	see p. 215 f.
No. 42,285.	Vol. II, pls. xxx–xxxiii.	Cr. Ser., Tabl. III, ll. 46–87.
No. 45,528+46,614.	,, pls. i–vi.	Cr. Ser., Tabl. I, ll. 1–48, 111–139.
No. 46,614.	see No. 45,528.	
No. 46,803.	Vol. II, pls. ix–xi.	Cr. Ser., Tabl. I, ll. 46–60, 62–67, 83–103.
No. 54,228.	,, pl. lxiii.	see App. I, pp. 175 ff.
No. 55,466+55,486+ 55,627.	,, pls. lxvii–lxxii	see App. III, pp. 208 ff.
No. 55,486.	see No. 55,466.	
No. 55,627.	see No. 55,466.	
No. 91,139+93,073.	Vol. II, pls. xxxviii–xlv.	Cr. Ser., Tabl. VII, ll. 3–40, 106–141.

REGISTRATION NO.	TEXT.	CONTENTS.
No. 92,629.	Vol. II, pls. xxxv–xxxvii.	Cr. Ser., Tabl. VI, ll. 1–21, 138–146.
No. 92,632+93,048.	„ pls. xxii–xxiv.	Cr. Ser., Tabl. II, ll. 14–29, (114)–(131).
No. 93,015 (82–7–14, 402).	Cun. Txts., XIII, pls. 1, 3.	Cr. Ser., Tabl. I, ll. 1–16, 124–142.
No. 93,016 (82–9–18, 3,737).	„ „ pls. 14–15.	Cr. Ser., Tabl. IV, ll. 1–44, 116–146.
No. 93,017 (88–4–19, 13).	„ „ pls. 10–11.	Cr. Ser., Tabl. III, ll. 47–105.
No. 93,048.	see No. 92,632.	
No. 93,051.	Cun. Txts., XIII, pl. 20.	Cr. Ser., Tabl. IV, ll. 42–54, 85–94.
No. 93,073.	see No. 91,139.	

III.

Glossary of Selected Words.

א

u, enclitic interrogative particle: *šab-ba-su-u*, p. 230, l. 52.

abubu, "deluge; thunder-bolt(?)": *a-bu-ba* (var. *bu*), Tabl. IV, l. 49 (p. 64); *a-bu-ba*, Tabl. IV, l. 75 (p. 68).

abāku, III 1, "to cause to bring, to cause to be brought": Imper. *šu-bi-ka*, Tabl. III, l. 6 (p. 38).

abālu, I 1, "to bring"; I 2, "to bring out, to proclaim(?)": *lit* (var. *li-it*)-*tab-bal*, Tabl. VII, l. 33 (p. 98); *lit* (var. *li-it*) -*ta-bal*, Tabl. VII, l. 122 (p. 110).

abāru, I 1, "to be strong"; I 2, do.: Perm. *it-bur-ti*, p. 224, l. 11.

itbaru, "strength": *it-ba-ru*, p. 224, l. 10.

ebēru, I 1: *e-bi-ru*, p. 167.

I 2, "to pass through, to force a way into": *i-tib-bi-ru*, Tabl. VII, l. 108 (p. 106).

abātu, II 2, "to be destroyed": *u-tab-ba-tu*, p. 206, l. 16.

agāgu, II 1, "to make angry": Perm. *ug-*[*g*]*u-ga*[*t*], Tabl. I, l. 43 (p. 184).

ugallu, "hurricane": Tabl. I, l. 122 (p. 18); Tabl. II, l. 28 (p. 26); Tabl. III, l. 32 (p. 42), l. 90 (p. 50).

adū, "age": plur. *a-di* (var. *a-di-i*), Tabl. I, l. 11 (p. 4).

ādū, "course, way, affair": *ad-di-ia*, p. 234, l. 95.

idu, "side"; *iduš*, "to the side of": *i-du-uš sa-pa-ra* (var. *ru*), Tabl. IV, l. 44 (p. 62).

idu, "to know; to choose (?)": *e-du-u*, Tabl. I, l. 135 (p. 20); Tabl. II, l. 41 (p. 26); Tabl. III, l. 45 (p. 44), l. 103 (p. 52).

uddu, "daylight."

uddakam, adv., "in the morning, every morning": *ud-da-kam*, p. 226, l. 26.

uddū, "trouble": plur. *ud-da-a-ti*, p. 232, l. 70.

edēlu, I 1, "to bolt."

III 2, "to be bolted": *liš-tam-di-lu*, p. 234, l. 90.

adāru, I 2, "to be troubled": Pret. *i-te-dir*, var. [. .]-*ti-di-ir*, Tabl. I, l. 53 (pp. 10, 186).

[azāmu], II 2, "to be angry(?)": Inf. *u-ta-az-zu-mi-šu*, p. 206, l. 9.

aḫāzu, I 1, "to take; to undertake, to begin": *i-ḫu-zu*, Tabl. IV, l. 18 (p. 60).
IV 1, "to be taken": *in-ni-ḫaz*, Tabl. IV, l. 100 (p. 70).

aḫulap, interrog. adv., "how long?": *a-ḫu-lap*, p. 228, ll. 46, 47, 48, 49, p. 230, l. 50; with suffix, *a-ḫu-lap-ki*, p. 226, ll. 27, 28, 29, 30; with *ḳibū*, by transference of meaning, "to cry 'It is enough!'": *a-ḫu-lap-ia ki-bi-ma*, p. 228, l. 45.

eṭū, "to be dark"; Inf. "darkness": *e-ṭu-u*, p. 234, l. 87.

ekiām, interrog. adv., "where?": *e-ki-a-am*, p. 224, ll. 15, 16, 17.

akū, "hungry, ravenous": *a-ku-u*, p. 230, l. 59.

akukūtu, "whirlwind": *a-ku-ku-u-tum*, p. 228, l. 37.

[**akālu**], "to be afflicted": Pres. *a-ka-la*, p. 146, n. 4; p. 148, l. 22.
ukkulu, "afflicted": *uk-ku-lu-ti*, p. 232, l. 72.

[**akāšu**], II 1, "to put an end to": Imper. *uk-ki-ši*, p. 230, l. 55.

ali, interrog. adv., "where?": *a-li*, Tabl. II, l. 56 (p. 30).

elū, "high"; fem. plur. *elāti*, "the height; the zenith (?)": *e-la-a-ti*, Tabl. V, l. 11 (p. 78).

alādu, I, "to bear."
II 1, do.: Part. *mu-al-li-da-at*, var. *mu-um-ma al-li-da-at* (= *muwallidat*), Tabl. I, l. 4 (p. 2).

alāku, "to go."
malaku, "going, gait": *ma-lak-šu*, Tabl. IV, l. 67 (p. 66).

ulinnu, "border (?) of a robe": *ulinni-šu*, p. 118, l. 16.

amu, "reed (?)": *a-mi*, p. 132, l. 18; *a-ma-am*, p. 132, l. 17.

[**amū**], "to speak."
amātu, "speech; thing, deed": *a-ma-tu-šu*, Tabl. VII, l. 31 (p. 98).

emū, I 1, "to be like."
III 1, "to make like; to create": *uš-ta-mu-u*, p. 126, l. 14; *šu-ta-mu-u*, p. 125, n. 5.

ūmu, "day"; *ištu ūmimma*, "henceforth": *iš-tu u-mi-im-ma*, Tabl. IV, l. 7 (p. 58).

ūmu, "tempest": Tabl. I, l. 123 (p. 18); Tabl. II, l. 29 (p. 26); Tabl. III, l. 33 (p. 42), l. 91 (p. 52); applied to Marduk's chariot, Tabl. IV, l. 50 (p. 64).

emēdu, IV 1, "to be established; to advance": *in-nin-du-ma*, var. [*in-nin-d*]*u u*[ ], Tabl. I, l. 21 (p. 4); *in-nin-du-ma*, Tabl. IV, l. 93 (p. 70).

imḫullu, "evil wind": *im-ḫul-lu* (var. *la*), Tabl. IV, l. 96 (p. 70); *im-ḫul-la*, Tabl. IV, l. 45 (p. 62), l. 98 (p. 70); *im-ḫul-lu*, p. 206, l. 15.

[amālu], II 1, intrans., "to be furious": Part. *mu-um-mil-tum*, p. 228, l. 38.

ammatu, "the sure earth": Tabl. I, l. 2 (p. 2).

unkennu, "might, strength, forces": *unken-na*, Tabl. I, l. 112 (p. 16); Tabl. II, l. 18 (p. 24); Tabl. III, l. 22 (p. 40), l. 80 (p. 50); *un-ki-en-na*, Tabl. III, l. 80 (var., p. 50, n. 5).

[esēḫu], "to despair": Pres. *is-si-ḫu*, p. 146, n. 4; p. 148, l. 22; *te-si-iḫ-ḫu*, var. *te-iš*(sic)-*si-iḫ-ḫu*, p. 152, l. 16.

asurakku, "bed of a river; depth": *a-sur-rak-ka*, p. 206, l. 19.

apu, "swamp": *a-pa*, p. 134, l. 32; *a-pu-um-ma*, p. 134, l. 27.

appunu, "huge": [*a*]*p-pu-na-a-ta*, Tabl. I, l. 126 (var., p. 18).

appunama, adv., "of huge size": *ap-pu-na-ma*, Tabl. I, l. 126 (p. 18); Tabl. II, l. 32 (p. 26); Tabl. III, l. 94 (var., p. 52); *ap-pu-un-na-ma*, Tabl. III, l. 36 (p. 42), l. 94 (p. 52).

epēḳu, II 1, "to cause to rage": *up-pa-ḳu*, p. 230, l. 62.

apparu, "marsh": *ap-pa-ri*, p. 134, ll. 25, 27.

upišu, "bewitchment": *u-pi-ša*, p. 230, l. 55.

aṣu, I 1, "to go out"; III 1, "to cause to go out; to take oneself off, to take to flight": *u še-ṣu-ma*, Tabl. IV, l. 109 (p. 72).

iṣṣimtu, "bone": *iṣ-ṣi-im-*[*tu*]*m*, Tabl. VI, l. 5 (p. 86).

eṣēpu, "to add to; to bring upon": Pret. *e-ṣip*, p. 148, l. 24.

uḳū: *u-ḳu-u*, p. 160.

II 2, "to pay homage, to worship": *u-tak-ḳu-u*, Tabl. VII, l. 4 (p. 92); *u-tuk-ḳu*, p. 224, l. 14.

aḳrab-amēlu, "scorpion-man": Tabl. I, l. 122 (p. 18); Tabl. II, l. 28 (p. 26); Tabl. III, l. 32 (p. 42), l. 90 (p. 50).

'āru, āru, "to set out, to set out against, to attack": *'-ir*, Tabl. III, l. 55 (p. 46), l. 113 (p. 54); *ia-ar-ka*, Tabl. II, l. 122 (p. 34).

arāku, I 1, "to be long, to endure": [*li-r*]*i-ik*, Tabl. VII, l. 114 (var., p. 108 f.).

II 1, "to lengthen; to be long": *ur-ri-ku*, varr. *u-ur-ri-ku*, *u-ri-ki*, Tabl. I, l. 13 (p. 4); [*u*]*-ri-ku-ma*, Tabl. II, l. 7 (p. 22).

urriš, adv., "by day": [*ur-r*]*iš*, Tabl. I, l. 50 (p. 10).

erēšu, "to desire."

erištu, "desire": *erišti* (ŠA-DI)-*ia*, p. 224, l. 11.

ešû, "to rage, to be in confusion; to destroy": Imper. *e-ši*-[. . .], Tabl. I, l. 49 (p. 10).

ašābu, I 2, "to seat oneself": Imper. *tiš-ba-ma*, var. *ti-iš-b*[*a*]-*ma*, Tabl. II, l. 137 (p. 36); *taš-ba-ma*, var. *ta-aš-ba-ma*, Tabl. III, l. 61 (p. 46 f.), l. 119 (p. 54); *ti-šam-ma*, Tabl. IV, l. 15 (p. 58).

ešgallu, "mansion": *eš-gal-la*, Tabl. IV, l. 144 f. (p. 76).

ùšumgallu, "monster-viper": *ušumgallē*^{pl}, Tabl. I. l. 117 (p. 16); Tabl. II, l. 23 (p. 24); Tabl. III, l. 27 (p. 42), l. 85 (p. 50).

ašamšutu, "hurricane": *a-šam-šu-tum*, Tabl. IV, l. 45 (p. 62).

ašāru, "to humble oneself": Pret. *i-šir*, Tabl. III, l. 70 (p. 48).

aširtu, "humiliation": *a-šir-ti*, p. 232, l. 75.

ašru, "place"; employed as synonym for "heaven": *aš-ru* = *ša-mu-u*, p. 168; *as-ri* (varr. *ra*, *ru*), Tabl. VII, l. 115 (p. 108).

ašriš, "towards": *aš-riš*, Tabl. IV, l. 60 (p. 66).

ašru, "shrine, sanctuary": *aš-ru-uk-ka*, Tabl. IV, l. 12 (p. 58).

uššu, "grass": *uš-šu*, p. 134, l. 25.

etilliš, "gloriously": *e-til-liš*, p. 232, l. 84.

[**atāru**], II 1, "to make exceeding strong": *u-wa*(i.e. PI)-*at-te-ir*, p. 146, n. 4.

atta'u, "fang (?)": Tabl. I, l. 115 (p. 16); Tabl. II, l. 21 (p. 24); Tabl. III, l. 25 (p. 40), l. 83 (p. 50).

ב

bēlu, "to rule, control, hold sway": *li-bil-ma*, var. *li-bi-el-ma*, Tabl. VII, l. 122 (p. 110); (?) *li-bi-il*, Tabl. VII, l. 114 (p. 108).

[**barû**], III^{II} 1, "to tend carefully": Inf. *šu-bar-ra-ai*, p. 232, l. 83.

III^{II} 2, "to abound in": *uš-ta-bar-ru-u*, p. 230, l. 50.

burumu, "heaven": *bu-ru-mi*, p. 206, l. 13; [*bu*]-*ru-mi*, p. 122, l. 2.

bašmu, "viper": Tabl. I, l. 121 (p. 18); Tabl. II, l. 27 (p. 24); Tabl. III, l. 31 (p. 42), l. 89 (p. 50).

batnu: *ba*(?)-*at-nu*, Tabl. IV, l. 36 (p. 62).

ג

guḫḫu: *guḫḫē*^{pl}, p. 144, l. 8; p. 150, l. 20.

gallū, "devil": *gal-li-e*, var. *gallē*, Tabl. IV, l. 116 (p. 72).

gisgallu, "station": *gi-is-gal-la-ša*, Tabl. V, l. 83 (p. 84).

gipāru, "field (?)," or possibly a kind of tree: *gi-pa-ra*, var. *gi-par-ra*, Tabl. I, l. 6 (p. 2).

gašāru, I 1, "to strengthen."

II 1, "to make very strong": Perm. *gu-uš-šur*, Tabl. I, l. 19 (p. 4).

magšaru, "might": Tabl. I, l. 142 (p. 20); Tabl. II, l. 48 (p. 28); Tabl. III, l. 52 (p. 44), l. 110 (p. 54).

ד

dabru, "mighty (?)": Tabl. I, l. 123 (p. 18); Tabl. II, l. 29 (p. 26); Tabl. III, l. 33 (p. 42), l. 91 (p. 52).

dālu, "to move about; to scout; to prowl round, to watch from hiding": Pret. *i-dul-lu*, Tabl. I, l. 57 (p. 186); *i-du-ul-[li]*, Tabl. I, l. 89 (p. 12); *ta-du-ul-l[i]*, Tabl. I, l. 99 (p. 14); *i-dul-lu-šu*, Tabl. IV, l. 63 f. (pp. 66, 186 f.).

dalābu, III 1, "to trouble": Perm. *šu-ud-lu-bu*, p. 228, l. 49.

dullu, "service (of the gods)": *dul-lu*, Tabl. VI, l. 8 (p. 88).

danninu, "firmness; the firm earth": *dan-ni-nu* = *irṣitim(tim)*, p. 168; *dan-ni-na*, Tabl. VII, l. 115 (p. 108).

dupšīmtu, pl. *dupšīmāti*, "the Tablets of Destiny": Tabl. I. l. 137 (p. 20); Tabl. II, l. 43 (p. 28); Tabl. III, l. 47 (p. 44), l. 105 (p. 52); Tabl. IV, l. 121 (p. 74); p. 209, l. 4.

durmaḫu, "ruler (?)": *dur-ma-ḫi*, p. 104 (Tabl. VII); *dur-ma-ḫu*, p. 165.

[dašū], II 1, "to cause to be fruitful": *lid-diš-ša-a*, var. *li-id-[di]-eš-ša-a*, Tabl. VII, l. 130 (p. 112).

III II, "to cause to abound in, to clothe with": Pret. *uš-daš-ša-a*, Tabl. I, l. 118 (p. 16); Tabl. II, l. 24 (p. 24); Tabl. III, l. 28 (p. 42), l. 86 (p. 50).

dittu, udittu, "rush": *di-it-ta*, p. 134, l. 25.

ז

zazāru: *i-za-az-ru-šu*, p. 134, l. 30.

zaḳāru, I 1, "to be high."

II 1, "to exalt": *u-zak-k[a-ru-šu]*, Tabl. VI, l. 146 (p. 90).

zaḳiḳu, "tempest": *za-ki-ḳu*, Tabl. I, l. 104 (p. 14).

[**zâru**], Pret. *izîr*, "to hate, to conceive a hatred for": Tabl. II, l. 11 (p. 22); Tabl. III, l. 15 (p. 40), l. 73 (p. 48).

[**zarbabu**], IV 1, "to fume, to rage": Perm. *na-zar-bu-bu*, Tabl. I, l. 111 (p. 16); Tabl. II, l. 17 (p. 24); Tabl. III, l. 21 (p. 40), l. 79 (p. 50).

ח

ḫabâṣu, "to be filled, to be bloated (?)": Perm. *ḫa-ba-ṣu*, Tabl. III, l. 136 (p. 56).

ḫalâḳu, III 1, "to destroy": Pres. (not as Prec.) *nu-uš-ḫal-laḳ* (= *nušaḫlaḳ*, Tabl. I, l. 45 (p. 185).

ḫamû, "to destroy (?)": *ḫa-mu-u*, p. 206, l. 21.

ḫasâsu, "to think, to know": Part. *ḫa-sis*, Tabl. I, l. 18 (p. 4), l. 60 (p. 12).

ḫipû, I 2, "to shatter, to burst": *iḫ-te-pi*, Tabl. IV, l. 101 (p. 70).

ḫâḳu, "to mingle together," intrans.: Pret. *i-ḫi-ḳu-u-ma*, Tabl. I, l. 5 (p. 2).

[**ḫarmamu**], III 1, "to destroy, to overcome (?)": *liš-ḫar-mi-im*, Tabl. I, l. 119 (p. 16); Tabl. III, l. 29 (p. 42).

IV 1, do. (?): *li-iḫ-ḫar-mi-im*, Tabl. II, l. 25 (p. 24); Tabl. III, l. 87 (p. 50).

ט

ṭâbu, "to be sound, to be healed": Pres. *i-te-ib-bi*, p. 228, l. 40.

ṭubtu, "joy": plur. *tu-ub-ba-a-ti*, Tabl. II, l. 115 (p. 32).

כ

kabâtu, II 1, "to make weighty; to oppress": *u-kab-bi*[*t*]-*ma*, Tabl. II, l. 1 (p. 22); *kub-bu-tu-ma*, Tabl. VI, l. 10 (p. 88).

kabittu, "midst (?)": *ka-bit-ti-ša-ma*, Tabl. V, l. 11 (p. 78).

kubuttû, "abundance": *ku-bu-ut-te-e*, Tabl. VII, l. 21 (p. 96); p. 161.

kâlu, II 1, "to uphold, to hold, to bring": *li-ki-il-lu*, Tabl. VII, l. 110 (p. 108); *mu-kil*, Tabl. VII, l. 19 (p. 96).

kalû, II 1, "to make an end of": *u-kal-la-an-ni*, p. 232, l. 74.

II 2, "to cease (?)": (?) *uk-ta-li* (var. *lu*), Tabl. VII, l. 114 (p. 108).

[**kalâmu**], II 1, "to inform."

taklimtu, "instruction": *ta*[*k*]-*lim-ti*, Tabl. VII, l. 137 (p. 114).

[kalmū], IV 1, "to look with anger upon, to persecute": Perm. *ni-kil-mu-u-in-ni-ma*, p. 230, l. 56.

kamū, IV 1, "to be taken captive": Pret. *ik-ka-mu-u*, Tabl. I, l. 98 (p. 14).

kamāru, I 2, Inf. *kitmuru*, "battle": Tabl. I, l. 142 (p. 20); Tabl. II, l. 48 (p. 28); Tabl. III, l. 52 (p. 44), l. 110 (p. 54).

kamāru, "snare."

kamāriš, "in the snare": *ka-ma-riš*, Tabl. IV, l. 112 (p. 72).

kanū, II 1, "to tend carefully."

taknītu, "fostering care, true worship": *tak-na-a-ti*, p. 206, l. 14.

kinūnu, "brazier": *ki-nu-ni*, p. 234, l. 87.

kisukku, "bondage."

kisukkiš, "in bondage": *ki-suk-kiš*, Tabl. IV, l. 114 (p. 72).

kusarikku, "ram": Tabl. I, l. 123 (p. 18); Tabl. II, l. 29 (p. 26); Tabl. III, l. 33 (p. 42), l. 91 (p. 52).

kupu, "trunk (?)": *šir ku-pu*, Tabl. IV, l. 136 (p. 76).

kipdu, "plan": [*ki*]*p-di-šu-nu*, Tabl. VII, l. 44 (p. 100).

kirimmu, "love": *ki-rim-ia*, p. 232, l. 83.

karru, "costly raiment (?)": Tabl. I, l. 132 (p. 20); Tabl. II, l. 38 (p. 26); Tabl. III, l. 42 (p. 44), l. 100 (p. 52).

kašāšu, "to collect (?)": Pret. *ik-ša-šu-nim-ma*, Tabl. III, l. 129 (p. 56).

katāmu, III 1, "to overcome": Perm. *šuk-tu-mat*, Tabl. II, 119 (p. 32).

ל

[li'ū], "to be strong; to be able."

la'ātu, "full extent": *a-na la-'-a-ti-su* (var. *ša*), Tabl. IV, l. 97 (p. 70).

[labābu], "to rage": Tabl. II, l. 12 (p. 22), l. 17 (p. 24); Tabl. III, ll. 16, 21 (p. 40), l. 74 (p. 48), l. 79 (p. 50); p. 226, l. 31.

labbu, "lion, lioness": *la-ab-bu*, p. 230 (l. 51).

labbu, "dragon": *lab-bi*, p. 118, ll. 17, 20, 24; p. 120, ll. 7, 9; *lab-ba*, p. 120, l. 4.

labānu, lebēnu, "to abase": Inf. *li-bi-en*, p. 234, l. 91.

luddu, a weapon: *lu-ud-di*, p. 146, l. 17.

lalū, I 1, "to be full."

II 1, "to make full": Perm. *lul-la-a*, Tabl. IV, l. 72 (p. 66).

lillu, "demon": *lil-lu*, p. 230, l. 59.

lamū, "to surround."

limītu, "circumference, circuit": pl. *li ma-a-ti*, p. 118, l. 10.

limēnu, I 2, "to plan evil": *il-te-im-na*, p. 220, n. 1.

II 1, "to do evil, to plan evil": Pret. *u-lam-mi-in*, Tabl. II, l. 3 (p. 22).

lumašu, "zodiacal constellation": *lu-ma-ši*, Tabl. V, l. 2 (p. 78).

lasāmu, "to be vigorous": *la-si-ma*, p. 226, l. 29.

lapātu, "to place, to set out (?)": *al-pu-t*[*u*], p. 144, l. 7; *al-p*[*u-t*]*u*, p. 150, l. 19.

מ

magāru, "to be favourable."

mitguru, "peaceful": *mit-gu-ru-ti*, p. 224, l. 9.

meḫū, "tempest": *me-ḫa-a*, var. *me-ḫu-u*, Tabl. IV, l. 45 (p. 62).

miḫḫu, "drink offering": *mi-iḫ-ḫa*, p. 236, l. 109.

maḫāṣu, III 2, "to render hostile, to cause hostility among": *muš-tam-ḫi-ṣa-at*, p. 224, l. 9.

maḫariš, "over against, before": *ma-ḫa-ri-iš* (var. *riš*), Tabl. II, l. 114 (p. 32); *ma-ḫa-ri-iš*, Tabl. IV, l. 2 (p. 58).

matū, I 1, "to lament"; *am-ṭi-ma*, p. 146, n. 4.

I 2, do.: *in-da-ṭa-a*, p. 116, l. 2.

miṭṭu, "club (?)": *iṣ*"*miṭ-ṭa*, var. *miṭ-ṭa*, Tabl. IV, l. 37 (p. 62); *mi-ṭi-šu*, Tabl. IV, l. 130 (p. 74); *miṭ-ṭa*, p. 175.

meku, "snarling, muttering": *me-ki-šu-un* (var. *nu*), Tabl. I, l. 60 (pp. 12, 187); *me-ku-uš*, Tabl. II, l. 81 (p. 30); *me-ki-šu*, Tabl. IV, l. 66 (p. 66).

malū, "to fill; to be full."

tamlū, "dam": *tam-la-a*, p. 134, l. 31.

millu, "troop (?)": *mi-il-la*, Tabl. IV, l. 116 (p. 72).

malmališ, adv., "corresponding with": *mal-ma-liš*, p. 125, n. 5.

mulmullu, "spear": *mul-mul-lum*, var. *mul-mul*, Tabl. IV, l. 36 (p. 62); *mul-mul*, p. 209, l. 1.

mummu, "chaos": Tabl. I, l. 4 (p. 2); = *rig-mu*, p. 162.

[maṣāru], II 1, "to divide": *u-ma-aṣ-ṣir*, Tabl. V, l. 3 (p. 78).

miṣru, "section (?)": plur. *mi-iṣ-ra-ta*, Tabl. V, l. 3 (p. 78).

[maṣāru], IV 1, "to be banded together (?)": *im-ma-aṣ-ru-nim-ma*, Tabl. I, l. 109 (p. 16); Tabl. II, l. 15 (p. 24); Tabl. III, l. 19 (p. 40), l. 77 (p. 48).

mukku, "affliction (?)": *muk-ku*, p. 230, l. 60.

marāru, "to be bitter."

namurratu, "anger, terrible splendour; fear (?)": *na-mur-ra-ti*, p. 128, l. 6; *na-mur-ra-tu*, p. 148, l. 4.

[**mēšu**], "to forgive": Imper. *mi-e-ši*, p. 232, l. 82.

mūšiš, "by night": *mu-šiš*, Tabl. I, l. 50 (p. 10).

mašdū, "flat (?)": *maš-di-e*, Tabl. IV, l. 137 (p. 76).

mašālu, I 1, "to be like."

II 2, "to make like": Pret. *um-taš-šil*, Tabl. I, l. 118 (p. 16), Tabl. III, l. 28 (p. 42), l. 86 (p. 50); *um-taš-ši-il*, varr. *um-ta-aš-ši-il*, *um-taš-ši-ir*, Tabl. II, l. 24 (p. 24 f.); *um-taš-ši-il*, Tabl. III, l. 86 (var., p. 51).

muttiš, "before": *mut-tiš*, Tabl. II, l. 75 (p. 30); *mut-ti-iš*, Tabl. III, l. 131 (p. 56).

nabū, "to name, to proclaim": Imper. *i-ba-a*, Tabl. II, l. 136 (p. 36); Tabl. III, l. 60 (p. 46), l. 118 (p. 54).

nabāṭu, "to blaze forth": *i-nam-bu-ṭu*, p. 206, l. 15.

nagū, I 1: *na-g[u-u]*, p. 169.

IV 2, "to be rejoiced": *i-te-en-gu*, var. *il-la-an-gu*, Tabl. VII, l. 118 (p. 110).

nagālu, IV 1, "to be made desolate": Perm. *na-an-gu-la-ku-ma*, p. 230, l. 65.

nadū, IV 1, "to be placed, to be established": Perm. *na-an-di-a-at* (fr. *nadū*, rather than IV 1, Perm. fr. *emēdu*), p. 228, l. 34.

[**nadāru**], "to rage."

nanduru, "afflicted, sorrowful": *na-an-du-ru-ti*, p. 232, l. 72.

niziḳtu, "misfortune": *ni-ziḳ-ti*, p. 232, l. 72.

niknaku, "censer": *nik-na-ki*, p. 138, l. 6.

nakāpu, I 2, "to violently attain": *mut-tak-ki-pat*, p. 224, l. 11.

namalu, "marsh (?)": *na-ma-la*, p. 134, l. 32.

namāru, "to be bright; to praise": *am-mir-ki*, p. 230, l. 60.

namurtu, "splendour": *na-mur-tum*, p. 129, n. 7.

nūn-amēlu, "fish-man": Tabl. I, l. 123 (p. 18); Tabl. II, l. 29 (p. 26); Tabl. III, l. 33 (p. 42), l. 91 (p. 52).

[**nannartu**], "light": *na-an-na-rat*, p. 222, l. 5.

nisū, I 1, "to remove, to carry away": *li-is-si-e-ma*, Tabl. VII, l. 114 (p. 108).

II 2, "to disappear, to depart": Pret. *ut-te-is-si* (var. *su*), Tabl. II, l. 116 (p. 34).

nasāḫu, "to carry off, to remove, to destroy": *is-su-ḫu*, Tabl. VII, l. 34 (p. 98).

nasāku, "to place; to place the hand upon, to grasp, to seize": *is-suk*, Tabl. IV, l. 101 (p. 70); *is-su-kam-ma*, p. 118, l. 7; *us-kam-ma*, p. 118, l. 4.

nasāsu, II 1, with *nissatu*, "to mourn bitterly": *u-na-as-sa-su*, p. 228, l. 49.

nassu, "sorrowful, grievous, lamenting": *na-as-si*, p. 228, l. 46; *na-as-sa-a-ti*, p. 228, l. 48.

nissatu, "mourning, lamentation": *nissati^pl*, p. 228, l. 49.

napāḫu, "to flame out; to roar against (of a wind)": *nap-ḫal*, p. 228, l. 37.

nipru, "offspring, child": *ni-ip-ri-šu*, Tabl. II, l. 2 (p. 22).

napāšu, II 1, "to make broad, to make merciful": Part. *mu-nap-pi-šu*, Tabl. II, l. 110 (p. 32).

niṣirtu, "treasure"; employed as synonym for "life": *ni-ṣir-ta-šu*, var. *na piš ta-šu*, Tabl. VII, l. 112 (p. 108).

nāḳu, I 1, "to lament."

III 2, "to cause lamentation": *mul-ta-nu-ḳa-a-ti*, p. 224, l. 9.

naḳū, II 2, "to be poured out": Pres. *ul-tak-ka* (?), Tabl. II, l. 130 (p. 36).

narāṭu, "to become weak, to falter": *i-nar-ru-ṭu*, p. 226, l. 21.

našū, IV 1, "to be raised on high": Perm. *na-an-še-a-al*, p. 228, l. 34.

našaku, III 1, "to remove from": *u-ša-as-si-ku* (var. *ka*), Tabl. VII, l. 28 (p. 96).

našāḳu, I 1, "to kiss": [*i*]*š-ši-iḳ*, Tabl. II, l. 116 (p. 34).

I 2, do.: *it-ta-šiḳ*, Tabl. V, l. 79 (p. 82).

IV 1, "to kiss one another": Pret. *in-niš-ḳu*, Tabl. III, l. 132 (p. 56).

našāḳu, II 1, "to give way beneath (?)": [*u*]*-na-ša-ḳu*, varr. *u-na-aš-ša*[*ḳ* . .], *u na-šaḳ*, Tabl. I, l. 54 (pp. 10, 186).

našāru, "to diminish": Perm. *na-ši-ir*, Tabl. I, l. 25 (p. 6).

ס

sagū, "to want, lack, need": Inf. *sa-gu-u*, p. 160; *sa-gi-šu-nu*, Tabl. IV, l. 12 (p. 58); *sa-gi-šu-nu-ma*, Tabl. VII, l. 10 (p. 94); *sa-gi-e-a*, p. 232, l. 75.

[**siḫū**], "to cease": Perm. *si-ḫa-ti*, Tabl. IV, l. 68 (p. 66).

sakāpu, "to lie down, to rest": Part. *sa-ki-pu*, Tabl. I, l. 110 (p. 16), Tabl. II, l. 16 (p. 24), Tabl. III, l. 20 (p. 40), l. 78 (p. 50); Perm. *sak-pu*, Tabl. I, l. 33 (p. 6).

[salū], II 1: "to pray, to supplicate": Inf. *su-lu-u-a*, p. 234, l. 99.

sinništu, "female, woman": *si-in-ni-ša-tum*, var. *si-in-ni-ša-at*, Tabl. II, l. 122 (p. 34).

[sapū], II 1, "to pray": Inf. *su-pu-u-a*, p. 234, l. 99.

sapāḫu, II 1, "to make of no effect, to cast down": Prec. *lu-sap-pi-iḫ*, Tabl. I, l. 39 (p. 84).

saparu, "net."

saparis, "in the net": *sa-pa-riš*, Tabl. IV, l. 112 (p. 72).

supuru, "fold": *su-pu-ri*, p. 234, l. 90.

sarāru, "to oppose, to resist (?)": *sa-ra-ar*, Tabl. IV, l. 9 (p. 58).

sarru, f. plur. *sarrāti*, "rebellion": *sar-ra-a-ti*, Tabl. IV, l. 72 (p. 66).

פ

pagru, "body"; *pa-ag-ri*, "my body, myself," p. 146 f., n. 4; cf. also *pūtu*.

palū, symbol of royalty, "ring(?)": *palū(a)*, Tabl. IV, l. 29 (p. 60).

[pēlu], III[II] 2, "to alter, annul": *uš-te-pi-il*, var. *uš-te-pi-el-l[u]*, Tabl. VII, l. 132 (p. 112).

palāsu, "to pay homage to (?)": *pal-su*[. .], Tabl. VII, l. 107 (p. 106); *pa-la-su*, p. 167.

[palsū], IV 1: *ni-pil-su-u*, p. 148, l. 4.

[palsaḫu], III 1, "to crush": Imper. *šu-pal-si-ḫi*, p. 234, l. 98.

[paltū], IV 1, "to succumb, to be defeated (?)": *ip-pal-tu-u*, Tabl. IV, l. 16 (p. 58).

pusummu, "bond (?)": *pu-su-um-me*, p. 226, l. 33.

pisannu, "treasure-chest": *pi-sa-an-na-ti-ka*, p. 154, l. 22.

[pāḳu], II 1, "to give heed to": *u-pa-ḳa*, p. 232, l. 79.

[paršadu], IV 1, "to escape": *na-par-šu-diš* (var. *di-iš*), Tabl. IV, l. 110 (p. 72).

pašāḫu, III 1, "to pacify"; Perm. "to rest": *šu-up-šu-ḫa-ak* (var. *ku*), Tabl. I, l. 38 (p. 8); *šup-šu-ḫa-at*, Tabl. I, l. 50 (p. 10).

[pešēḳu], "to be in trouble": Pret. *ip-še-iḳ*, p. 232, l. 68.

pašāru, I 2, "to divulge (?)": *ip-ta-šar* (?): Tabl. II, l. 4 (p. 22).

pūtu, "front; person": *pu-ut-ka*, p. 154, l. 25; *pag-ri u pu-u-ti* (var. *pu-ti*), "my own person, myself," p. 140, l. 8, p. 148, l. 2.

pitḳu, "handiwork": *pi-ti-iḳ-šu*, Tabl. II, l. 1 (p. 22).

צ

ṣabātu, I 1, "to take."
I 2, Inf. *tiṣbutu*, "to begin": Tabl. I, l. 130 (p. 18); Tabl. II, l. 36 (p. 26); Tabl. III, l. 40 (p. 42), l. 98 (p. 52).
IV 1, "to be held fast, to be held in remembrance": *li-iṣ-ṣab-tu-ma*, var. [*li-iṣ*]-*ṣa-ab-tu*, Tabl. VII, l. 125 (p. 110).

ṣabāru, I 2, "to attain (?)," or "to understand(?)": Inf. *ti-iṣ-bu-ru*, Tabl. III, l. 5 (p. 38).
III 1, "to impart to, to make known to": Pret. *u-ša-aṣ-bi-ra-an-ni*, Tabl. III, l. 14 (p. 40), l. 72 (p. 48); *u-ša-aṣ-bir-an-ni*, Tabl. III, l. 72 (var., p. 48 f.).

ṣalālu, "to lie down, to lie down to rest": Pret. *ni-iṣ-lal*, Tabl. I, l. 40 (p. 8), l. 46 (but cf. p. 185), ll. 100, 102 (p. 14); Pres. *ni-ṣa-al-lal*, Tabl. I, l. 96 (p. 14); Perm. *ṣal-la-*[*at*], Tabl. I, l. 50 (p. 10); *ṣa-al-la-ku*, Tabl. I, l. 38 (p. 184).

ṣallūtu, "plague": *ṣal-lu-tum*, p. 206, l. 21.

ṣimru, "fulness": *ṣi-im-ri*, Tabl. VII, l. 21 (p. 96); *ṣi-im-ru*, p. 161.

ṣuṣū, "marsh": *ṣu-ṣa-a*, var. *ṣu-ṣa-'*, Tabl. I, l. 6 (p. 2).

[ṣāru ?], II 1, "to cover (?)": *u-ṣir*, Tabl. V, l. 14 (p. 78).

ṣīriš, "unto": *ṣi-ri-iš*, var. *ṣi-riš*, Tabl. I, l. 32 (p. 6); *ṣi-ri-iš*, Tabl. IV, l. 128 (p. 74).

ṣirmaḫu, plur. *ṣirmaḫē*, "monster-serpent": Tabl. I, l. 114 (p. 16); Tabl. II, l. 20 (p. 24); Tabl. III, l. 24 (p. 40), l. 82 (p. 50).

ṣirritu, "sceptre": *ṣir-rit*, p. 226, l. 32.

ṣirruššu, "dragon": Tabl. I, l. 121 (p. 18); Tabl. II, l. 27 (p. 24); Tabl. III, l. 31 (p. 42), l. 89 (p. 50).

ק

ḳablu, "midst, inward parts": *ḳab-lu-uš Ti-a-ma-ti*, Tabl. IV, l. 65 (p. 66).

ḳudmiš, "before": *ḳu-ud-mi-iš*, var. *ḳud-meš*, Tabl. I, l. 33 (p. 6).

ḳuddušu, "pure, holy": *ḳud-du-šu*, p. 226, l. 28.

ḳāpu, I 2, "to entrust to": *iḳ-ti-pa*, Tabl. V, l. 12 (p. 78).

[ḳaṣābu], III 2: Imper. *šu-taḳ-ṣi-ba-am-ma*, Tabl. V, l. 20 (p. 80).

ḳaṣāru, I 1, "to collect, to take": *lu-uk-ṣur-ma*, Tabl. VI, l. 5 (p. 86).
I 2, "to make, to fix, to form, to contrive": Pret. [*iḳ*]-*ta-ṣar*, Tabl. II, l. 2 (p. 22); Perm. *ki-iṣ-ṣu-ra*, Tabl. I, l. 6 (p. 2).
II 1, do.: Perm. *ku-zu-ru*, Tabl. I, l. 6 (var., p. 2).

ḳarābu, I 2, Inf. *ḳitrubu*, "battle."
ḳitrubiš, "to the battle": [*ḳi*]*t-ru-bi-iš* (var. *biš*), Tabl. II, l. 111, p. 32.

ḳirbu, "midst, inward parts": *kir-biš* (var. *bi-iš*) *Ti-amat*, Tabl. IV, l. 41 (p. 62), l. 48 (p. 64); *kir-biš Tam-tim*, p. 106; *kir-biš* (var. *i-na kir-bi*) *Ti-amat*, Tabl. VII, l. 108 (p. 106); *a-ḫi-zu*(var. *iz*) *kir-bi-šu*, a title of Marduk, Tabl. VII, l. 109 (p. 108); *kir-bu*, pp. 107, 168.

ḳarbāti, plur., "fields": *ḳar-ba-a-ti-ia*, p. 232, l. 76.

ḳīšu, "forest": *ki-šu*, p. 134, l. 25.
ḳīštu, "forest": plur. *ki-ša-tu-ma*, p. 134, l. 29.

ר

ra'ābu, "to rage": Perm. *ra-'-ba-ti-ma*, p. 234, l. 94.

rābu, "to quake": *i-ru-ub-bu*, p. 206, l. 8; p. 226, l. 20; *i-ru-bu*, p. 226, l. 21.

rabū, III 2, "to make pre-eminent": Imper. *šu-te-ir-ba-'*, Tabl. II, l. 136 (var., p. 36 f.).

[**rabābu**], II 1, "to make great": *li-ra-ab-bi-ib*, Tabl. III, l. 52 (p. 45).
III II 1, do.: *liš-rab-bi-ib*, Tabl. I, l. 142 (p. 20); Tabl. II, l. 48 (p. 28); Tabl. III, l. 52 (p. 44), l. 110 (p. 54).

ridū, "to follow, pursue"; Inf. "pursuit, occupation": *ri-du-u-a*, p. 230, l. 58.

raṭu, "water-channel (on land); current, movement (in water)": *ra-ṭu-um-ma*, p. 132, l. 11.

rakābu, III 2, "to sling on (a spear)": *uš-tar-ki-ba*, Tabl. IV, l. 36 (p. 62).

rakāsu, "to fix, to lay": *ir-ku-us*, p. 132, l. 17.
riksu, "limit, bound (?)": *rik-si-šu-un*, Tabl. V, l. 6 (p. 78).
markasu, "band": [*m*]*ar-kas*, p. 104; *mar-ka-su*, p. 165.

ramū, II 1, "to set free": Inf. "deliverance": *ru-um-mi-ia*, p. 232, l. 83.

rēsu, II 1, "to smite, to crush (?)": *li-ra-i-su*, Tabl. IV, l. 16 (p. 58).

rūḳu, "distant; wide, compassionate (of the heart)": *ru-u-ḳu*, Tabl. VII, l. 135 (p. 112), p. 173.

rēšu-arkāt, "the Beginning and the Future": *rēšu-arkāt*, Tabl. VII, l. 107 (p. 106); *ri-e-šu ar-kat*, p. 167; cf. also *ša ina ri-e-ši u ar-ka-[ti . . .]*, p. 178, l. 19.

ש

šē'u, "to take wing, to fly": *i-ša-'*, p. 230, l. 63.

še'ū, "to seek, to look for: to perceive, to behold": *i-še'-a*, Tabl. I, l. 60 (p. 12), Tabl. IV, l. 66 (p. 66); *i-še-'-am-ma*, Tabl. II, l. 81 (p. 30); *te-še-'-e-ma*, var. *te-eš-[. . .]*, Tabl. IV, l. 83 (p. 68); Perm. *še-'* (= *še'i*), Tabl. I, l. 6 (p. 2).

ša'ālu, I 1, "to ask."

II 1, "to demand, to cry out for": *u-ša-'-lu*, var. *u-ša-'-a-lu*, Tabl. IV, l. 92 (p. 70).

šabū, I 2, "to overwhelm": *i-sa-am-bu-'*, p. 206, l. 17.

šabāšu, "to turn, to pervert (?)": *šab-šu*, p. 140, l. 7.

[**šudu**], con. st. *šud*, "height, supremacy"; *šud tamḫari*, "command in battle": Tabl. I, l. 131 (p. 20); Tabl. II, l. 37 (p. 26); Tabl. III, l. 41 (p. 42), l. 99 (p. 52).

šadādu, "to drag": Pres. *i-šad-da-[ad]*, p. 118, l. 12.

[**šaḫādu**], I 2, "to rear up": *liš-taḫ-ḫi-dam-ma*, Tabl. I, l. 120 (p. 16); Tabl. III, l. 30 (p. 42), l. 88 (p. 50); *liš-taḫ-ḫi-da-am* (var. *dam*)-*ma*, Tabl. II, l. 26 (p. 24).

šuḫarruru, "to be afflicted": Pret. *uš-ḫa-ri-ir-ma*, Tabl. II, l. 6 (p. 22); Perm. *šu-ḫar-ru-ur*, *šu-ḫar-ru-rat*, p. 232, l. 75.

šaḫāṭu, I 1, "to rage."

III 1, "to cause to rage, to stir up": *u-ša-aš-ḫi-iṭ*, p. 120, l. 5; *šu-uš-ḫi-iṭ*, p. 120, l. 2.

šiklu, "sense (?)": *ši-ik-la-šu*, p. 140, l. 7.

šikkatu, "supremacy, control"; *rab-šikkati*, "chief"; *rab-šikkatūtu*, "chieftainship": Tabl. I, l. 131 (p. 20); Tabl. II, l. 37 (p. 26); Tabl. III, l. 41 (p. 42), l. 99 (p. 52).

šakānu, "to set; to provide."

šukuttu, "provision": *šu-ku-us-su*, Tabl. VII, l. 8 (p. 92).

šakāru, "to drink"; Perm. "to be drunk (?)": *ši-ik-ru* (poss. subs., "carouse"), Tabl. III, l. 136 (p. 56).

šalummatu, "glory, pride": *ša-lum-mat*, p. 148, l. 3.

šalāḳu, "to cut out, to cut off."

šulluḳtu, "cutting off, destruction": *šul-lu-uḳ-ti*, p. 228, l. 37; p. 232, l. 69.

šumu, "name," plur. *šumē*: *šu-mi-e-šu*, Tabl. VII, l. 124 (var., p. 110).

šemū, I 1, "to hear."
IV 1, "to be heard": (?) *liš-ši-ma* (or *našū*, I 1; cf. var. fr. *nisū*, p. 109, n. 17), Tabl. VII, l. 114 (p. 108).
šamāru, I 2, "to rage": *iš-tam-ma-ru*, p. 230, l. 58.
šumurratu, "confusion, rage, anger": *šu-mur-ra-tu*, Tabl. VII, l. 42 (p. 100).
šitmuriš, "wildly": *šit-mu-riš* (var. *ri-iš*), Tabl. IV, l. 89 (p. 70).
šanū, "to repeat"; Inf. *šanū*, "version": *š[a]-n[i]-[e]*, p. 126, l. 8.
šanānu, "to rival."
šinnatu, "rivalry": *šin-na-as-su*, p. 206, l. 12.
šasū, I 2, "to cry": *il-ta-si*, Tabl. I, l. 42 (p. 8).
šipru, "business, occupation": *ši-pir*, p. 152, l. 19.
šuḳammumu, "to roar": Perm. [*šu*]-*ḳa-am-mu-m*[*a*]-*a*[*t*], Tabl. I, l. 26 (p. 6).
šaḳummiš, šaḳummeš, adv., "in sorrow": [*ša-ku-um*]-*mi-iš*, var. [*ša*]-*ku-um-meš*, Tabl. I, l. 58 (pp. 10, 186); *ša-ku-um-mi-iš*, Tabl. II, l. 6 (p. 22).
šaḳāšu, "to destroy."
šaḳšu, "violent, unruly": *šaḳ-šu*, p. 226, l. 26.
šāru, "wind": *šār arba'i*, "the fourfold wind"; *šār sibi* (var. VII - *bi* - *im*), "the sevenfold wind"; *šāra ēšā*, "the whirlwind"; *šāra la šanān*, "the wind which had no equal," Tabl. IV, l. 46 (p. 62).
[šāru], "to oppose (?)": Part. *ša-'-ir-ru*, p. 206, l. 11.
šērtu, "punishment": *še-rit-su*, Tabl. IV, l. 114 (p. 72).
šarbabu, "terror (?)": *šar-ba-ba*, Tabl. I, l. 119 (p. 16); Tabl. III, l. 29 (p. 42), l. 87 (p. 50); *šar-ba-bi-iš* (probably with pron. suff., not adv.), Tabl. II, l. 25 (p. 24).
šarāḳu, "to present, to furnish": *iš-ruḳ-*[*ku*], p. 128, l. 5; *iš-ru-uḳ-ku*, p. 129, n. 7; *iš-ru-ku-nik-kim-ma*, p. 128, l. 7.
šarūru, "light": *ša-ru-ur*, p. 228, l. 35.
šurišam, adv. (?): *šu-ri-šam*, Tabl. IV, l. 124 (p. 74).
šašmu, "battle, fight."
šašmeš, "to the fight": *ša-aš-meš*, Tabl. IV, l. 94 (p. 70).
šutummu, "storehouse": *šu-tum-mu*, p. 226, l. 28.

ת

tabinu, "power, might": *ta-bi-ni*, p. 232, l. 78.
tubuḳtu, "enclosing wall": *tub-ḳa-a-ti*, p. 154, l. 24.
taḫāzu, "battle."
taḫāziš, "to the battle": *ta-ḫa-zi-iš*, Tabl. IV, l. 94 (p. 70).

IV.

Index to names of Deities, Stars, Places, etc.

Adad, god : ^{ilu}*Adad*, p. 198, l. 5.

Adu-nuna, title of Marduk : ^{ilu}*A-du-nun-na*, Tabl. VII (K. 8,519 and comm. K. 4,406, Rev., col. ii, l. 23), pp. 104 f., 166; p. 173, l. 20; p. 178, l. 21.

Aga-azag, title of Marduk : ^{ilu}*Aga-azag*, Tabl. VII, l. 25 (p. 96 f.).

Agi[l . . .], title of Marduk : ^{ilu}*A-gi[l . . .]*, Tabl. VII (K. 13,761), p. 102 f.; var. ^{ilu}GIL[ ], p. 163.

Akkadū, Akkad : *Ak-ka-di-i*, p. 147, note, l. 20; ^{mâtu}*Akkadū*^{KI}, p. 212, l. 26; ^{mâtu}*Akkadī*^{KI}, p. 211, l. 18; *ṣi-ri Ak-ka-di-i*, p. 147, note, l. 16.

Aḳrabu, Scorpio: *Aḳrabu*, p. 213, ll. 6, 13, 14.

Alim-nuna, possibly shorter form of *Asaru-alim-nuna*, title of Marduk : [. . . A]LIM-NUN-NA, p. 216.

Almanu, deity : ^{ilu}*Al-ma-nu*, p. 218, l. 10.

Ana, the god Anu : AN-NA, p. 124, l. 1; p. 126, l. 6; see also **Anu**.

Anbanini, mythical king: *An-ba-ni-ni*, p. 142, l. 18.

Anšar, god : *An-šar*, Tabl. I, ll. 12, 15 (p. 4 f.); Tabl. II, ll. 8, 9 (p. 22 f.), l. 49 (p. 28 f.), l. 72 (p. 30, restore *An-šar*), l. 79 (p. 30 f.), ll. 83, 114, 115 (p. 32 f.), l. 119 (p. 34 f.); Tabl. III, l. 1 (p. 38 f.), l. 13 (p. 40 f.), l. 71 (p. 48 f.), l. 131 (p. 56 f.); Tabl. IV, l. 125 (p. 74 f.); p. 195; p. 198, l. 30, l. 15 (Rev.); p. 199, l. 23; = Ἀσσωρός, see Introduction.

Anu, god : ^{ilu}*A-nu*, Tabl. I, l. 14 (p. 4 f.); ^{ilu}*A-num*, Tabl. I, l. 14 (var., p. 5), ll. 15, 16 (p. 4 f.), l. 85 (p. 12 f.); Tabl. II, l. 81 (p. 30 f.); Tabl. III, l. 53 (var., p. 46); Tabl. IV, ll. 4, 6 (p. 58 f.), l. 146 (p. 76 f.); Tabl. V, l. 8 (var. for ^{ilu}*E-a*, K. 13,774, p. 190 f.), l. 78 (p. 82 f.), p. 126, l. 8, p. 224, l. 18; ^{ilu}*A-nu-um*, Tabl. I, l. 16 (var., p. 5); Tabl. III, l. 53 (p. 46 f.), l. 111 (p. 54 f.); ^{ilu}*A-nim*, Tabl. IV, l. 44 (p. 62 f.); Tabl. VII, l. 6 (p. 92 f.); [^{ilu}] *A-nam*, Tabl. II, between ll. 85 and 104 (K. 10,008, p. 190); ^{ilu}*Anu*, p. 216, l. 2, p. 218,

l. 8; AN-NA = *ilu A-nu*, p. 138, l. 13 f.; = 'Ἀνός, see Introduction.

Anunitu, goddess: *ilu A-nu-ni-tum*, p. 144, l. 10; p. 150, l. 22.

Anunnaki, the spirits of the earth: *ilu A-nun-na-ki*, Tabl. I, l. 136 (p. 20 f.); Tabl. III, l. 46 (p. 44 f.), l. 104 (p. 52 f.); Tabl. VI, l. 20 (p. 88 f.), p. 140, l. 5, p. 206, l. 22, p. 226, l. 21; [(DINGIR)A]-NUN-NA-GE-E-NE = *ilu A-nun-na-ki*, p. 132, l. 15; see also **Enukki**.

Anūtu, the power of Anu: *ilu A-nu-ti*, Tabl. I, l. 139 (p. 20 f.); Tabl. II, l. 45 (p. 28 f.); Tabl. III, l. 49 (var. *e-nu-ti*, "lordship," p. 44), l. 107 (p. 54 f.); *ilu An-nu-ti*, Tabl. IV, l. 82 (var. *ilu A*-[. . .], p. 68 f.).

Apsū, (1) primeval water-god: *Ap-su-u*, Tabl. I, l. 97 (p. 14 f.); *Ap*-[. . . .], Tabl. I, l. 47 (var., p. 9); *Apsū(u)*, Tabl. I, l. 3 (var., p. 2); *Apsū*, Tabl. I, l. 3 (p. 2 f.), ll. 22, 25, 29, 35 (p. 6 f.), l. 47 (p. 8 f.), l. 51 (p. 10 f.); Tabl. II, l. 3 (p. 22 f.), l. 55 (p. 28 f.), between ll. 85 and 104 (K. 10,008, p. 189), p. 175; = 'Ἀπασών, see Introduction; (2) the Deep, not personified: *ap-su-u*, p. 206, l. 9; *ap-si-i*, p. 128, l. 4; *apsi*, Tabl. IV, ll. 142, 143 (p. 76 f.); ABZU = *ap-su-u*, p. 130, l. 8, p. 132, l. 13, p. 138, l. 8 f.; *bāb ap-si-i*, "the Gate of the Deep," p. 209, l. 5.

Aruru, goddess: (DINGIR)A-RU-RU, p. 134, l. 21.

Asari, title of Marduk: *ilu Asar-ri*, Tabl. VII, l. 1 (pp. 92 f., 158); p. 177, l. 6; in title of composition, p. 169.

Asaru-alim, title of Marduk: *ilu Asaru-alim*, Tabl. VII, l. 3 (pp. 92 f., 159).

Asaru-alim-nuna, title of Marduk: *ilu Asaru-alim-nun-na*, Tabl. VII, l. 5 (pp. 92 f., 160); DINGIR ASARU-ALIM-NUN-NA, p. 181, l. 2; [. . . . . ALI]M-NUN-NA, p. 216, l. 2.

Aššur, city: *alu Aššur KI*, p. 199, l. 37.

Bābilu, Babylon: [*Bāb*]*ilu KI*, p. 220, n. 1; *Bābili KI*, p. 172, ll. 17, 18, p. 212, ll. 24, 27; [KA-DINGIR-RA](KI) = *Bābilu KI*, p. 132, l. 14.

Barsip, Borsippa: *Bar-sip KI*, p. 236, l. 112.

Bēl, Enlil, Illil, the elder Bēl: *ilu Bēl*, Tabl. IV, l. 146 (p. 76 f.); Tabl. V, l. 8 (p. 78 f.); Tabl. VII, l. 6 (p. 92 f.), l. 116 (p. 110), p. 116, l. 7, p. 126, l. 8, p. 172, l. 12, p. 195, p. 216, l. 2, p. 218, l. 8, p. 224, l. 18; = Ἴλλινος, see Introduction.

Kingu, god: *ilu Kin-gu*, Tabl. I, l. 128 (p. 18 f.), l. 139 (p. 20 f.); Tabl. II, l. 34 (p. 26 f.), l. 45 (p. 28 f.), l. 56 (p. 30 f.), between ll. 85 and 104 (p. 190); Tabl. III, l. 38 (p. 42 f.), l. 49 (p. 44 f.), l. 96 (p. 52 f.), l. 107 (p. 54 f.); Tabl. IV, l. 66 (p. 66 f.), l. 81 (p. 68 f.), l. 119 (p. 74 f.), p. 209, ll. 2, 4, p. 213, l. 3, p. 218, ll. 8, 9; *ilu Kin-gi*, p. 213, ll. 5, 9; [*ilu Ki*]-*in-gu*, Tabl. I, l. 136 (var., p. 21).

Kišar, deity: *Ki-šar*, Tabl. I, l. 12 (p. 4 f.); = Κισσαρή, see Introduction.

Kutū, Cuthah: *Kutū KI*, p. 152, l. 12.

Laḫamu, (1) deity: *ilu La-ḫa-mu*, Tabl. I, l. 10 (p. 4 f.); Tabl. III, l. 4 (p. 38 f.), l. 68 (var., p. 48), l. 125 (p. 56 f.), p. 195, p. 198, n. 4; *ilu La-ḫa-me*, Tabl. III, l. 68 (p. 48 f.); = Λαχή (for Δαχή), see Introduction; (2) monster: *ilu La-ḫa-mu*, Tabl. II, l. 27 (p. 24 f.); *ilu La-ḫa-mi*, Tabl. I, l. 121 (p. 18 f.); Tabl. III, l. 31 (p. 42 f.), l. 89 (p. 50 f.).

Laḫḫa, Laḫmu: *Laḫ-ḫa*, Tabl. III, l. 125 (p. 56 f.).

Laḫmu, deity: *ilu Laḫ-mu*, Tabl. I, l. 10 (p. 4 f.); Tabl. III, l. 4 (p. 38 f.), l. 68 (p. 48 f.); p. 198, l. 13; = Λαχός (for Δαχός), see Introduction.

Lugal-ab[. . . .], title of Marduk: *ilu Lugal-ab*-[. . .], Tabl. VII (K. 13,761), p. 102 f.

Lugal-dul (or **du**)**-azaga**, title of Marduk: *ilu Lugal-dul-azag-ga*, Tabl. VII (K. 8,519), p. 106 f.; (DINGIR)LUGAL-DUL-AZAG-GA = *ilu Lugal-dul-azag-ga*, p. 132, l. 13; *ilu* LUGAL-DUL-AZAG-GA, p. 220, n. 1.

Lugal-durmaḫ, title of Marduk: *ilu Lugal-dur-maḫ*, Tabl. VII (K. 8,519, and comm. K. 4,406, Rev., col. ii, l. 8), pp. 104 f., 165.

Lugal-en-ankia, title of Marduk: *ilu* LUGAL-EN-AN-KI-A, p. 173, l. 19.

Lu-ku-mal, star: *kakkabu* LU-KU-MAL, p. 212, l. 30; p. 218, l. 9.

Marduk, god: *ilu Marduk*, Tabl. II (K. 10,008), between ll. 85 and 104 (p. 190); Tabl. III, l. 10 (p. 38 f.), l. 55 (p. 46 f.), l. 113 (p. 54 f.), l. 138 (p. 56 f.); Tabl. IV, ll. 5, 13 (p. 58 f.), ll. 20, 28 (p. 60 f.), l. 93 (p. 70 f.), l. 126 (p. 74 f.); Tabl. VI, l. 1 (p. 86 f.); Tabl. VII, l. 129 (p. 112 f.), l. 139 (p. 114 f.), p. 134, l. 31, p. 178, l. 17, p. 180, l. 1, p. 181, ll. 2, 3, 4, 5, 6, p. 205, l. 7, p. 211, ll. 8, 12, 13, p. 213, l. 2, p. 214, l. 24, p. 218; *ilu Marduk* (AN-ASAR-LU-ŠAR), p. 128, l. 7; (DINGIR)ASAR-LU-ŠAR

Supplementary Texts.

Preface.

In this volume is published for the first time the texts from a group of tablets, inscribed in the Neo-Babylonian character, and containing new portions of the great series of Creation Legends, to which the Assyrians and Babylonians gave the title *Enuma elish*. The group includes :—1. Portions of four copies of the First Tablet of the series, together with two extracts from the text, inscribed upon rough "practice-tablets" by the pupils of Babylonian scribes; 2. Portions of two copies of the Second Tablet of the series; 3. Part of a copy of the Third Tablet, and fragments of three "practice-tablets" inscribed with portions of the text, which I have joined to other similar fragments already published in *Cuneiform Texts from Babylonian Tablets, etc., in the British Museum*, Part XIII (1901); 4. Part of a copy of the Sixth Tablet, which is of peculiar interest inasmuch as it refers to the Creation of Man, and settles the disputed question as to the number of Tablets, or sections, of which the Creation Series was composed; and 5. Portions of two copies of the Seventh Tablet of the series.

A "practice-tablet," which is inscribed in the Sumerian and Babylonian languages with texts relating to the Creation of the Moon and of the Sun, is also included.

The Appendices contain texts which, for the most part, are closely connected with the interpretation of the Creation Legends. They include :—1. A number of Assyrian commentaries on the Seventh Tablet of the Creation Series, together with fragments of texts which are similar in character to that composition ; 2. A Neo-Babylonian duplicate of the tablet which has been supposed to belong to the Creation Series and to contain the instructions given to man after his creation, but which is now shown by the new duplicate to be part of a tablet of moral precepts and to have no connection whatsoever with the Creation Series ; 3. Part of a large astrological text of the period of the Arsacidae, in which some of the chief personages of the Creation-story appear in astrological characters, and the story itself is interpreted on astrological lines ; and 4. The text of the legend which was at one time commonly, but erroneously, believed to contain an Assryian version of the story of the Tower of Babel. The last appendix contains a "Prayer of the Raising of the Hand to Ishtar," which belongs to the series of similar compositions already published in my *Babylonian Magic and Sorcery* (1896); both from the beauty of its language and from its perfect state of preservation, it must be regarded as one of the finest and most complete Babylonian religious texts which have hitherto been recovered.

After the plates in this volume had been printed off, and whilst I was engaged in making a hand-list of the smaller fragments in the Kuyunjik Collections, I identified ten additional fragments of the Creation Series, belonging to copies of the First, Second, Fifth, and Seventh Tablets of the composition. The texts of these fragments, as well as those of some other closely allied Assyrian and Neo-Babylonian tablets, are published by means of outline blocks in the first volume of this work.

L. W. KING.

LONDON, July 29th, 1902.

45528 + 46614.

OBVERSE.

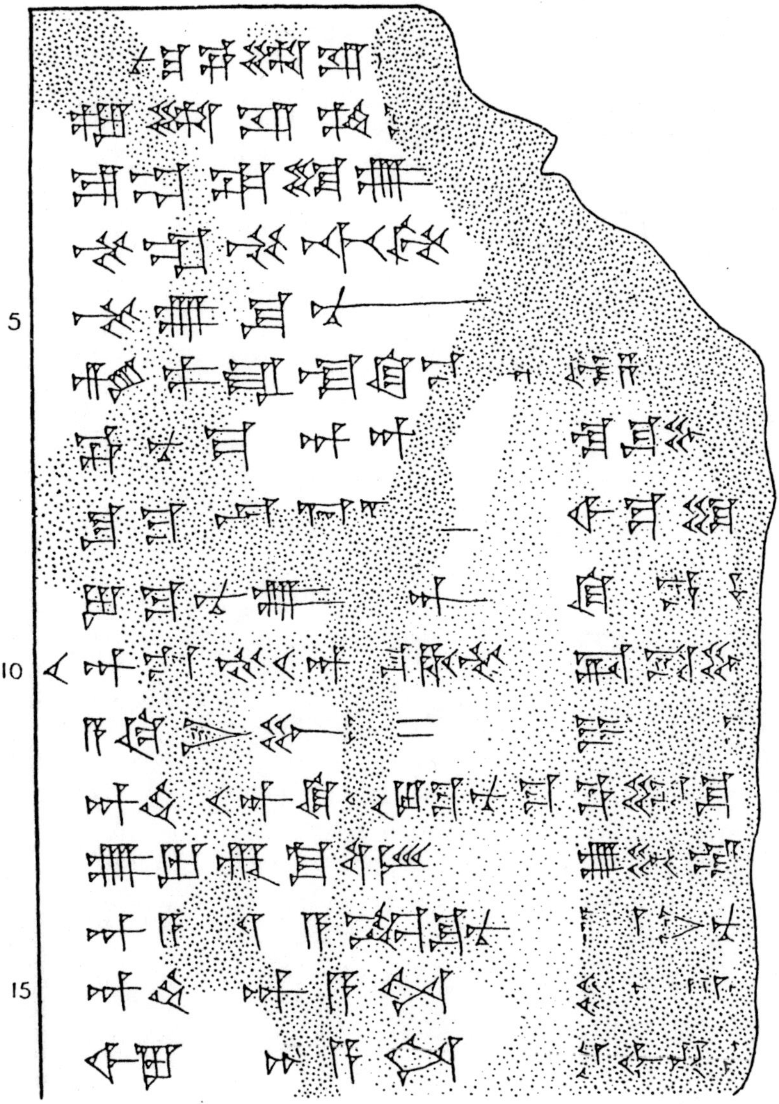

45528 + 46614.

OBVERSE (Cont.).

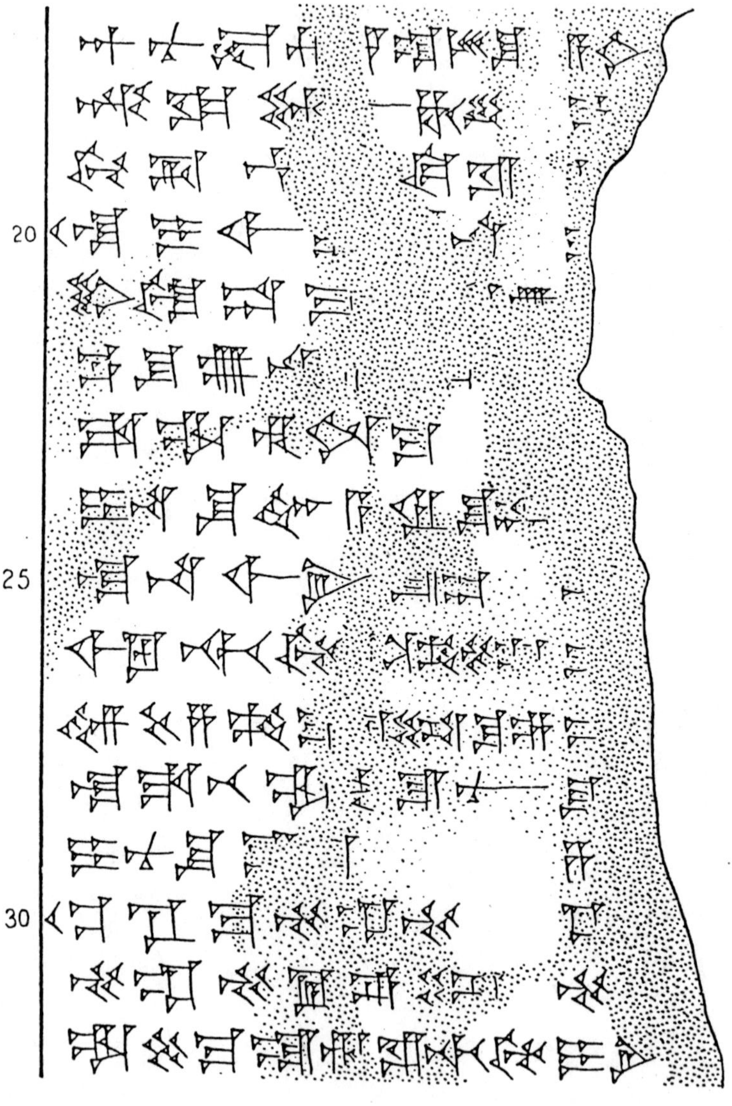

45528 + 46614.

OBVERSE (Cont.).

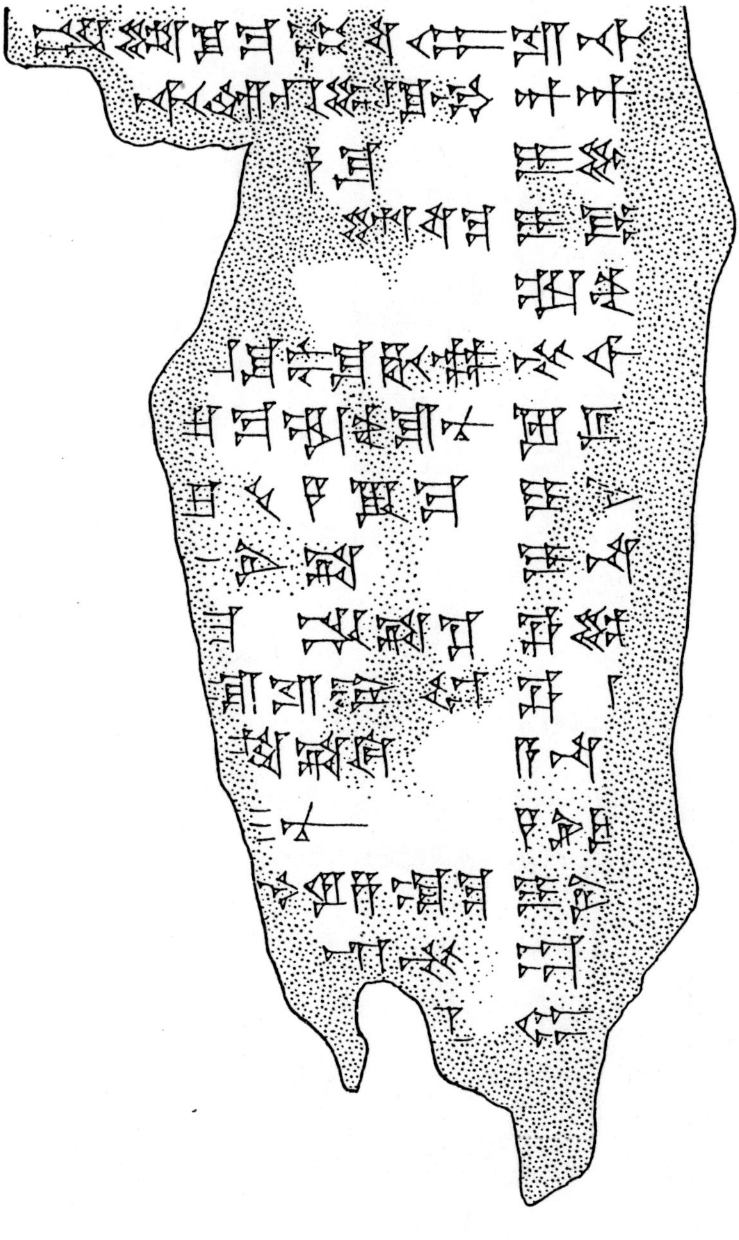

45528 + 46614.

REVERSE.

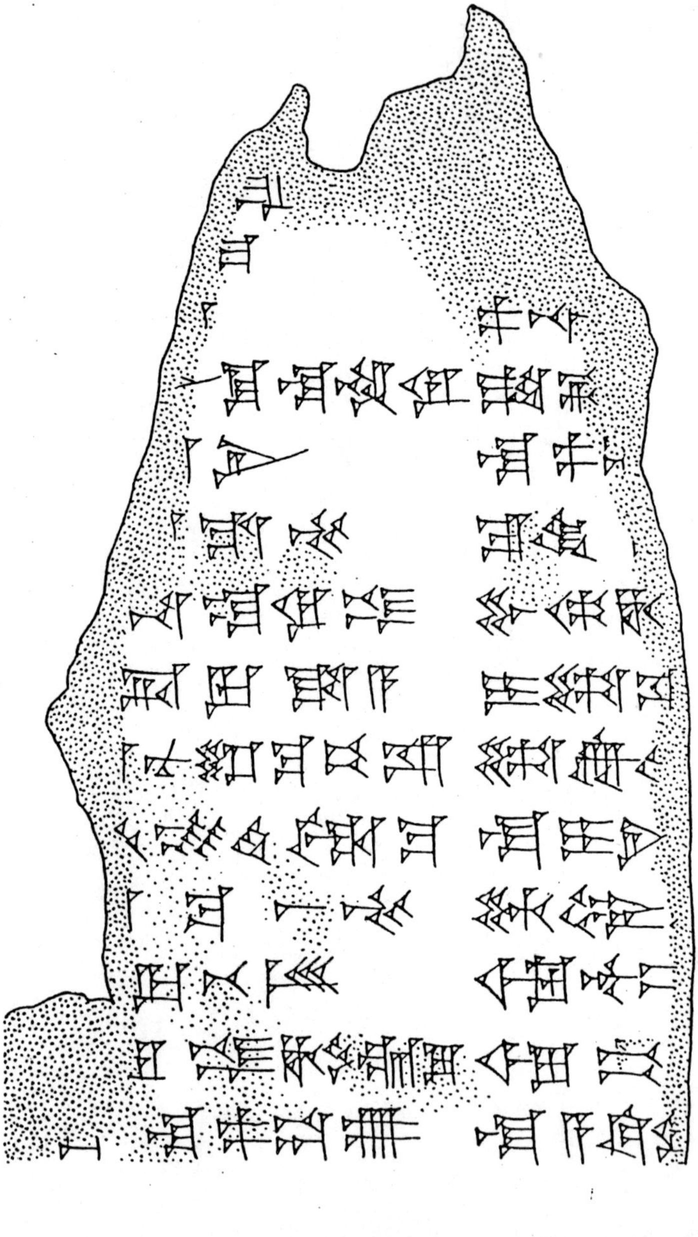

45528 + 46614.

REVERSE (Cont.).

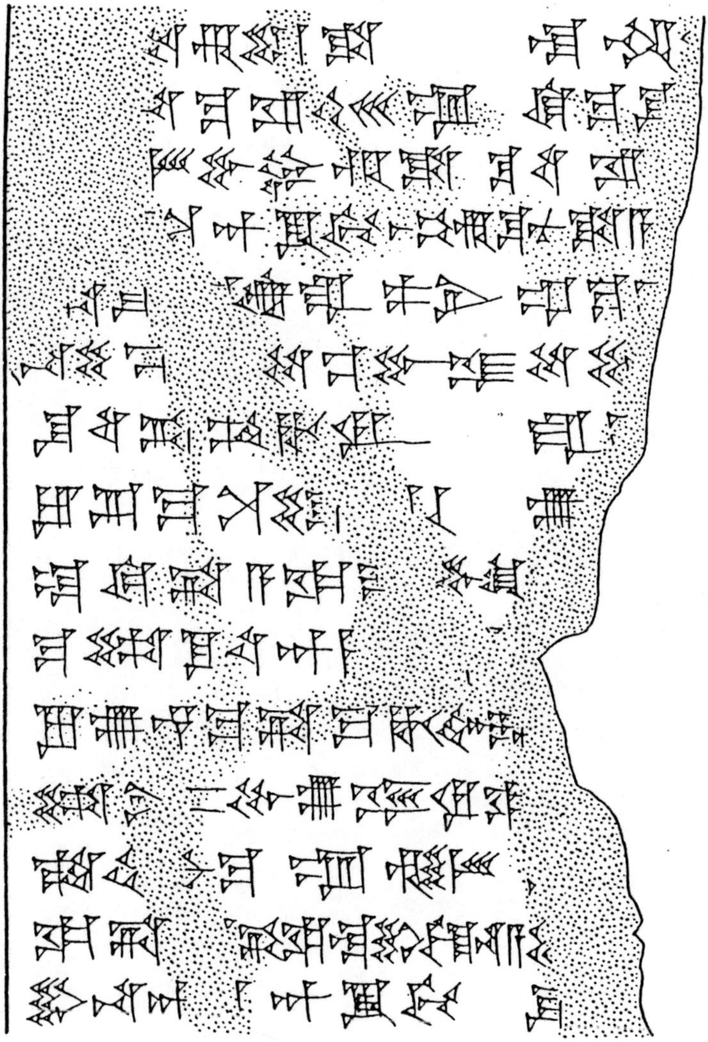

45528 + 46614.

REVERSE (Cont.).

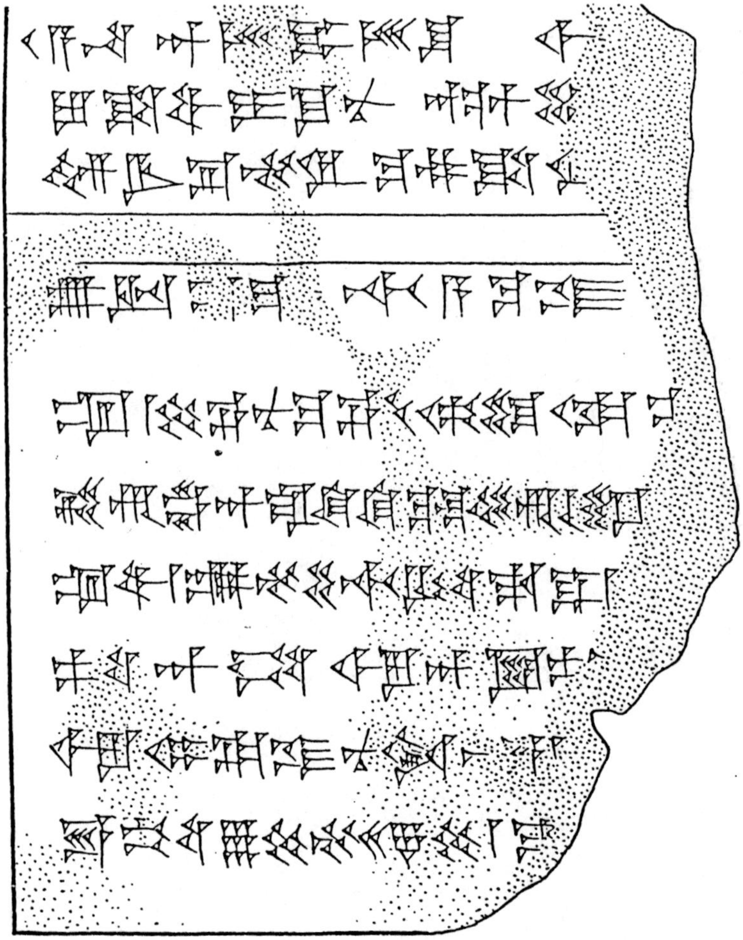

35134.

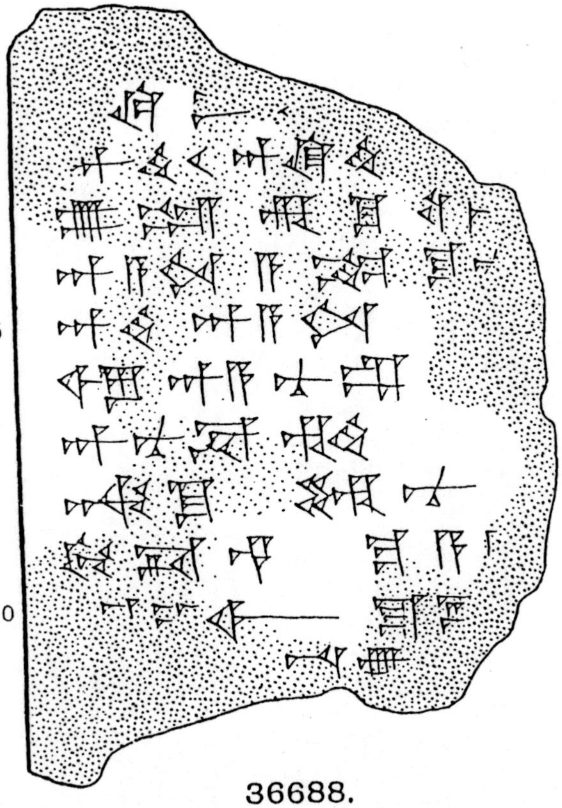

36688.

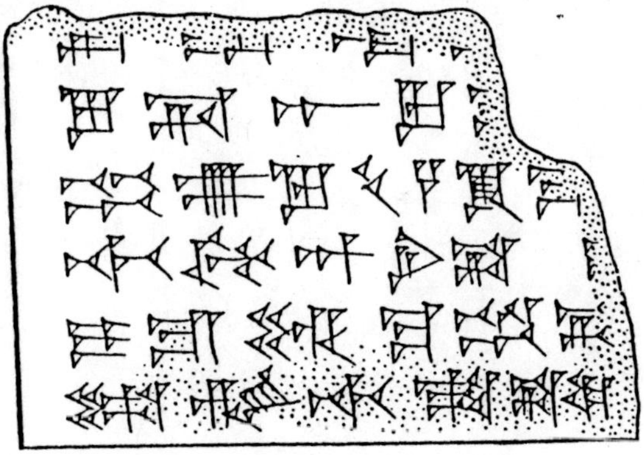

The text is an extract from a practice-tablet.

36726.

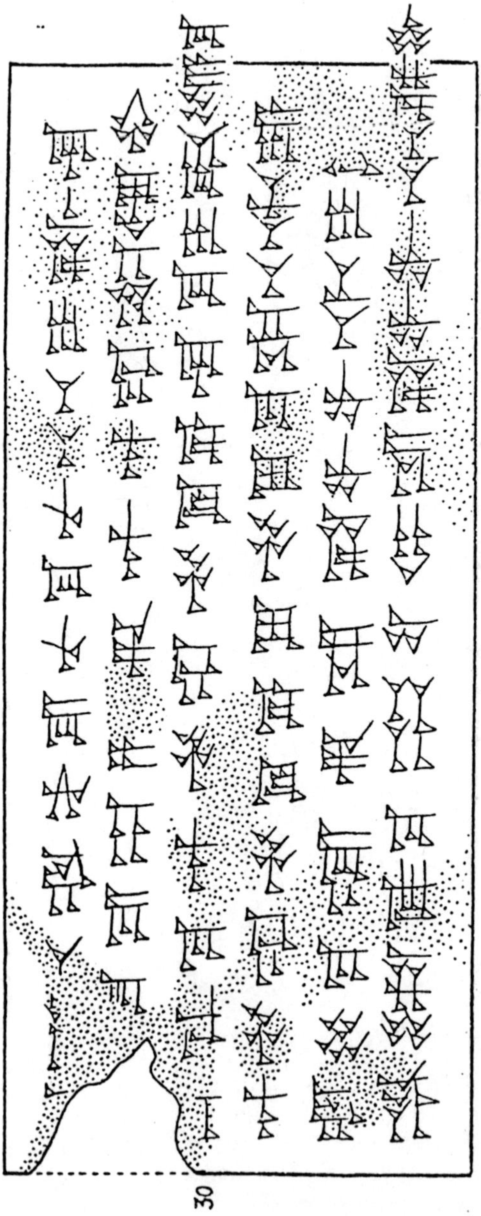

The text is an extract from a practice-tablet.

46803.

OBVERSE.

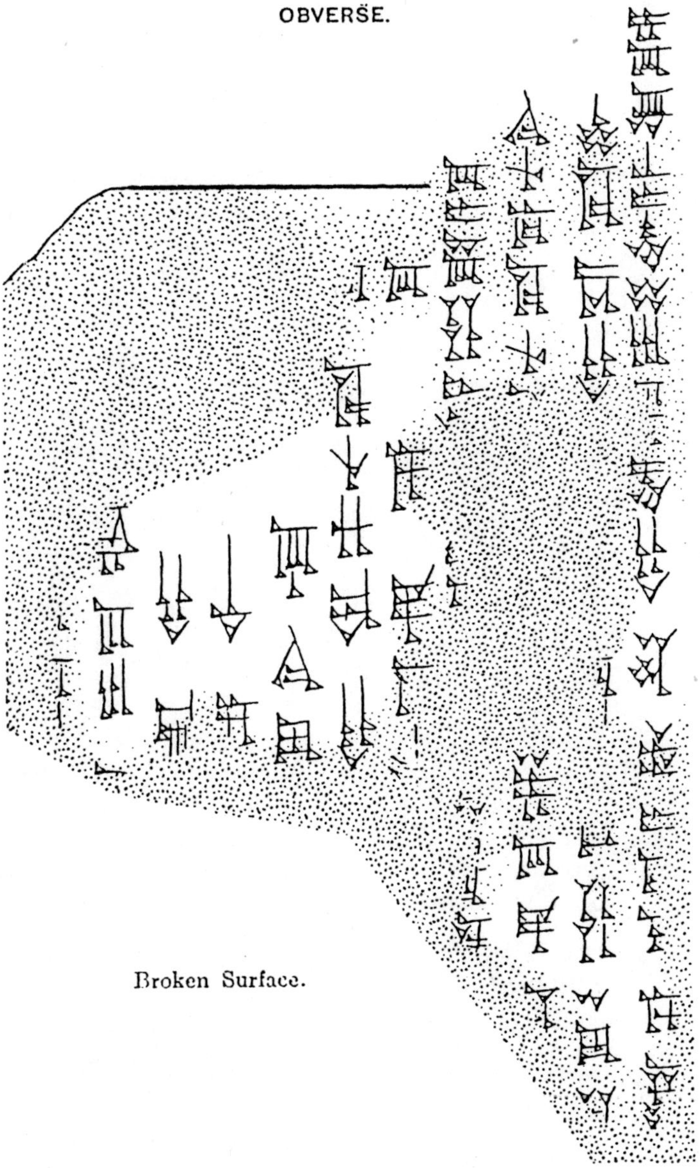

Broken Surface.

46803.

OBVERSE (cont.). & REVERSE

OBVERSE (Cont.)

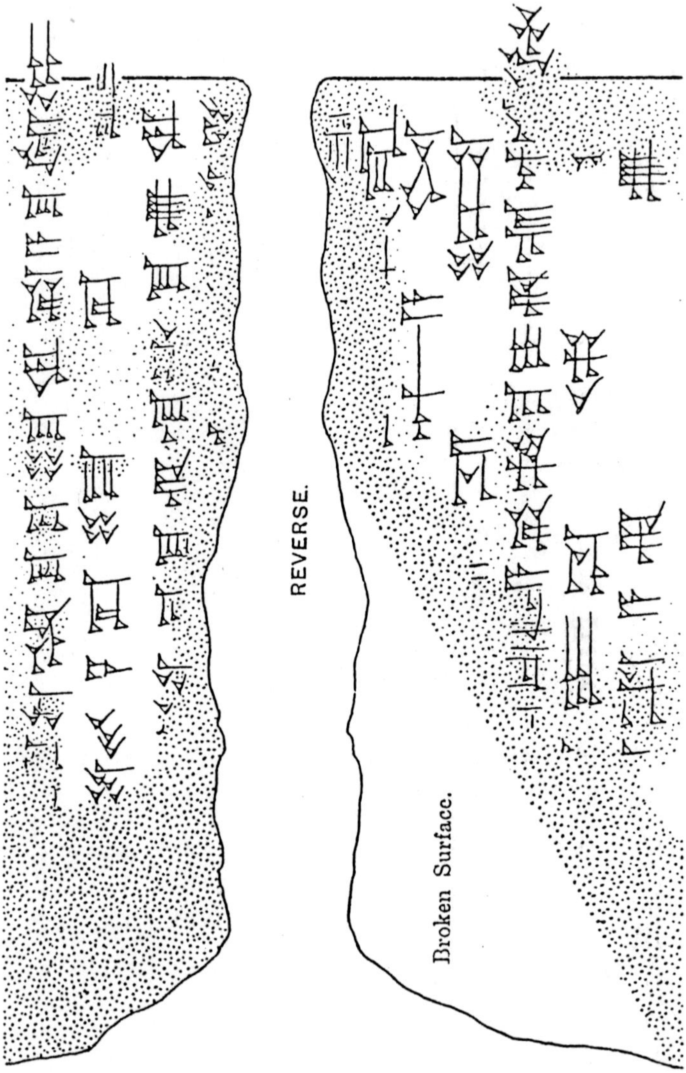

46803.

REVERSE (cont.).

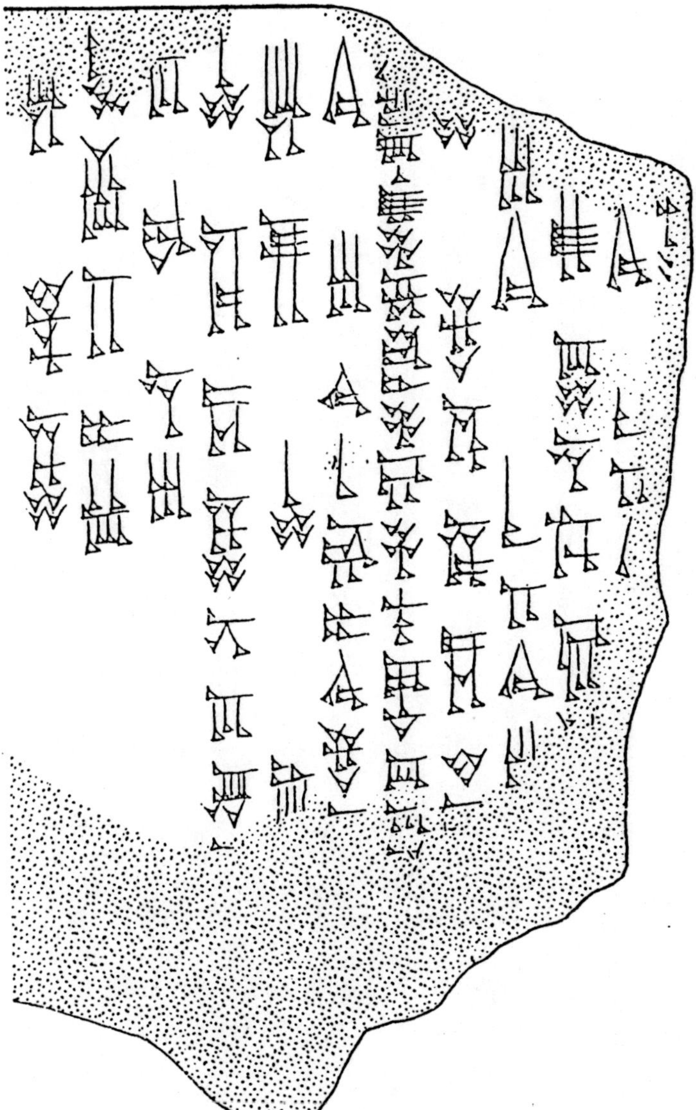

82-9-18, 6879.

REVERSE.

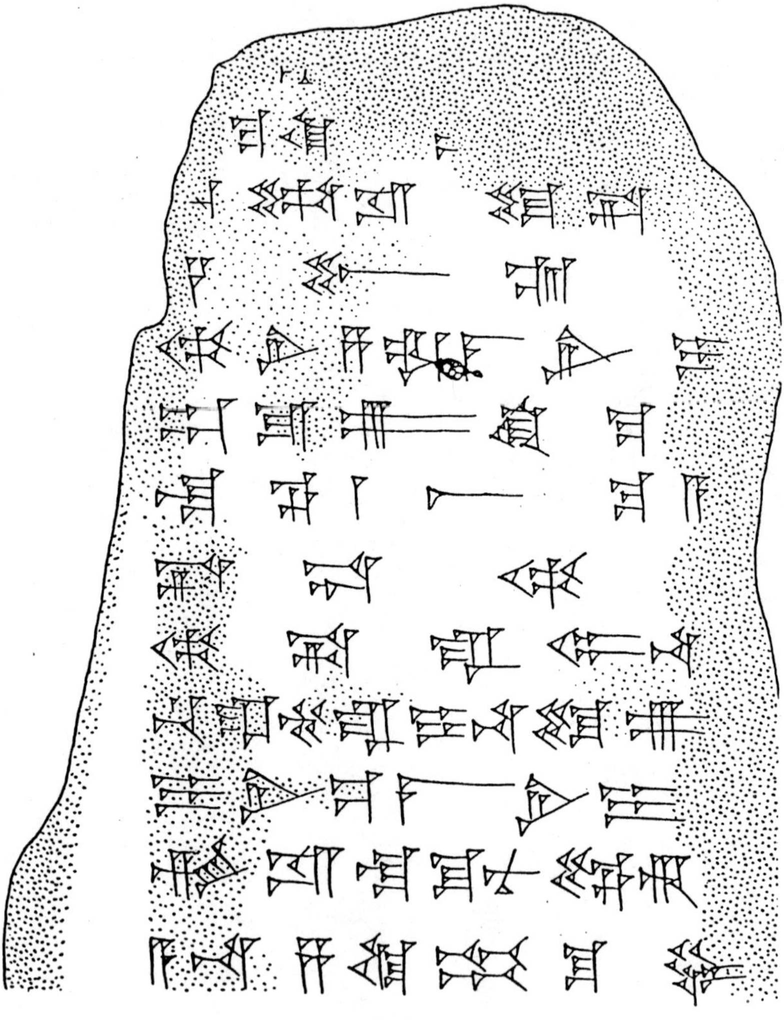

The Obverse of the fragment is missing.

82-9-18, 6879.

REVERSE (cont.).

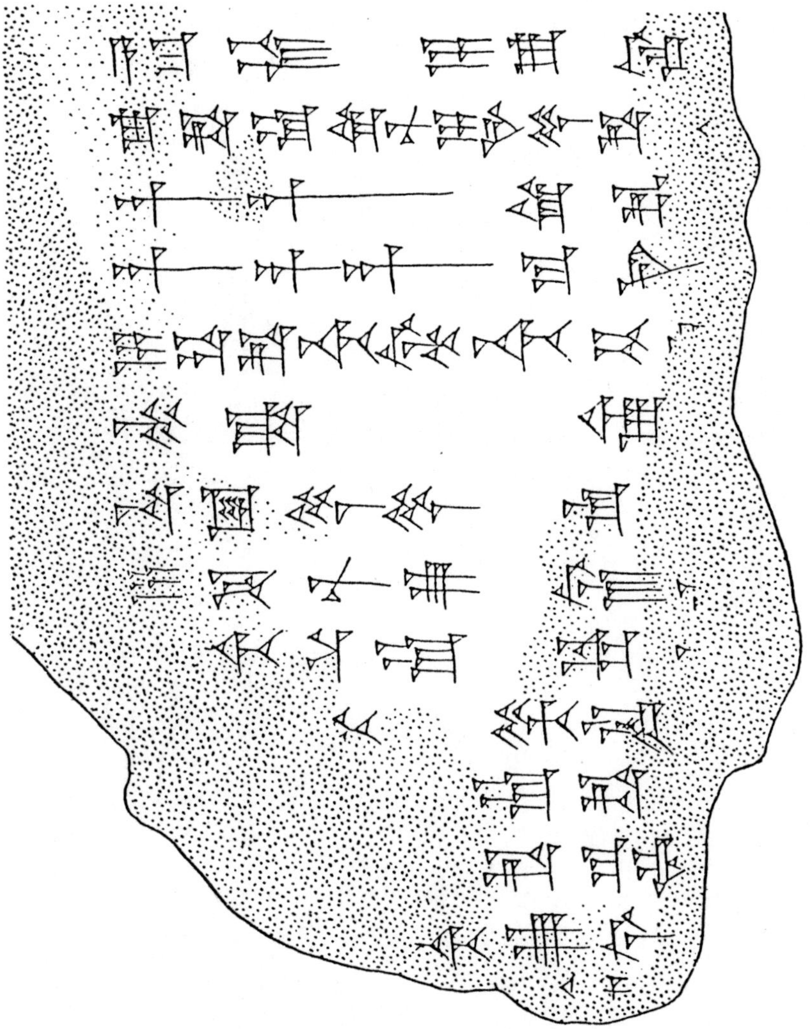

40559.

OBVERSE.

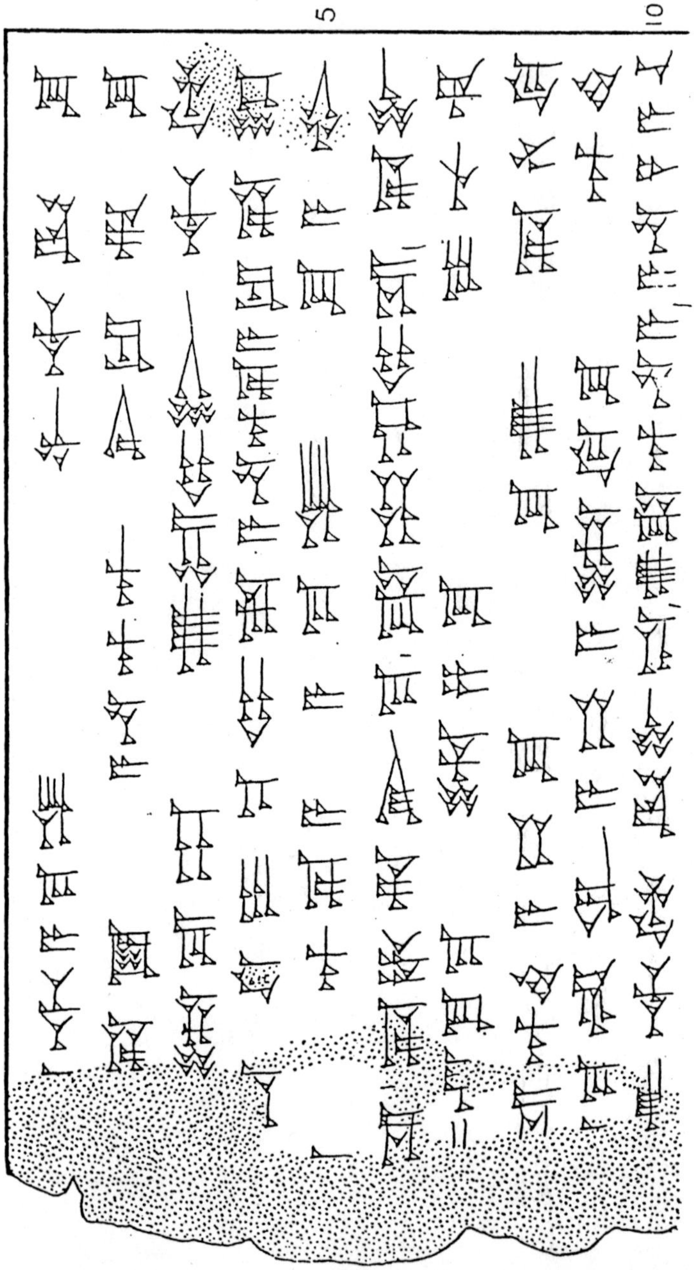

40559.

OBVERSE (cont.).

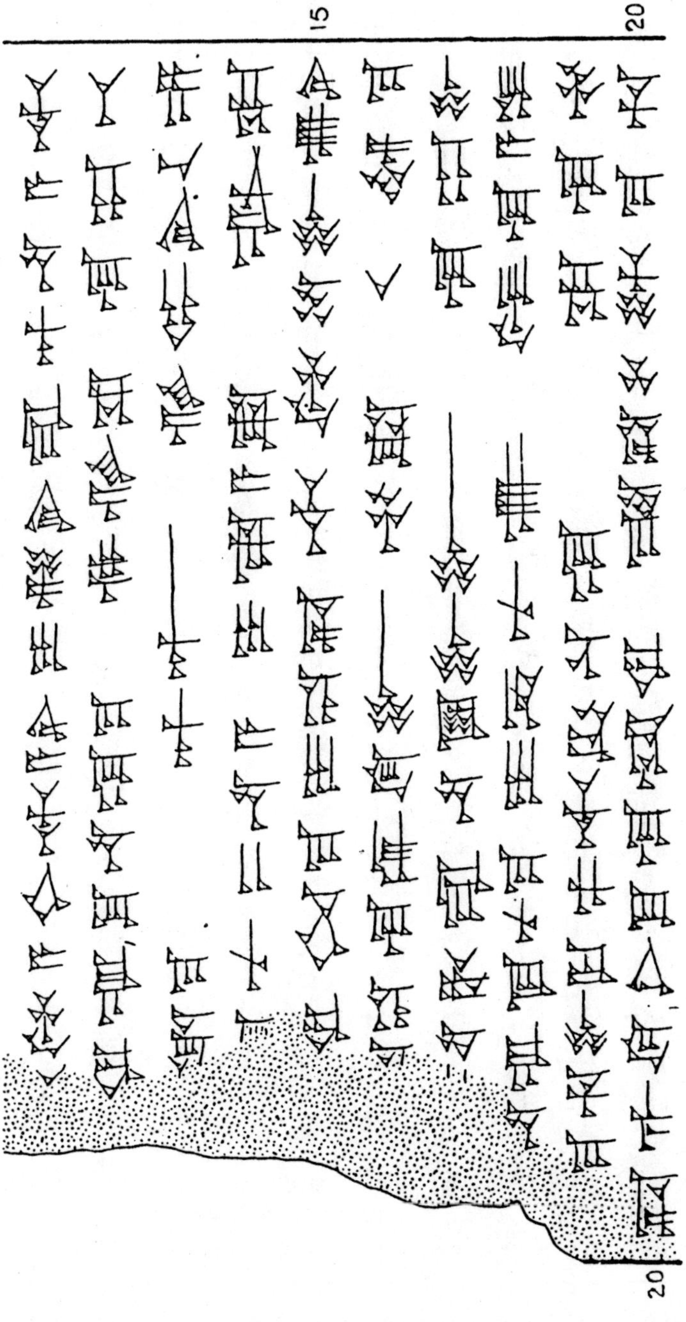

40559.

OBVERSE (cont.).

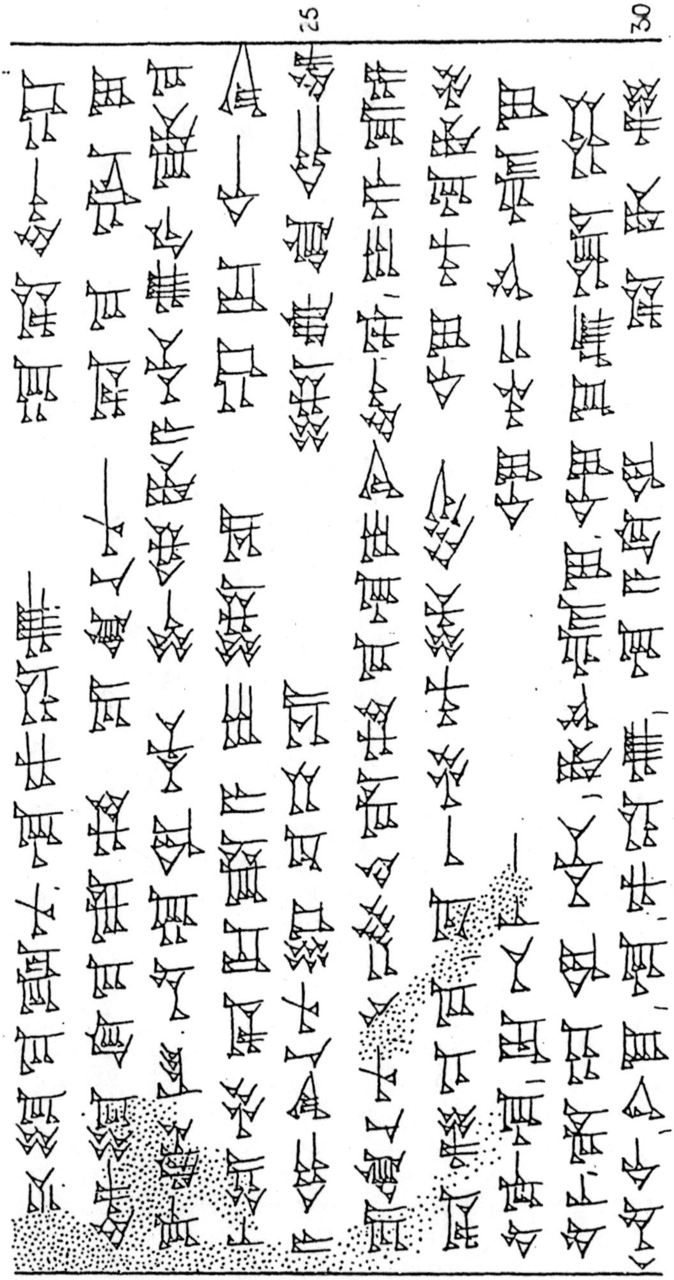

40559.

OBVERSE (cont.).

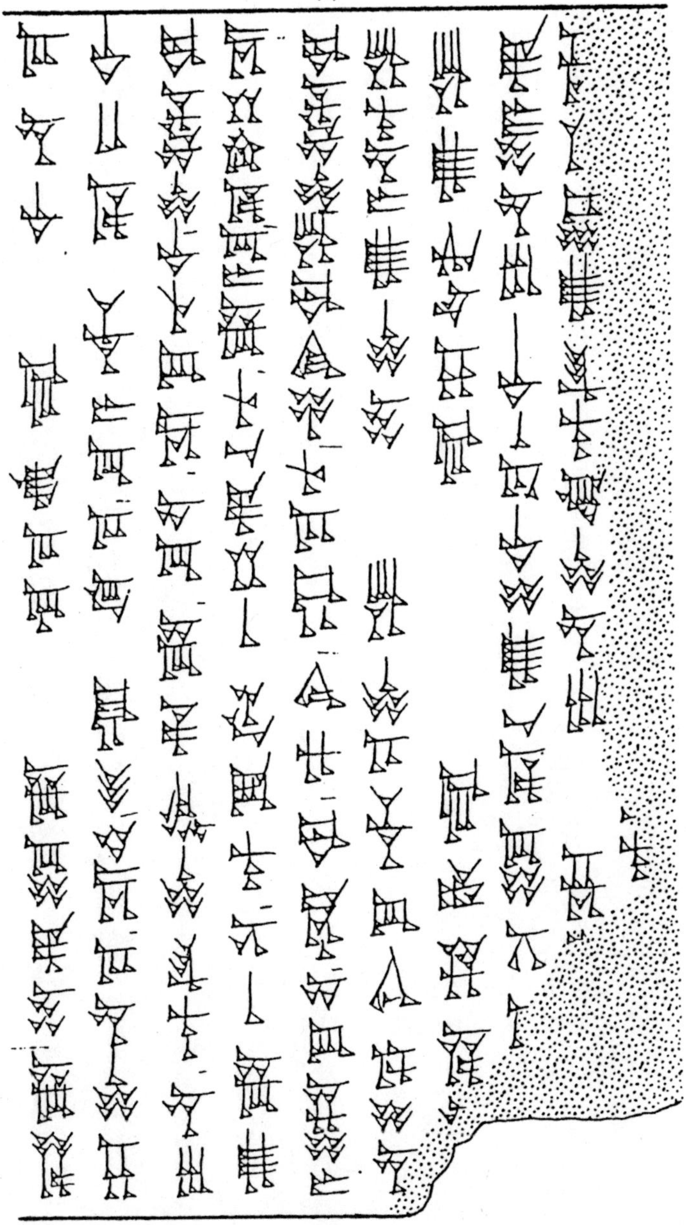

40559.

REVERSE.

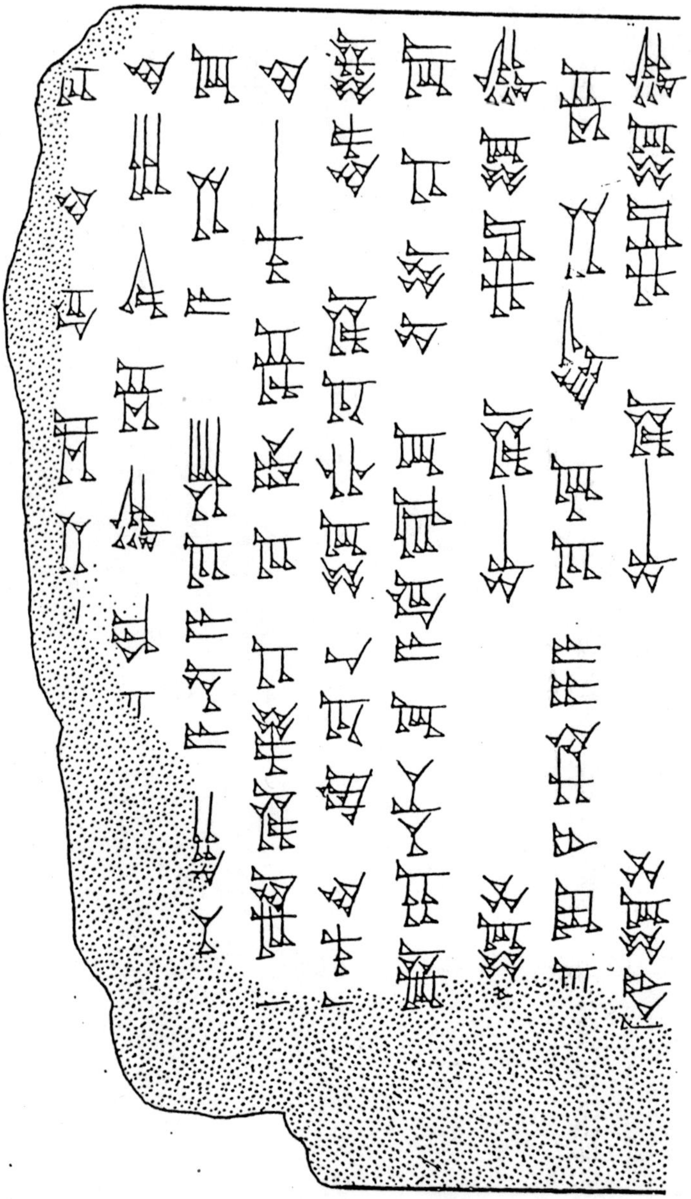

40559.

REVERSE (cont.).

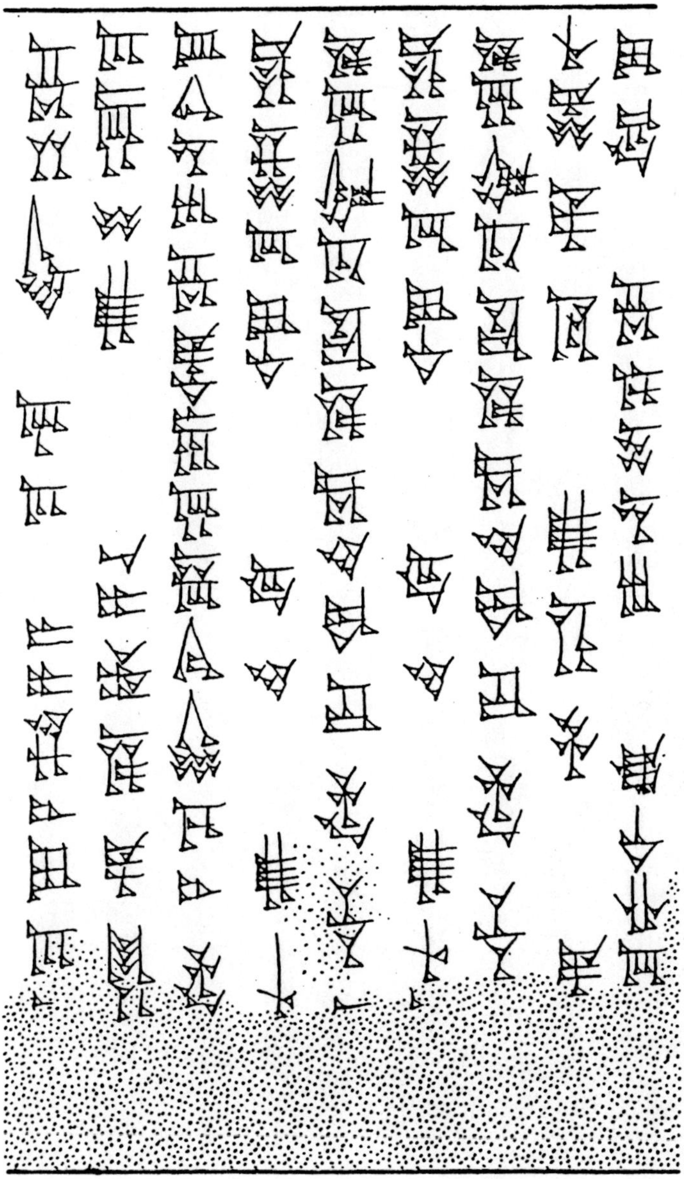

40559.

REVERSE (Cont.).

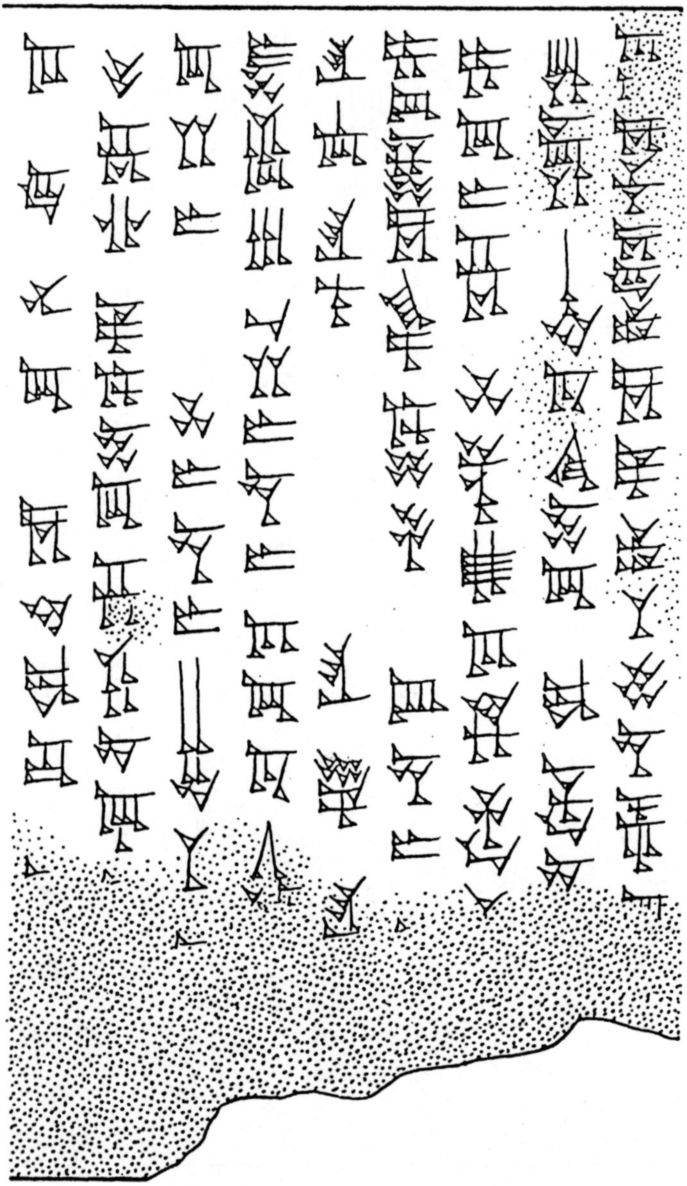

40559.

REVERSE (cont.).

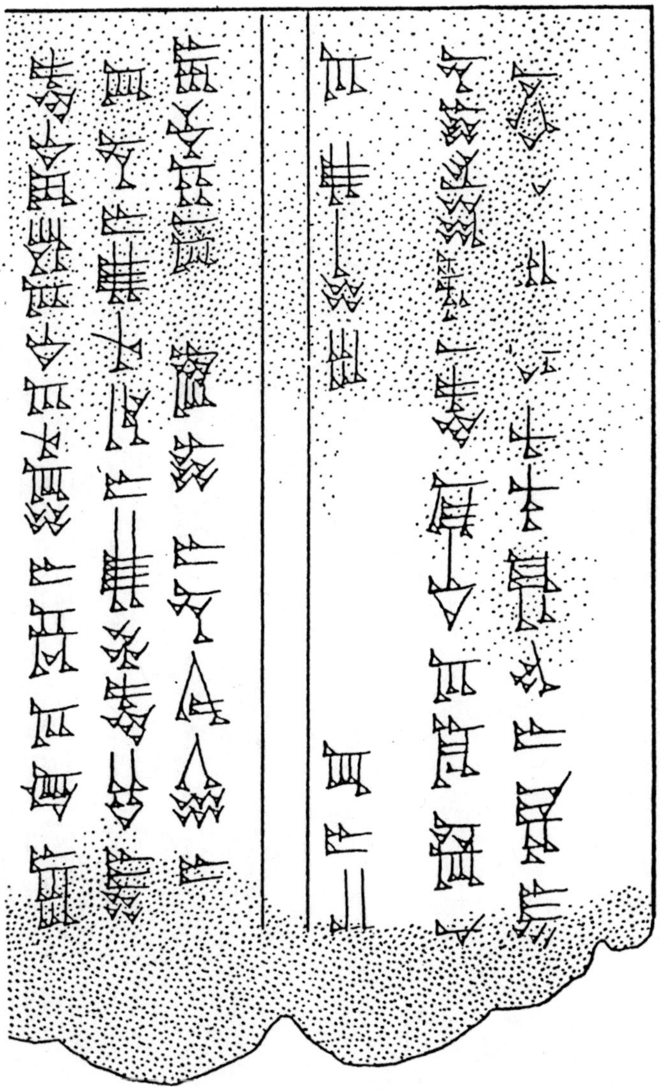

92632 + 93048.

OBVERSE.

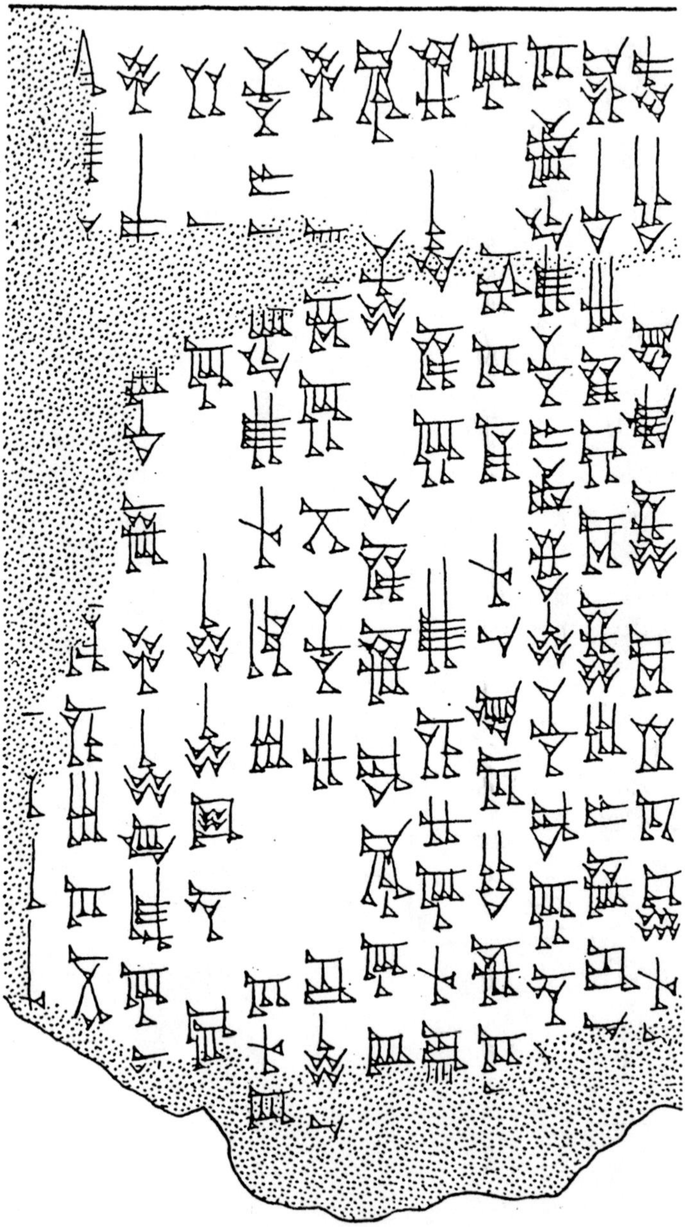

92632 + 93048.

OBVERSE (cont.).

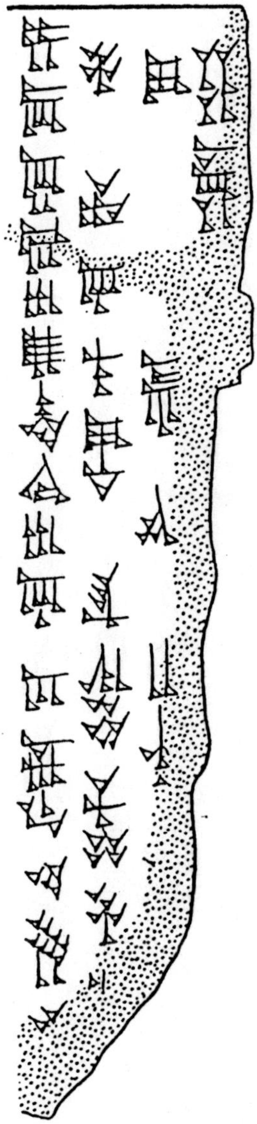

REVERSE.

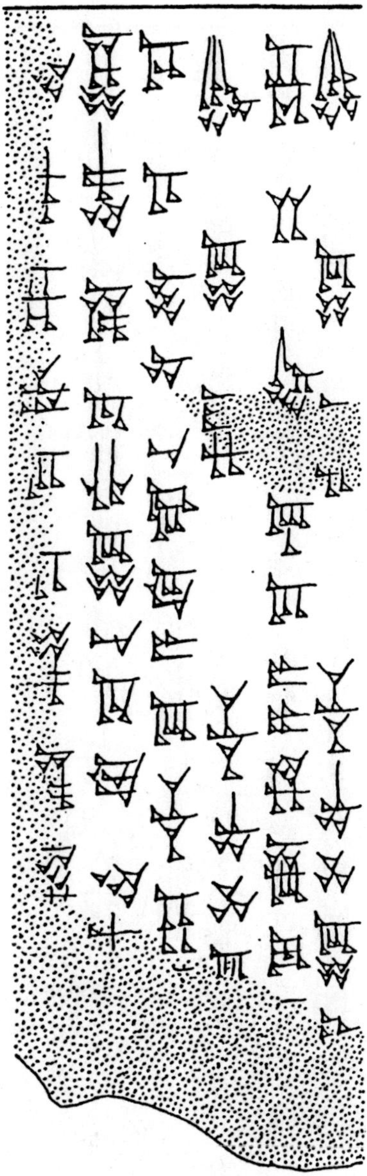

92632 + 93048.

REVERSE (cont.).

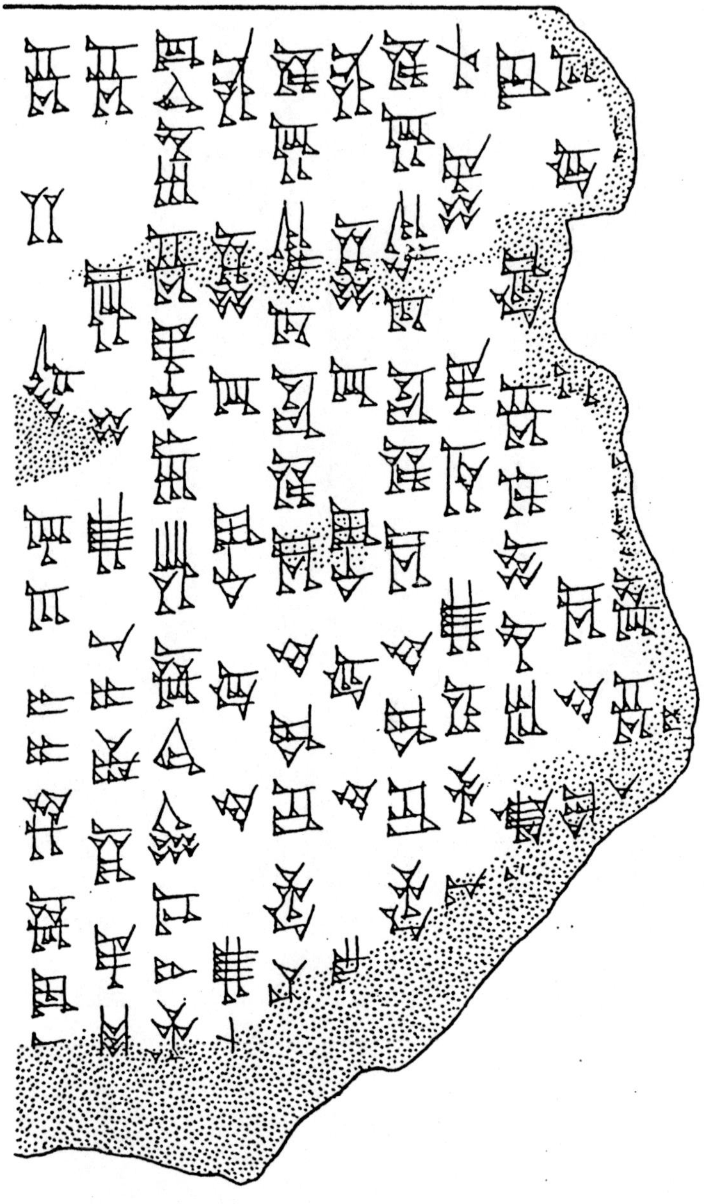

82-9-18, 1403 + 6316.

OBVERSE.

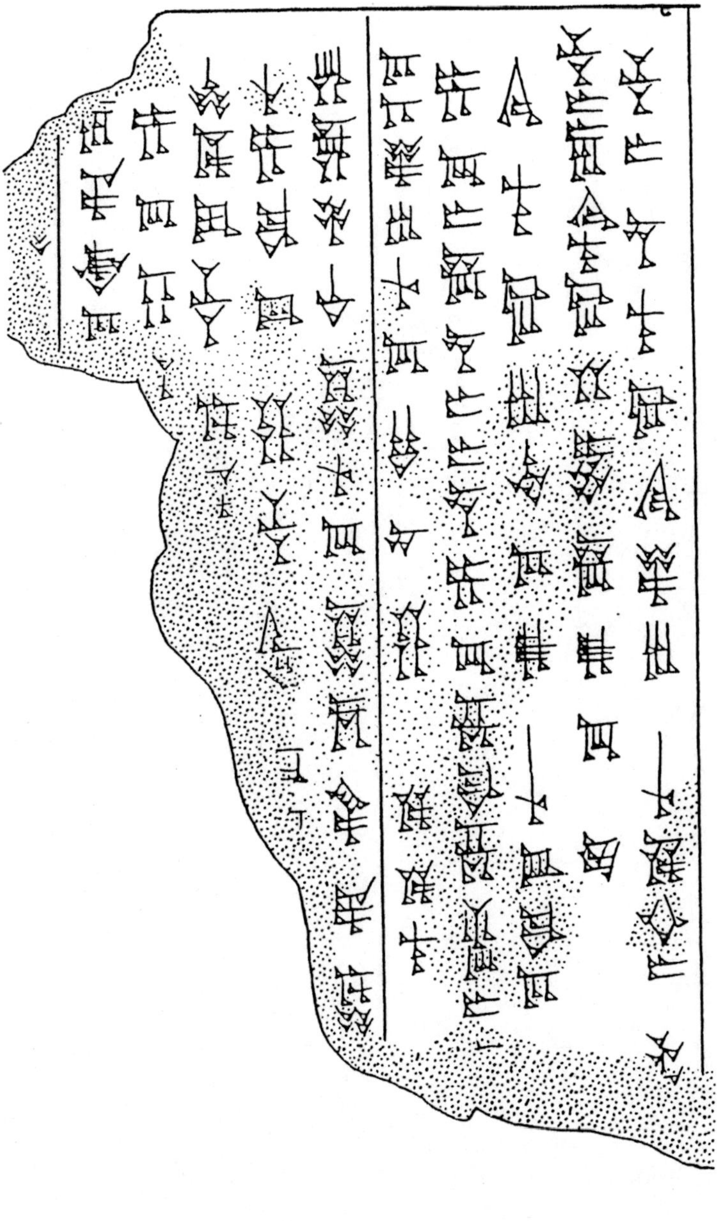

82-9-18, 1403 + 6316.

OBVERSE (Cont.).

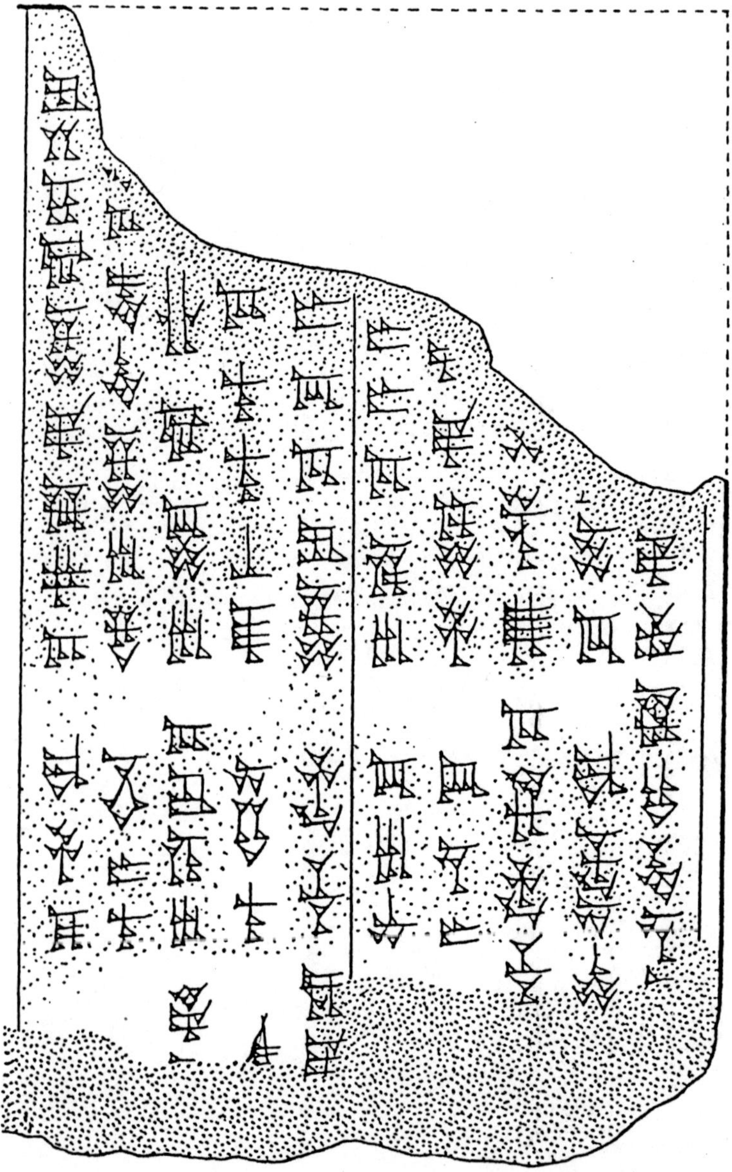

82-9-18, 1403 + 6316.

REVERSE.

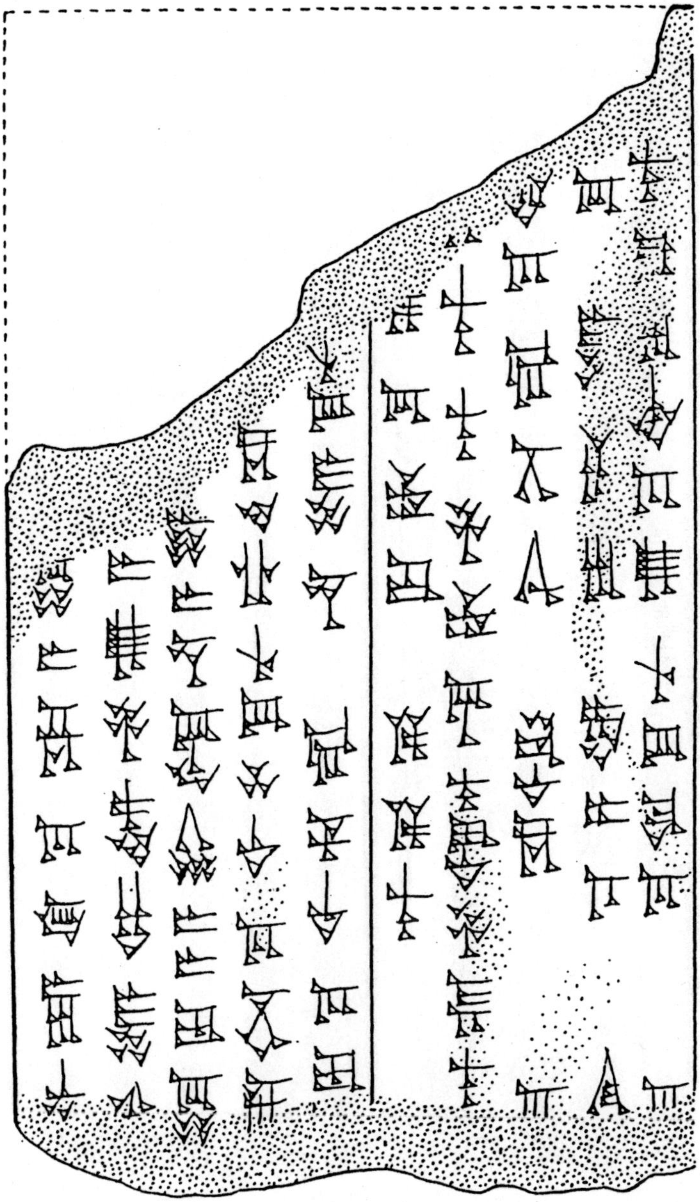

82-9-18, 1403 + 6316.

REVERSE (Cont.).

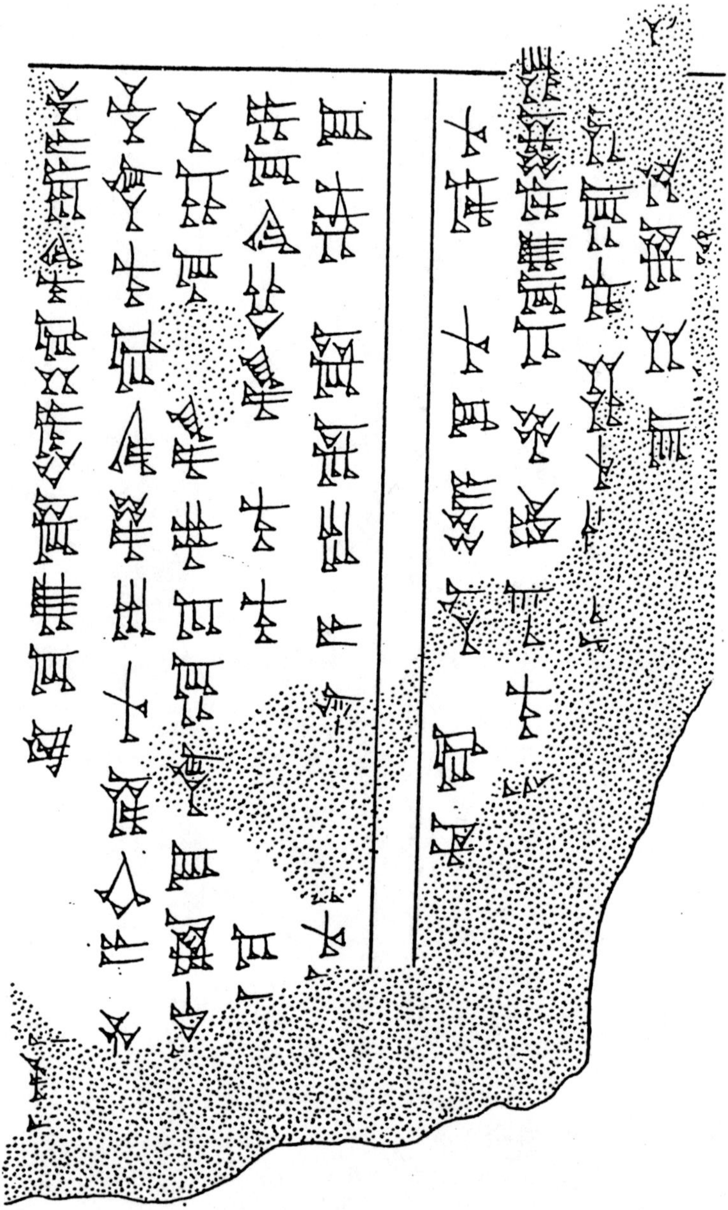

82-9-18, 6950 + 83-1-18, 1868.

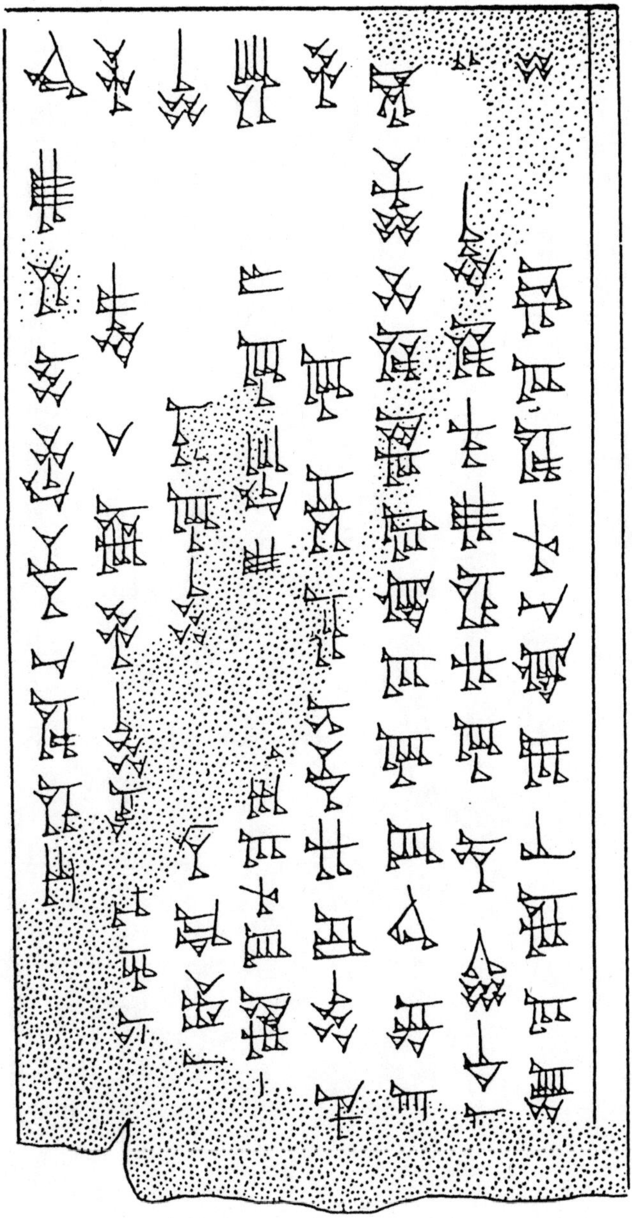

The text is an extract from a practice-tablet.

42285.

OBVERSE.

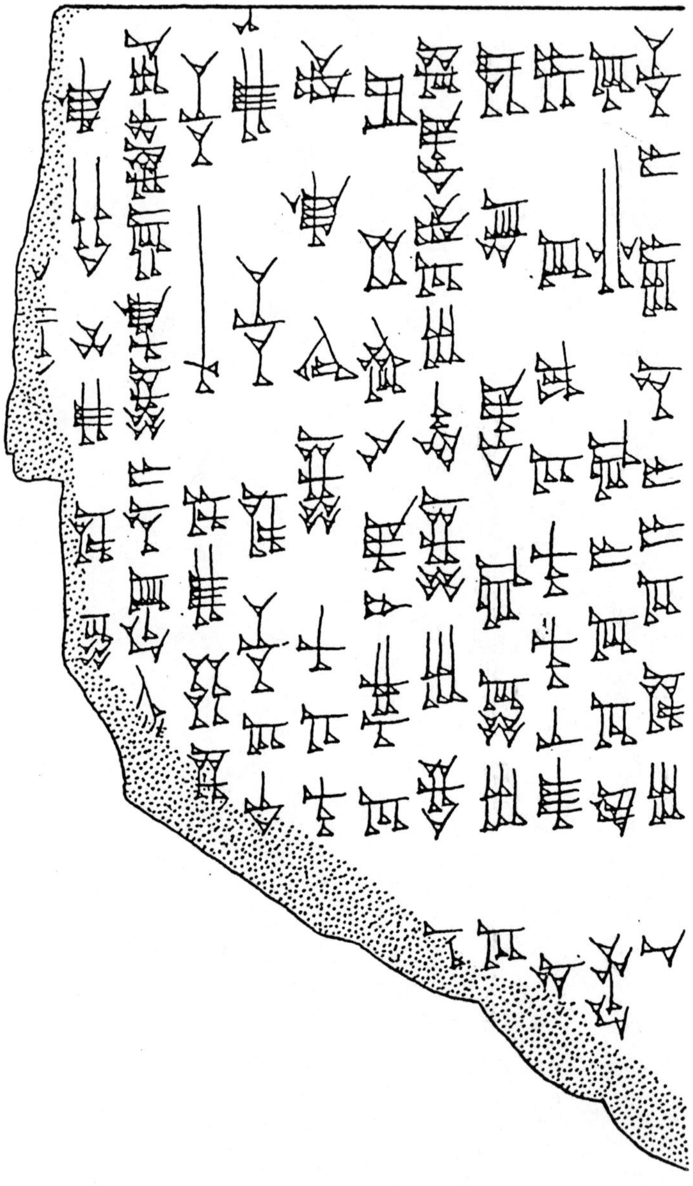

42285.

OBVERSE (Cont.).

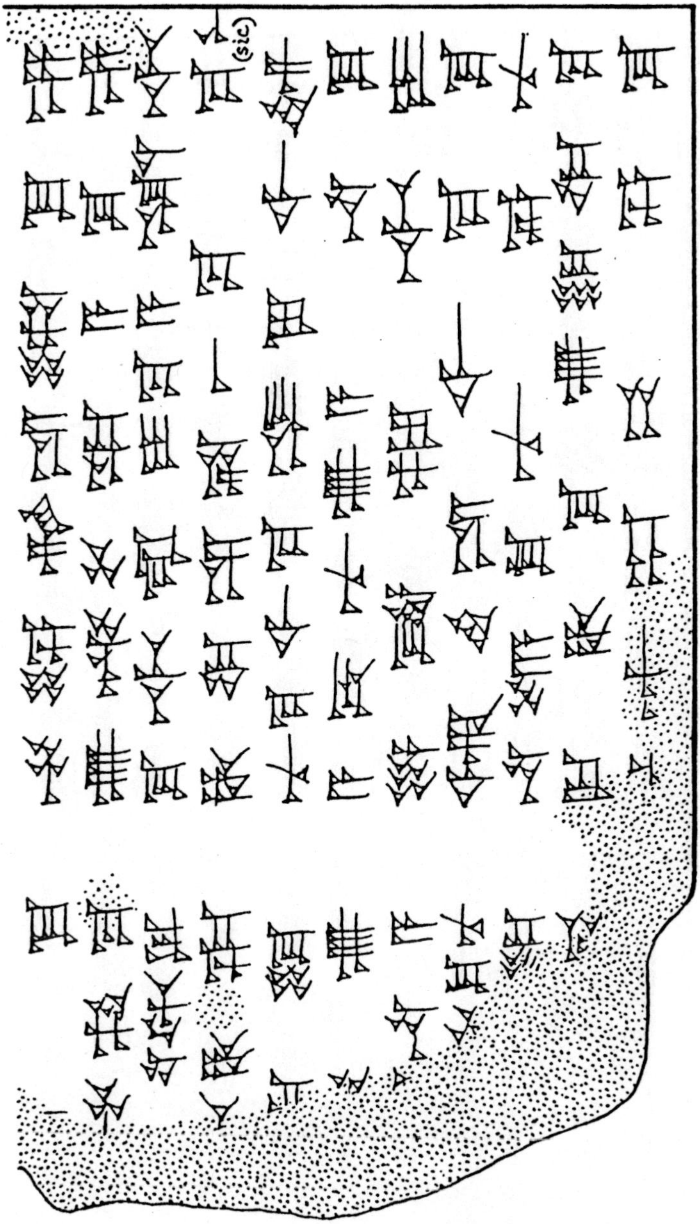

42285.

REVERSE.

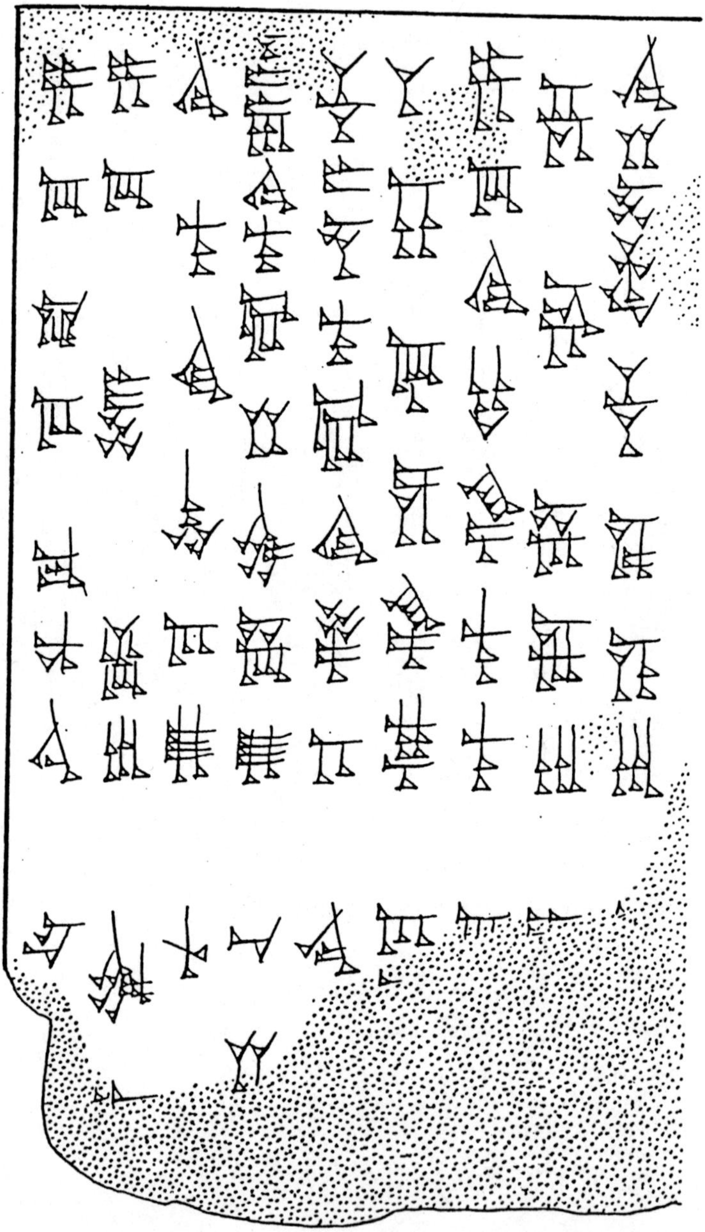

42285.

REVERSE (Cont.).

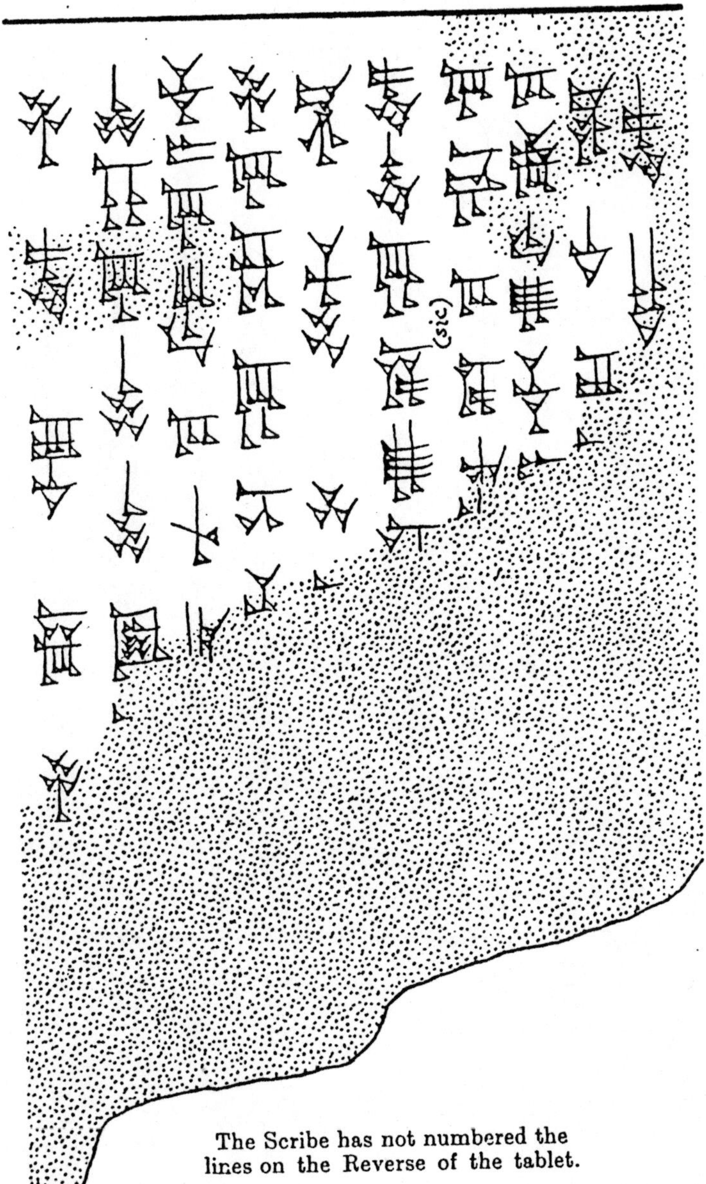

The Scribe has not numbered the lines on the Reverse of the tablet.

82-9-18, 5448 + 83-1-18, 2116.

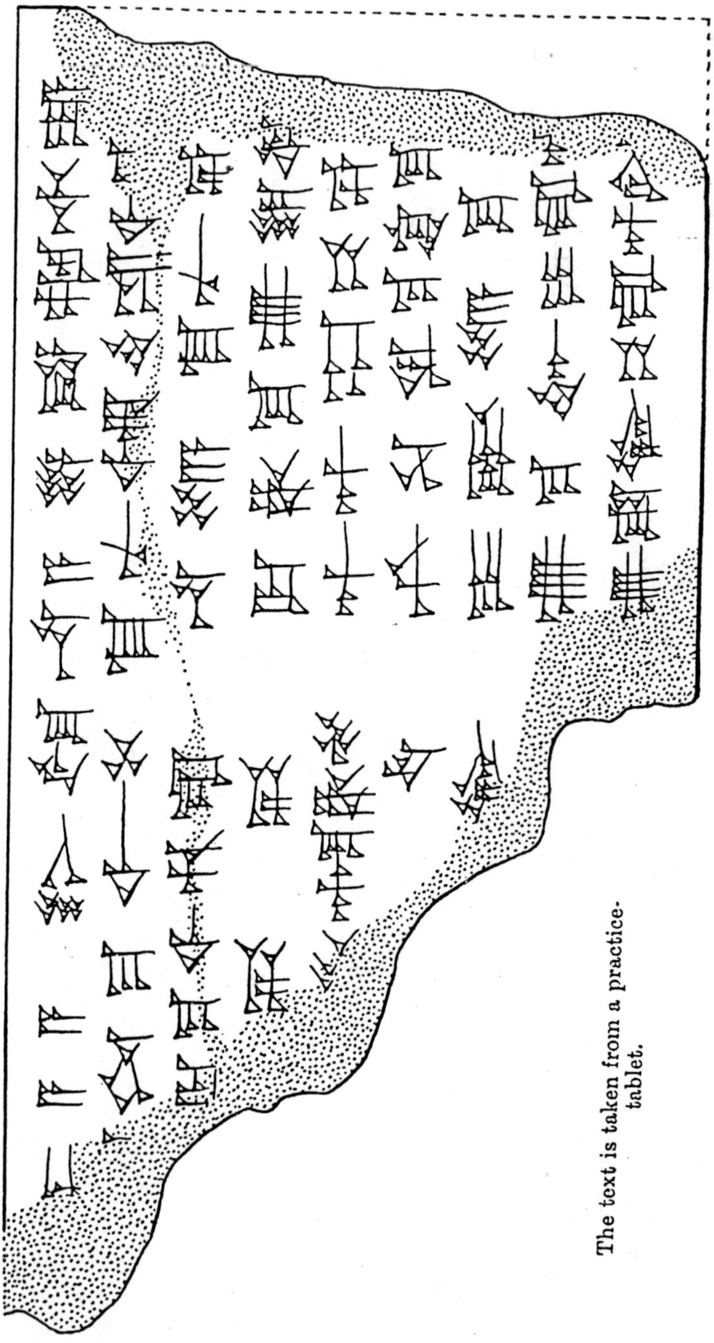

The text is taken from a practice-tablet.

92629.

OBVERSE.

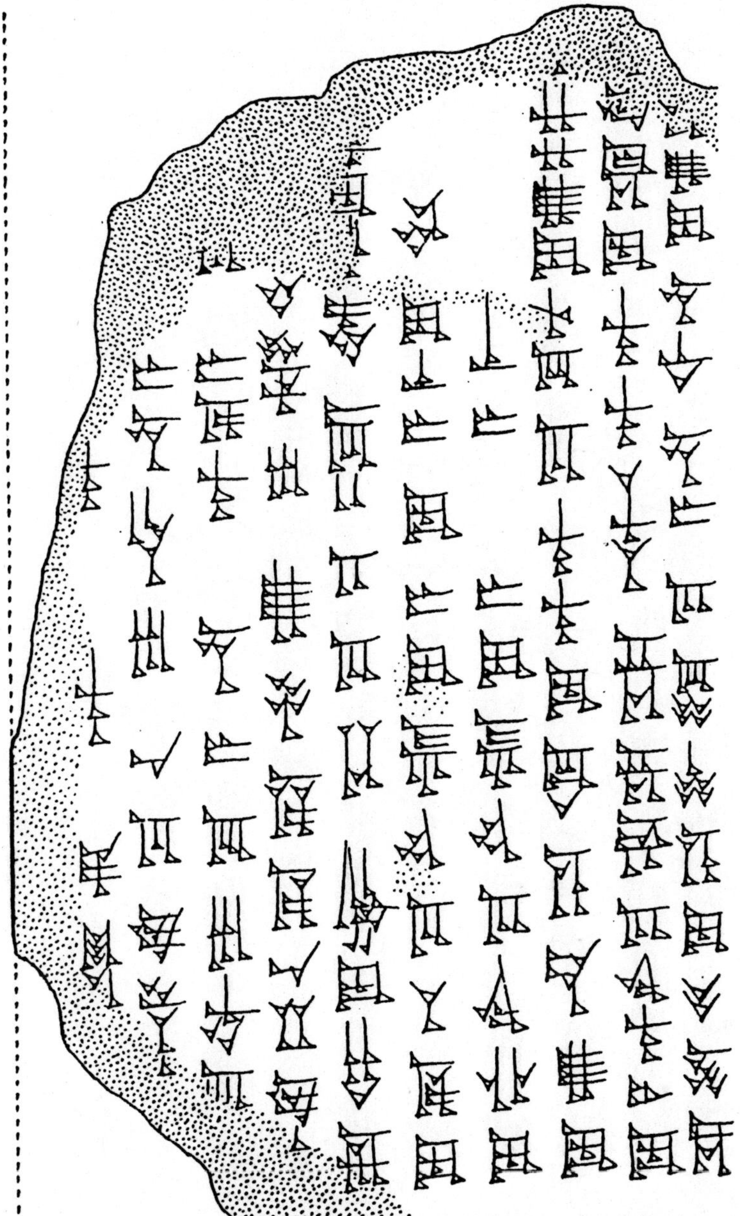

92629.

OBVERSE (cont.).

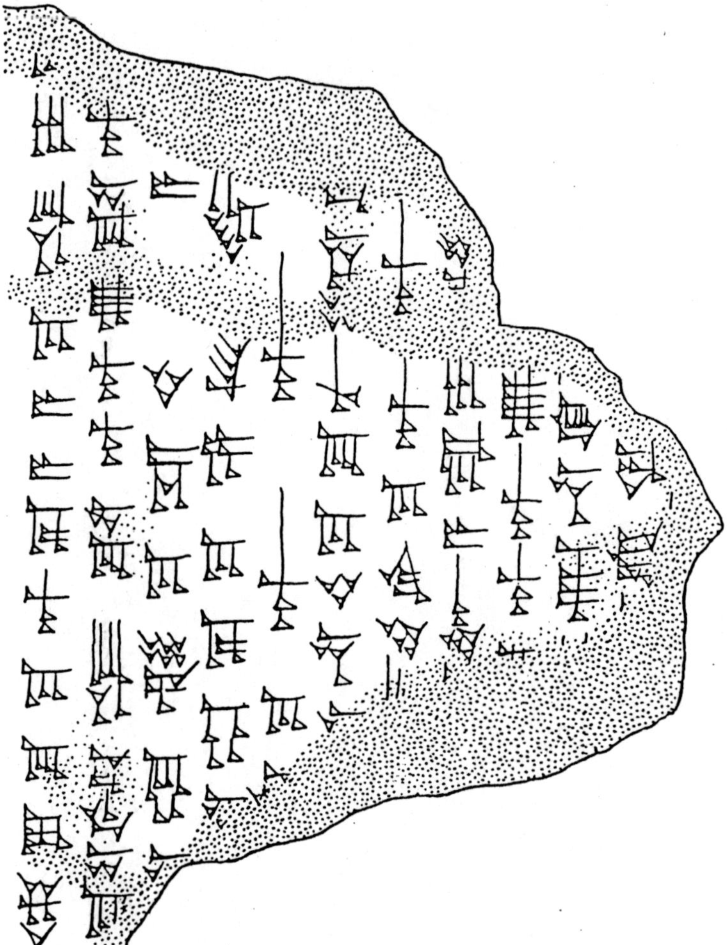

92629.

REVERSE.

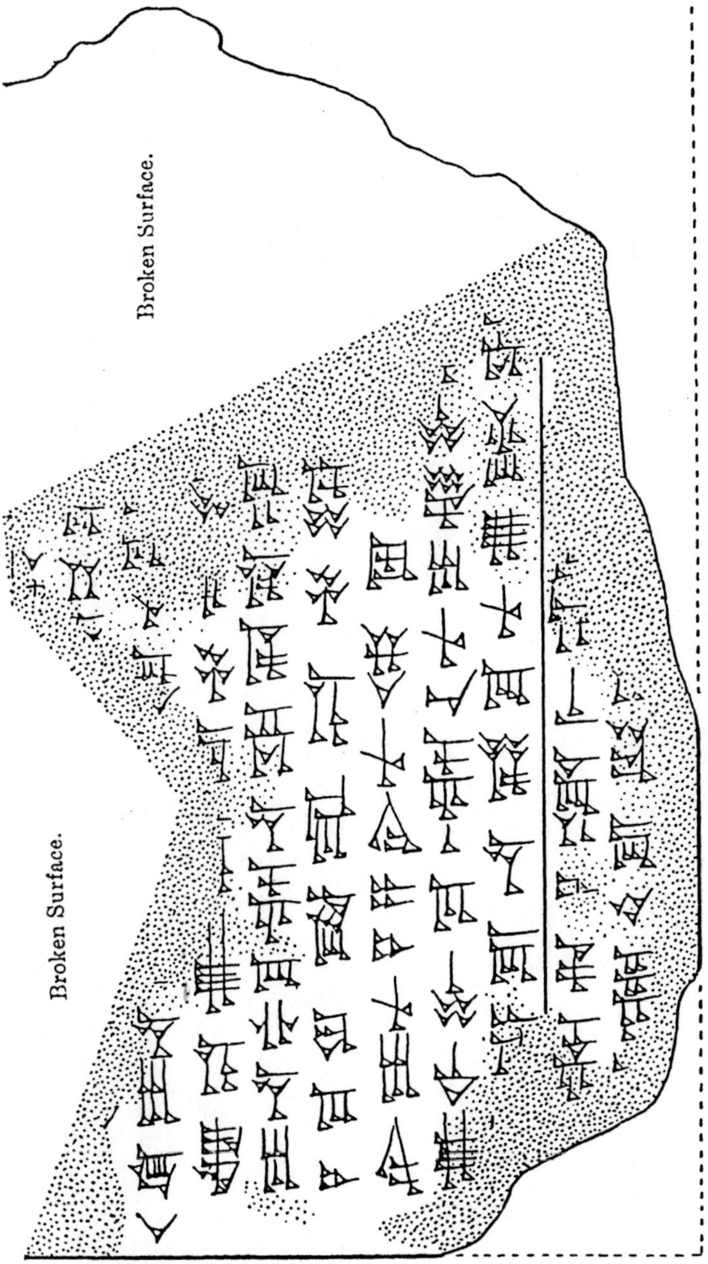

91139 + 93073.

OBVERSE.

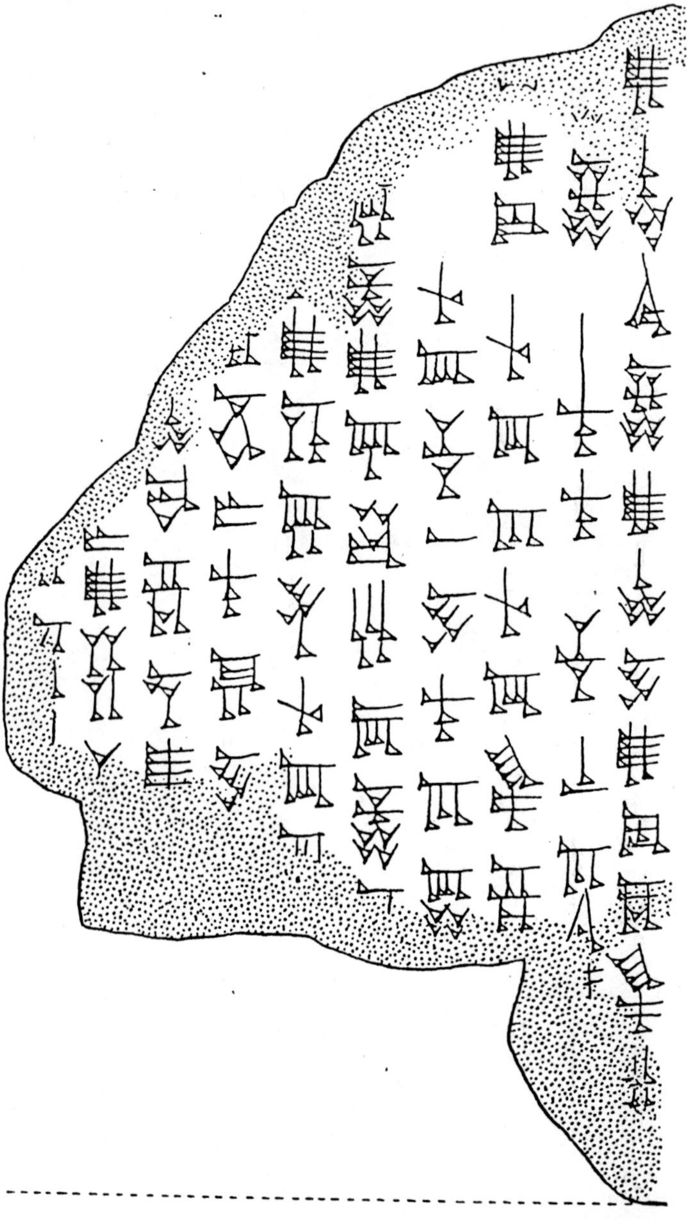

91139 + 93073.

OBVERSE (cont.).

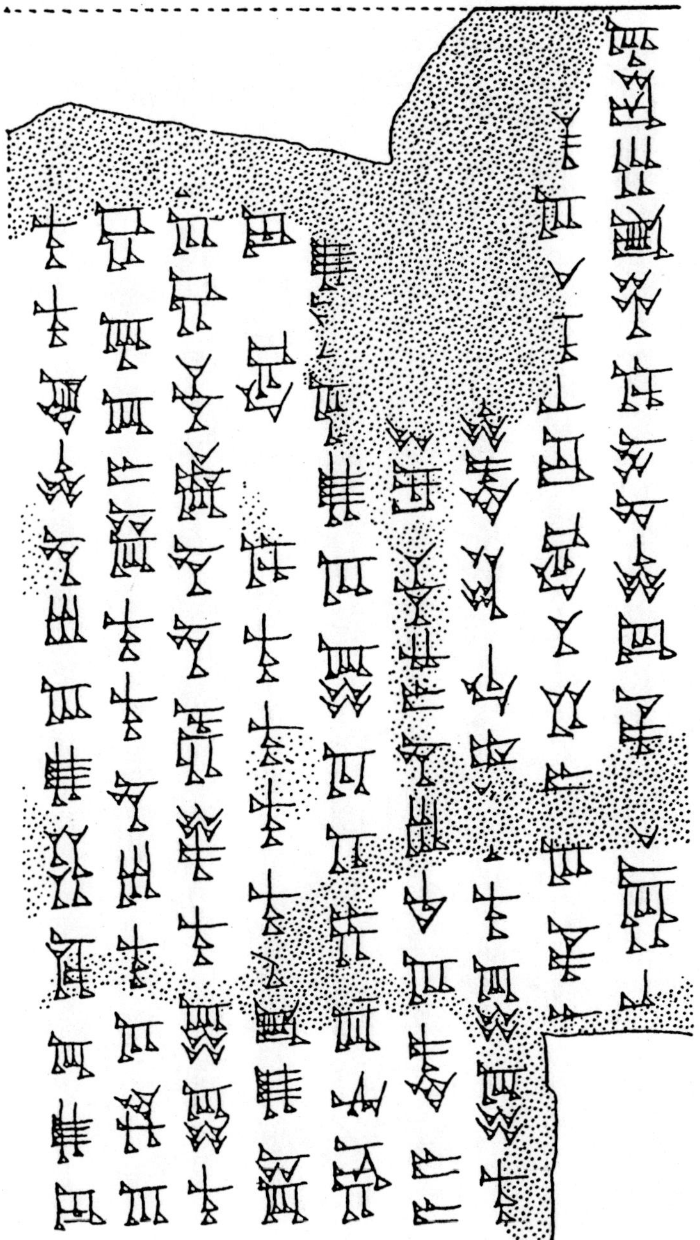

91139 + 93073.

OBVERSE (cont.).

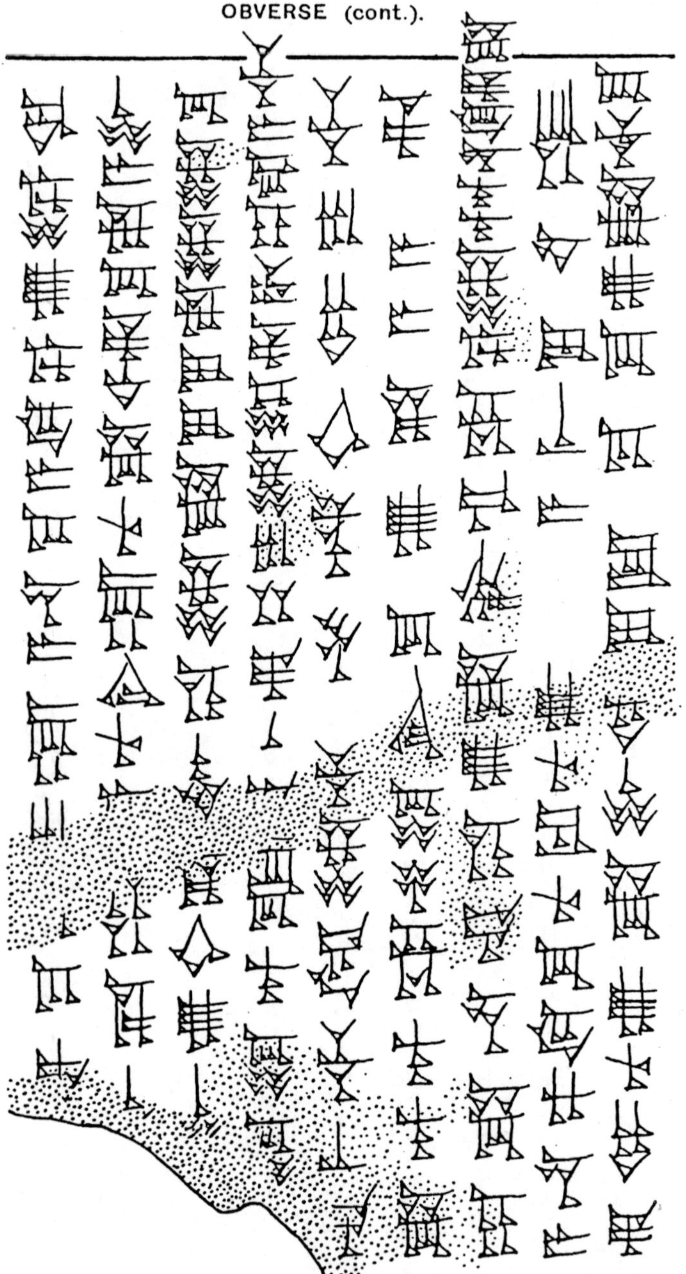

91139 + 93073.

OBVERSE (Cont.).

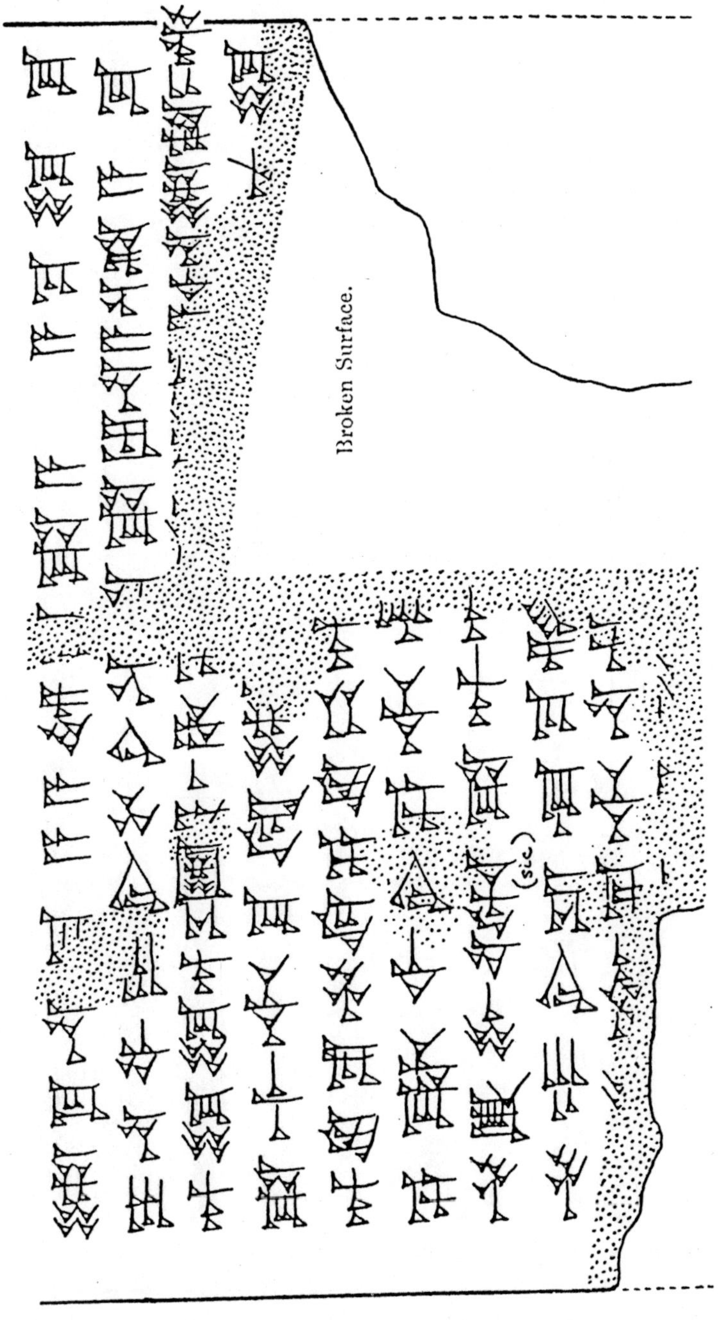

91139 + 93073.

REVERSE.

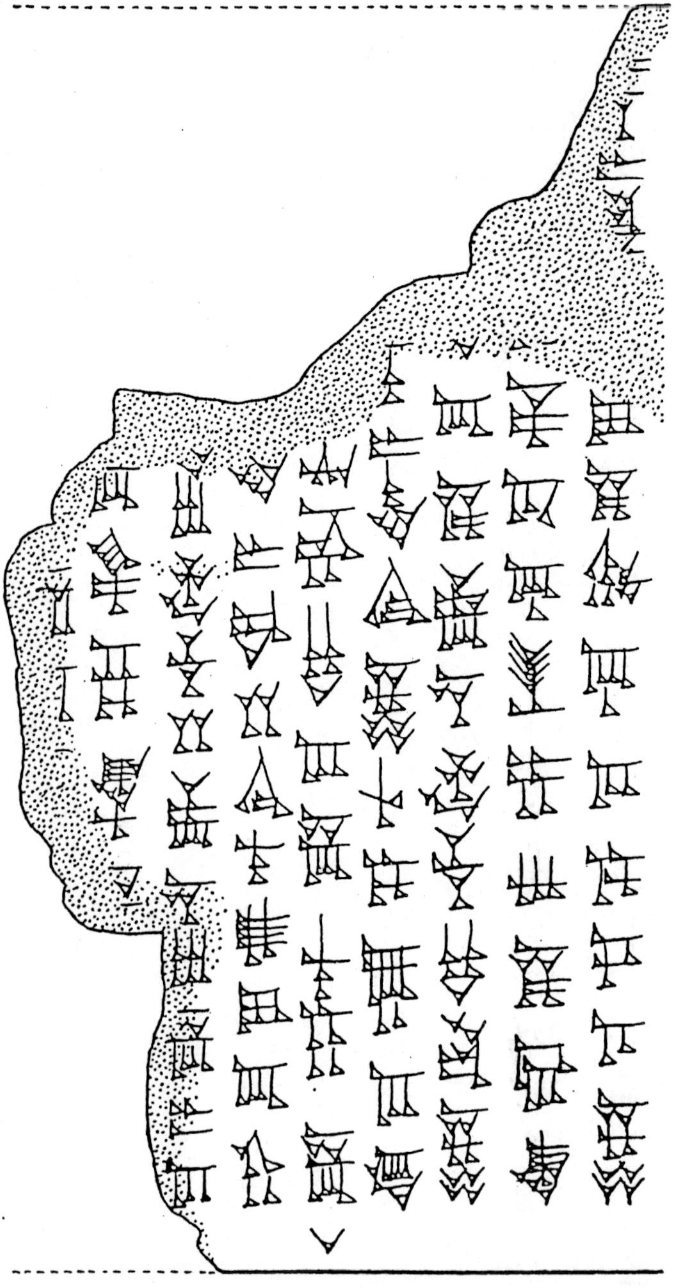

91139 + 93073.

REVERSE (cont.).

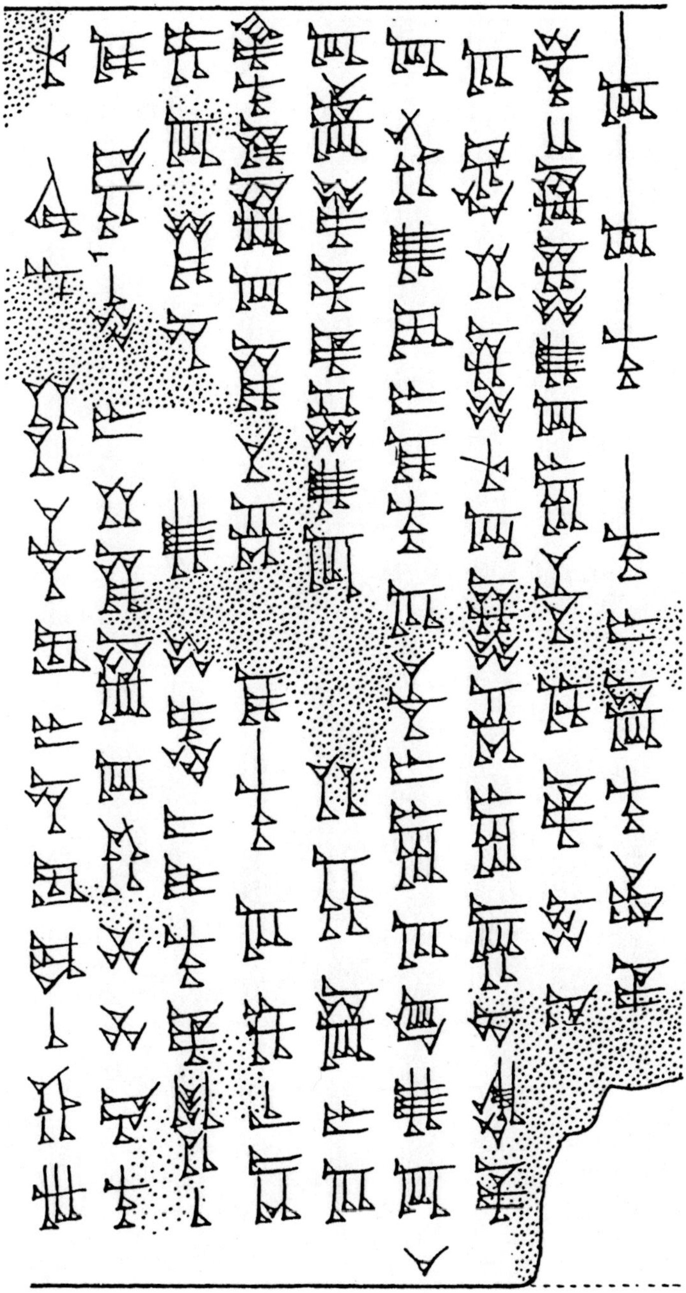

1. Erasure by the Scribe.

91139 + 93073.

REVERSE (cont.).

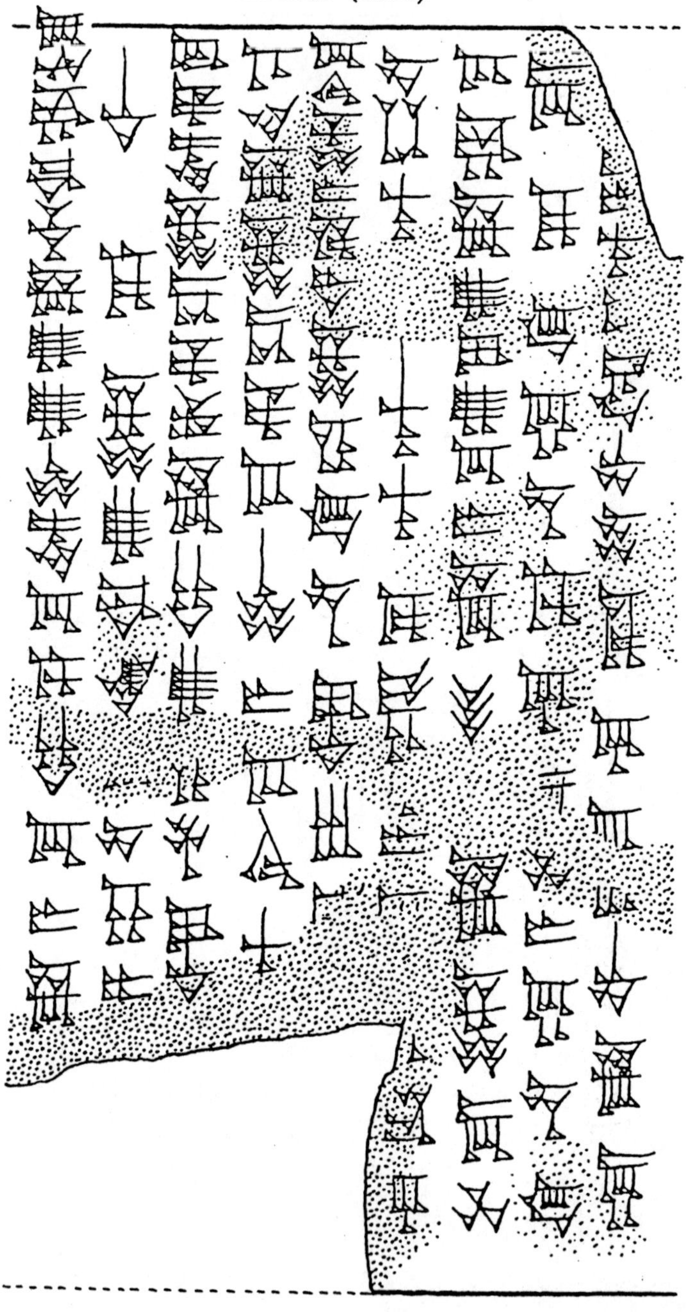

91139.+93073.

REVERSE (cont.).

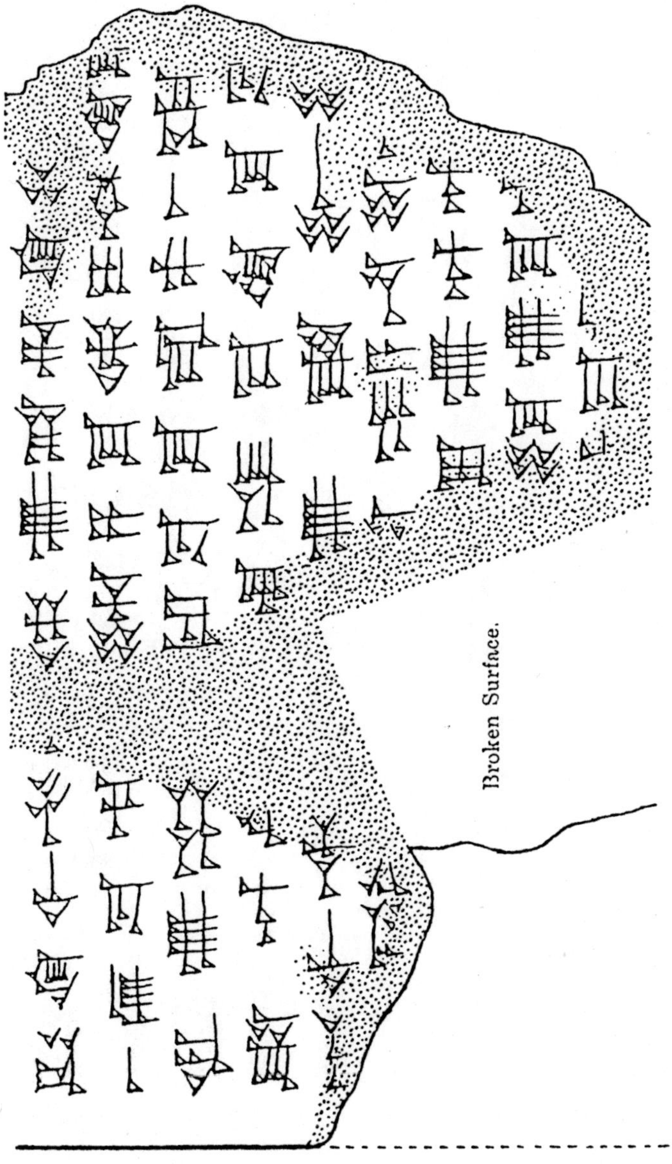

35506.

OBVERSE.

35506.

OBVERSE (Cont.).

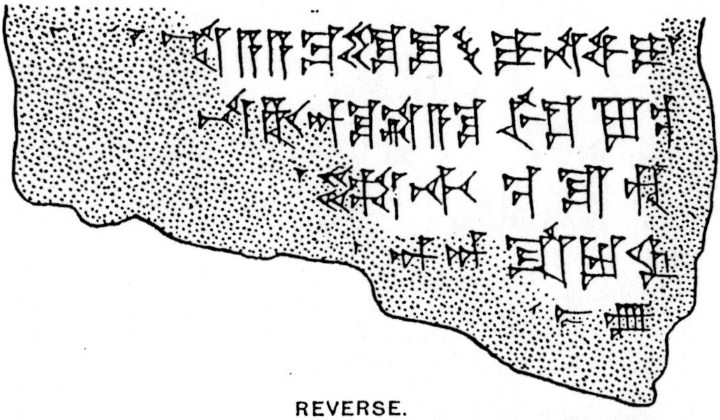

REVERSE.

35506.

REVERSE (Cont.).

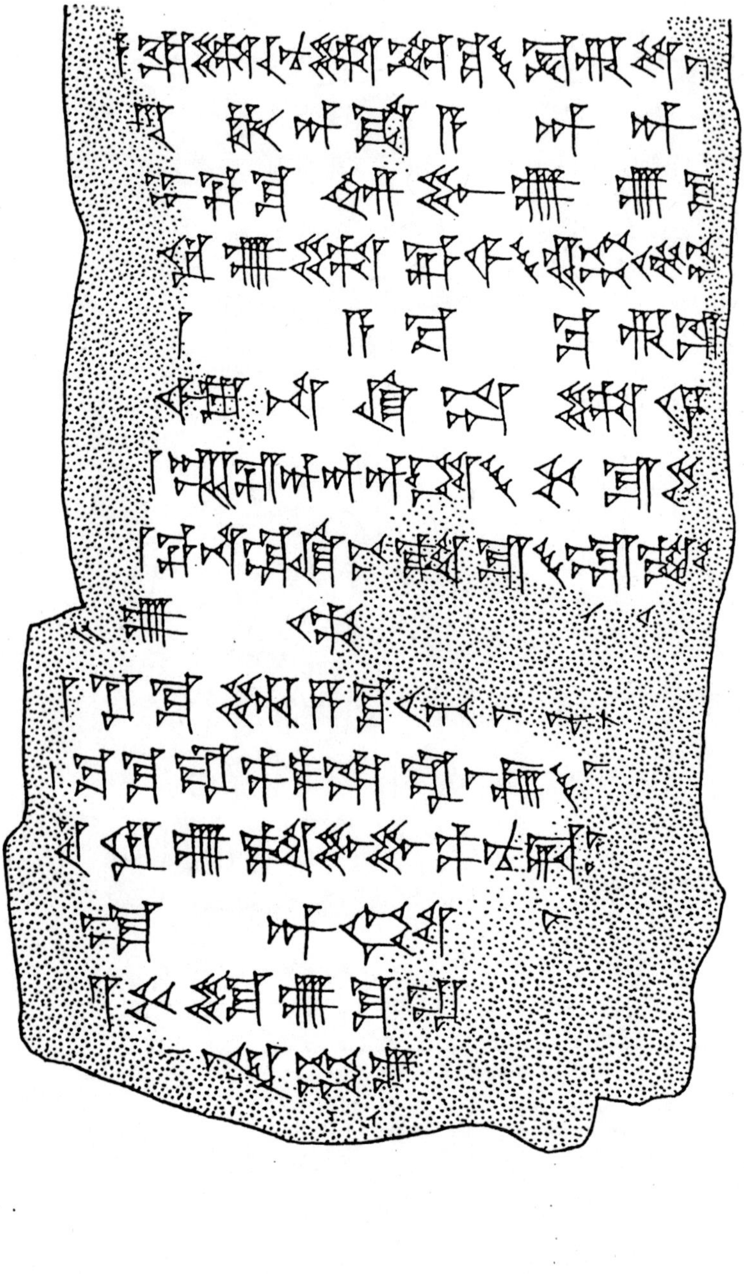

82-7-14, 4005.

OBVERSE.

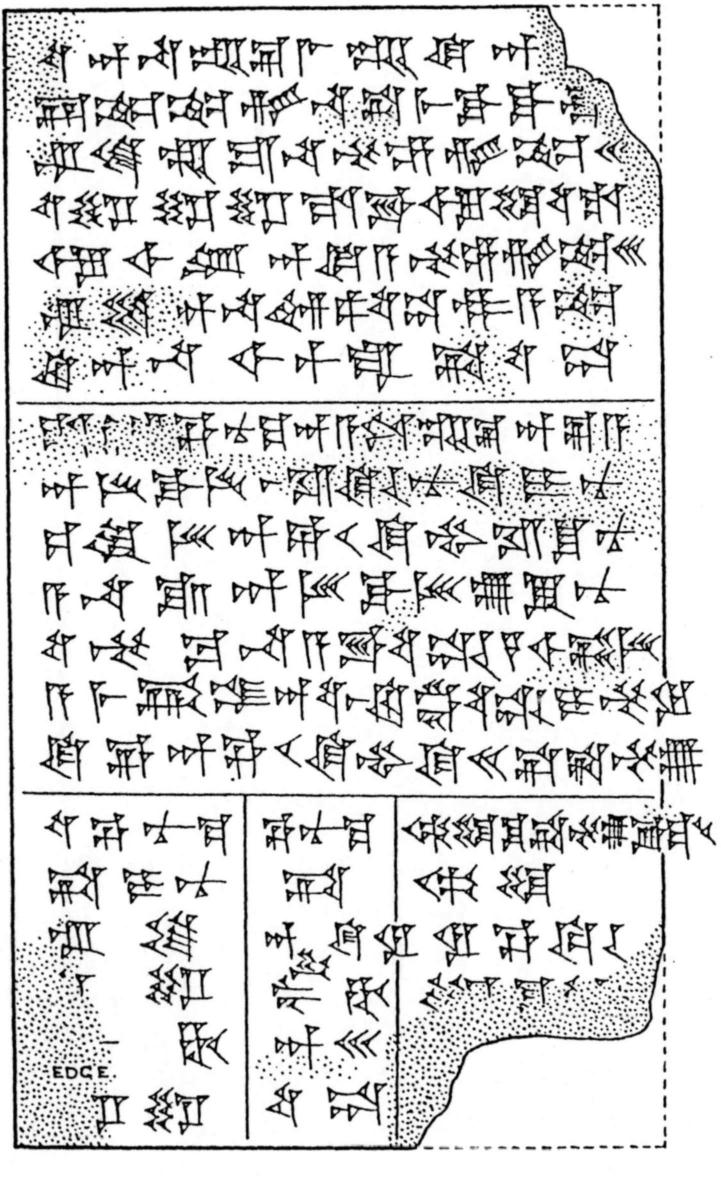

82-7-14, 4005.

REVERSE.

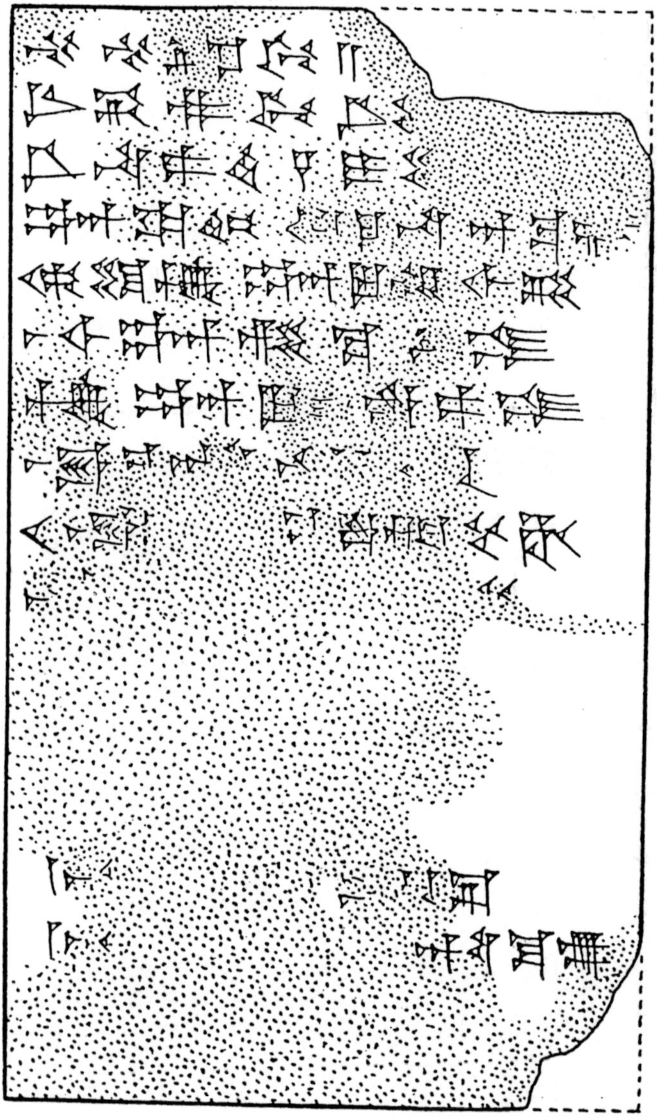

APPENDIX I. PLATE LI.

S. 11 + S. 980.

OBVERSE.

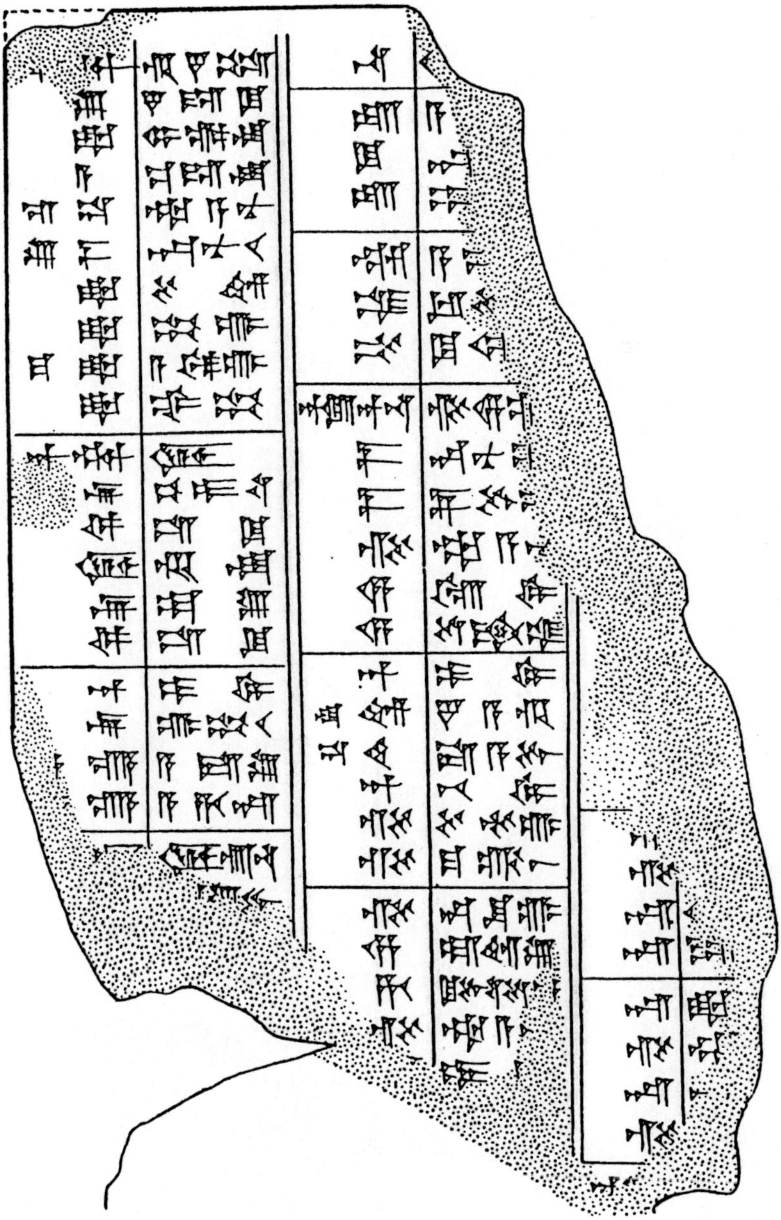

S. 11 + S. 980.

REVERSE.

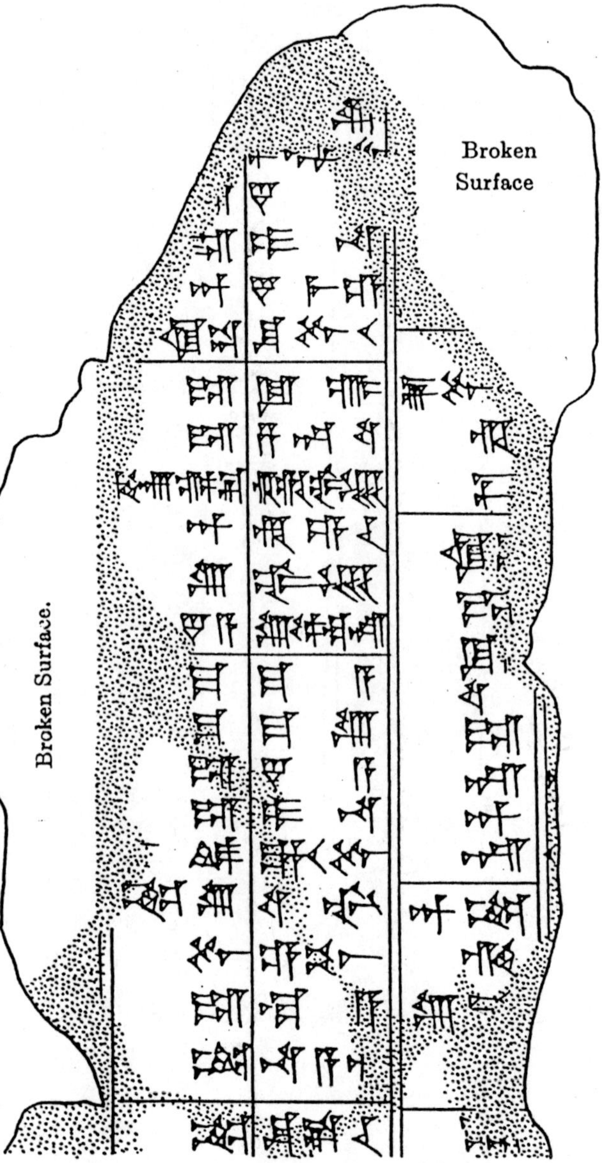

S. 11 + S. 980.

REVERSE (Cont.).

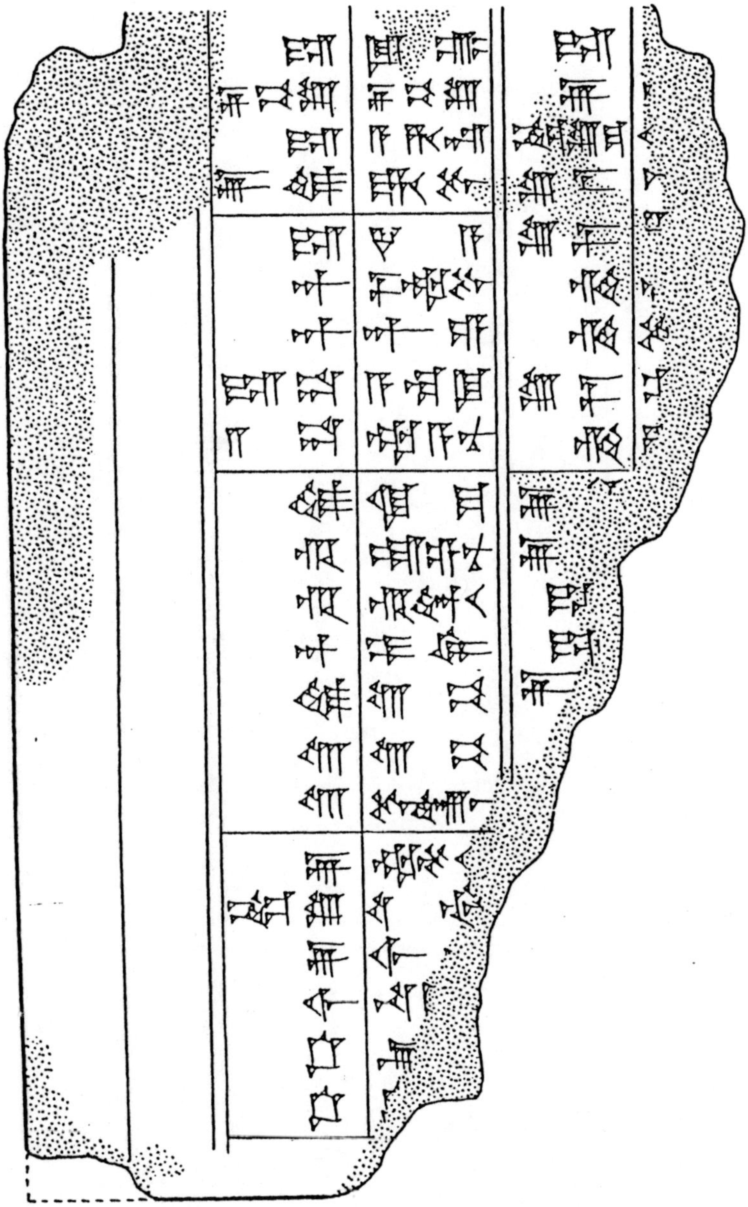

K. 4406.

REVERSE.

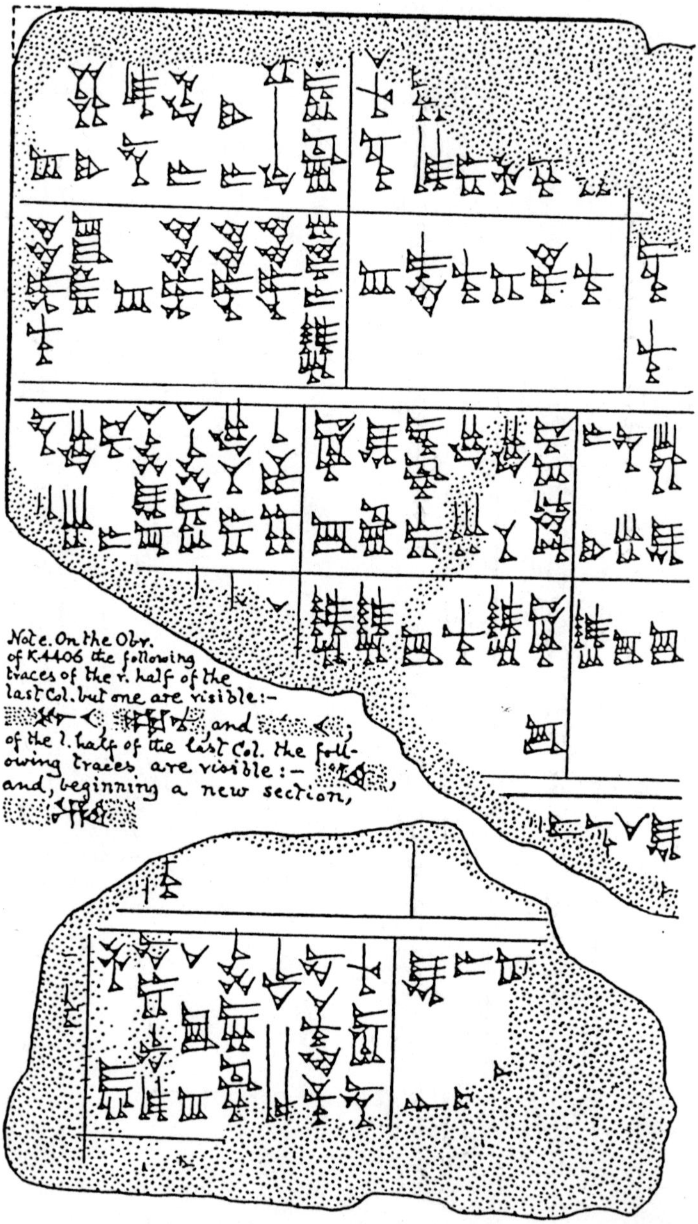
Note. On the Obv. of K.4406 the following traces of the r. half of the last Col. but one are visible:- and ; of the l. half of the last Col. the following traces are visible:- , and, beginning a new section,

82-3-23, 151.

K. 4406.

REVERSE (Cont.).

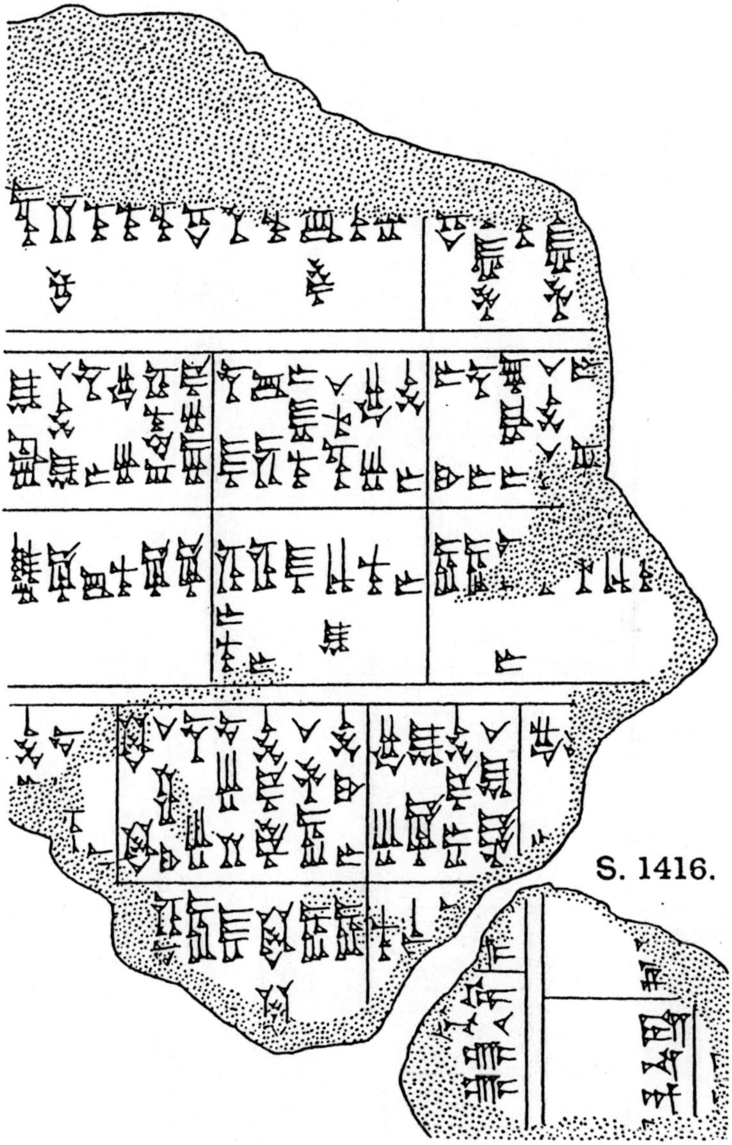

S. 1416.

R. 366 + 80-7-19, 293.

OBVERSE.

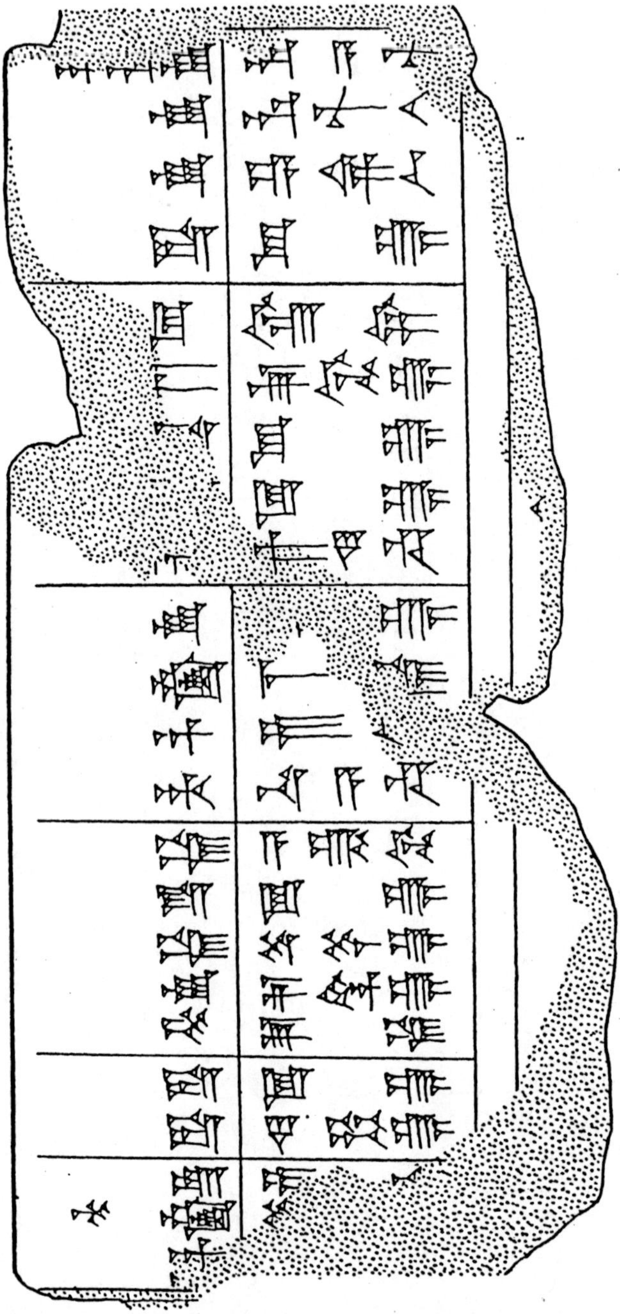

R. 366 + 80-7-19, 293.

REVERSE.

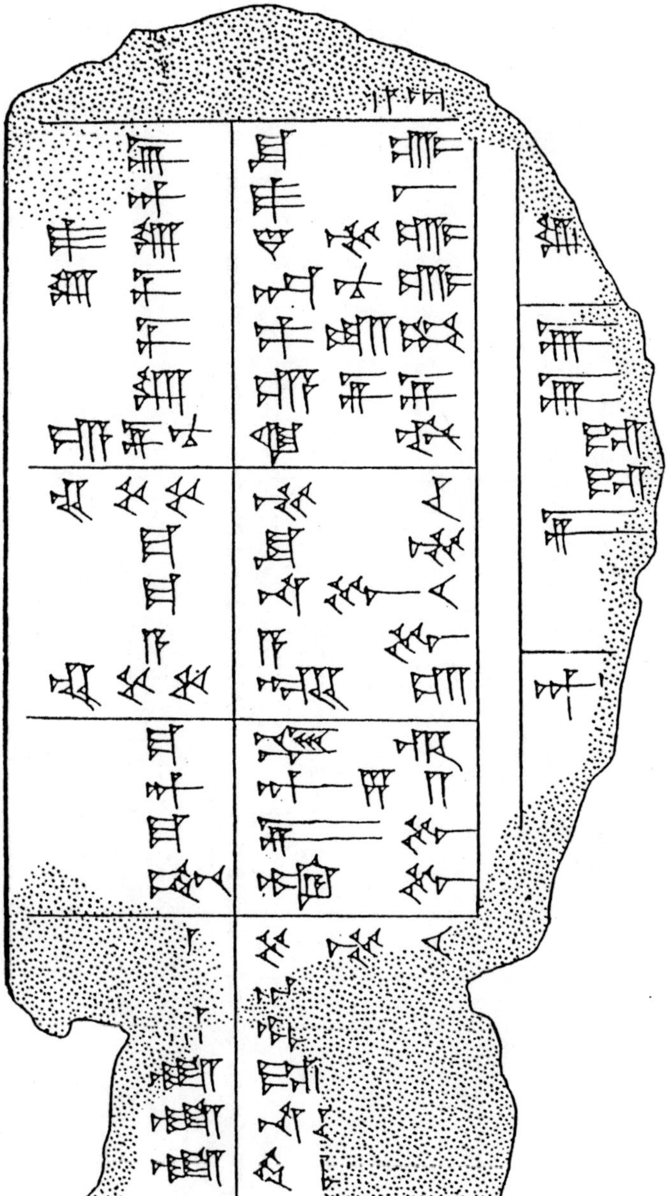

R. 366 + 80-7-19, 293.

REVERSE (cont.).

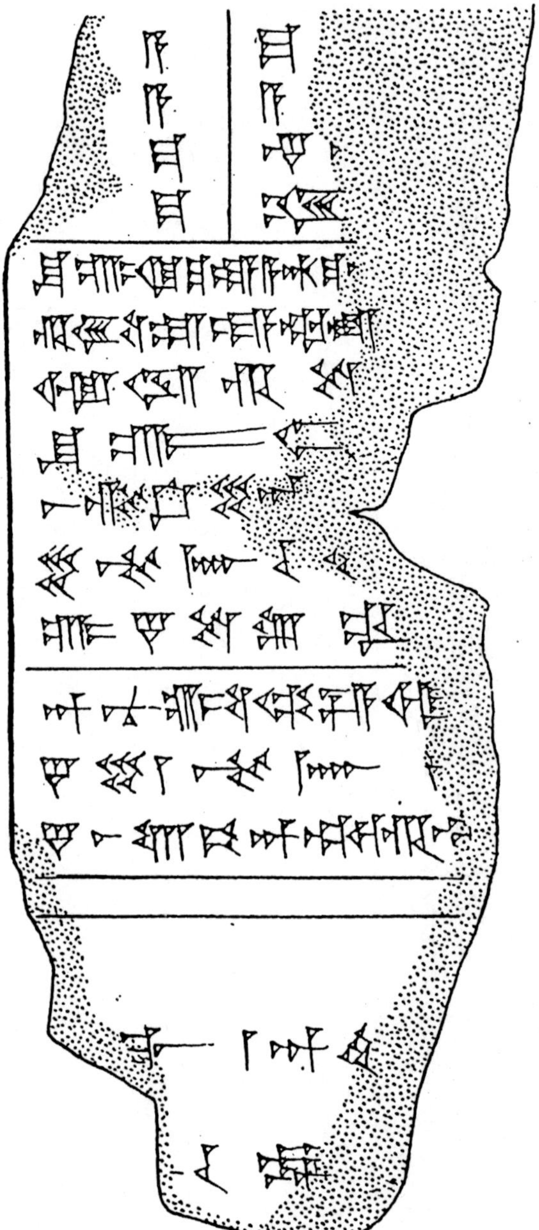

K. 2053.

OBVERSE.

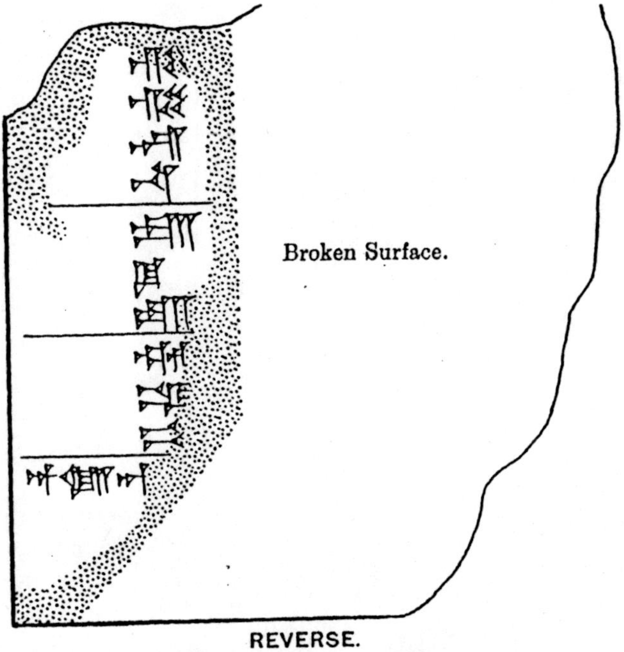

REVERSE.

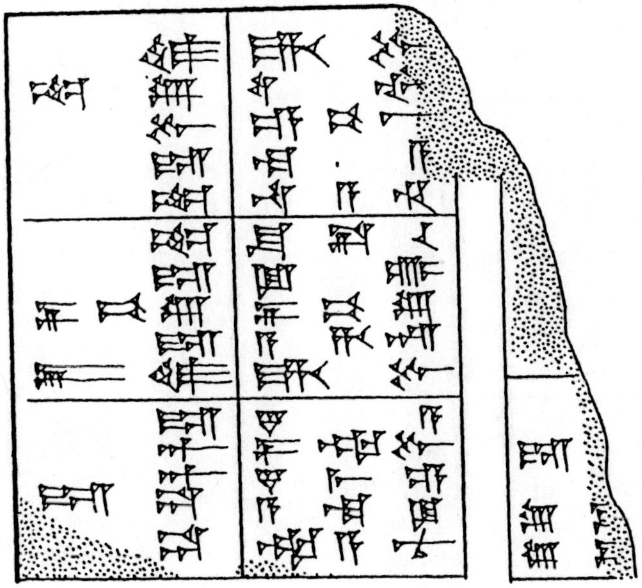

K. 2053.

REVERSE (cont.).

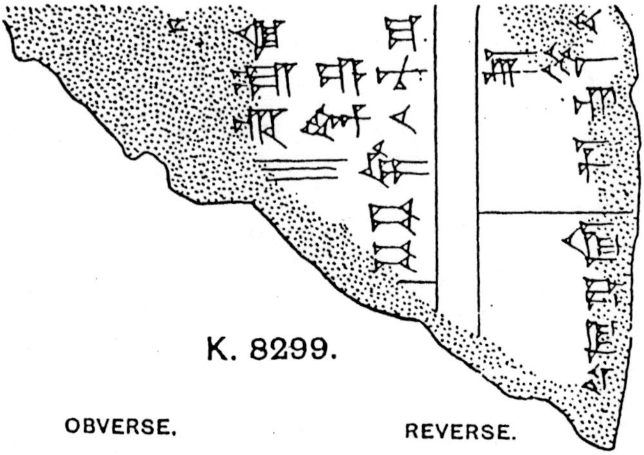

K. 8299.

OBVERSE.

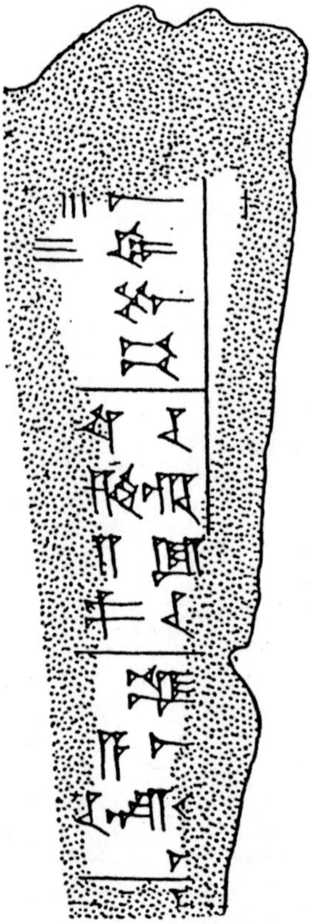

REVERSE.

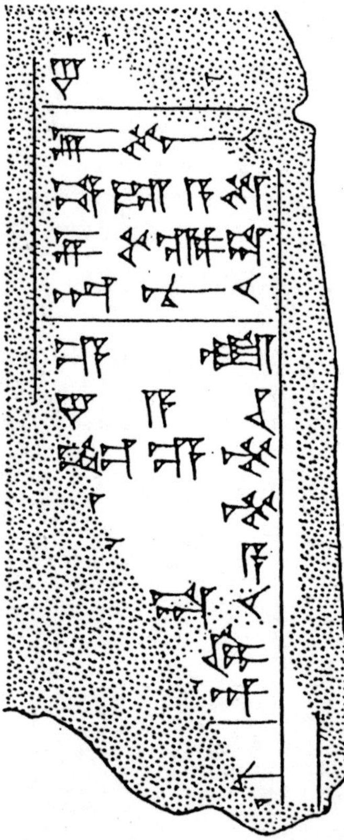

K. 2107 + K. 6086.

OBVERSE.

The Reverse of the Tablet is inscribed with a list of Temples.

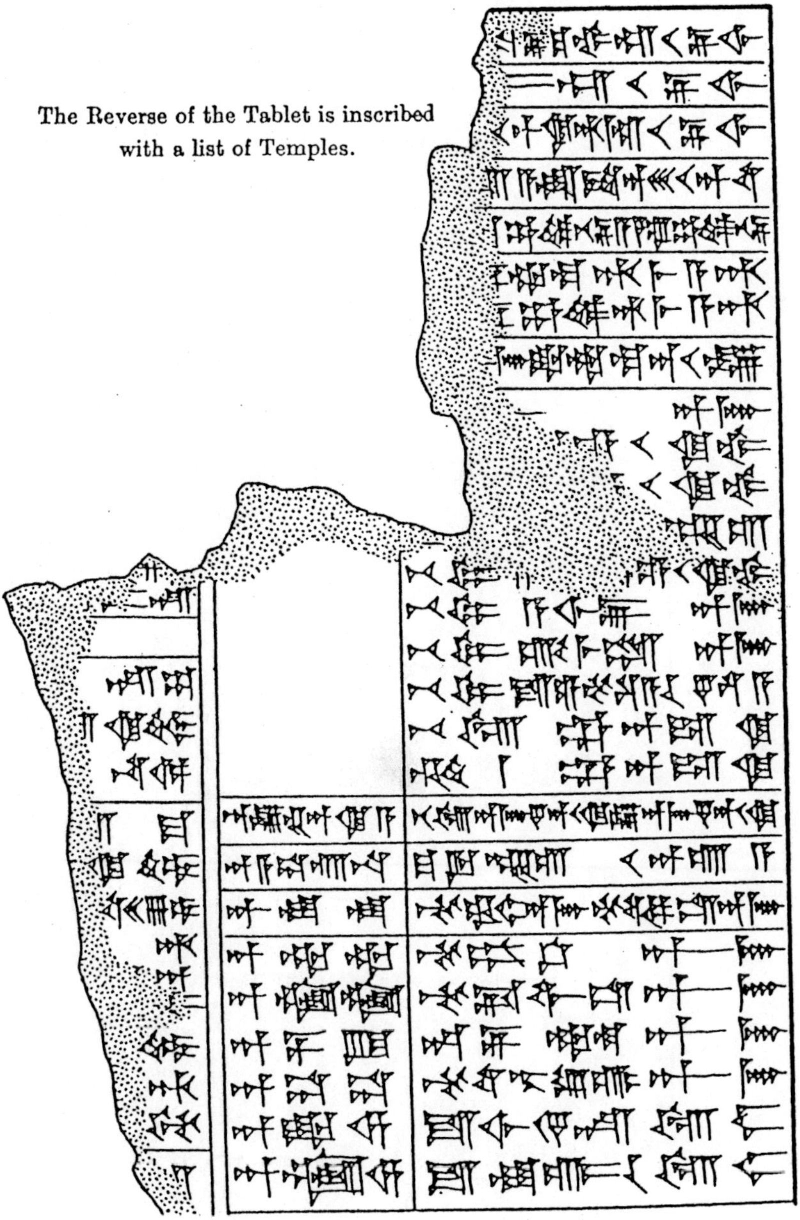

K. 2107 + K. 6086.

OBVERSE (Cont.).

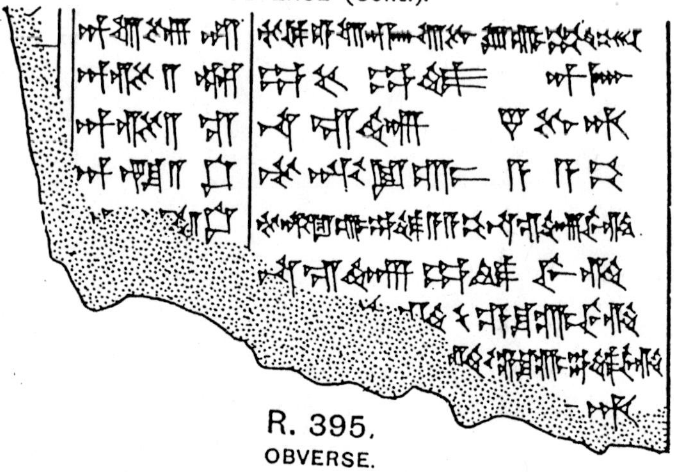

R. 395.

OBVERSE.

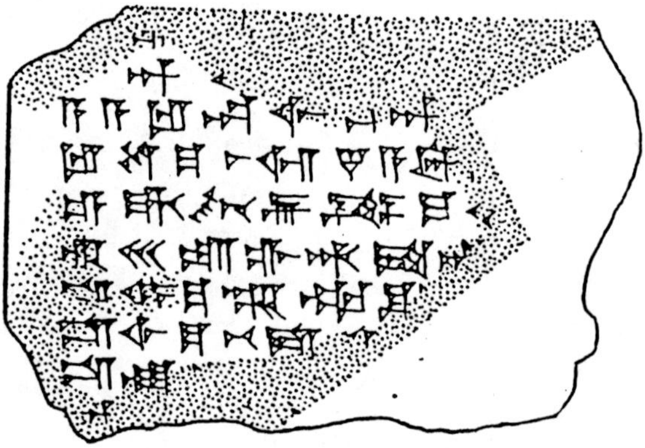

REVERSE.

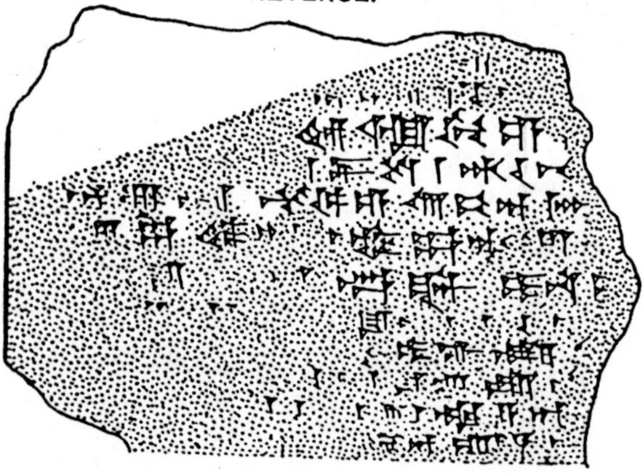

54228.

33851.

OBVERSE.

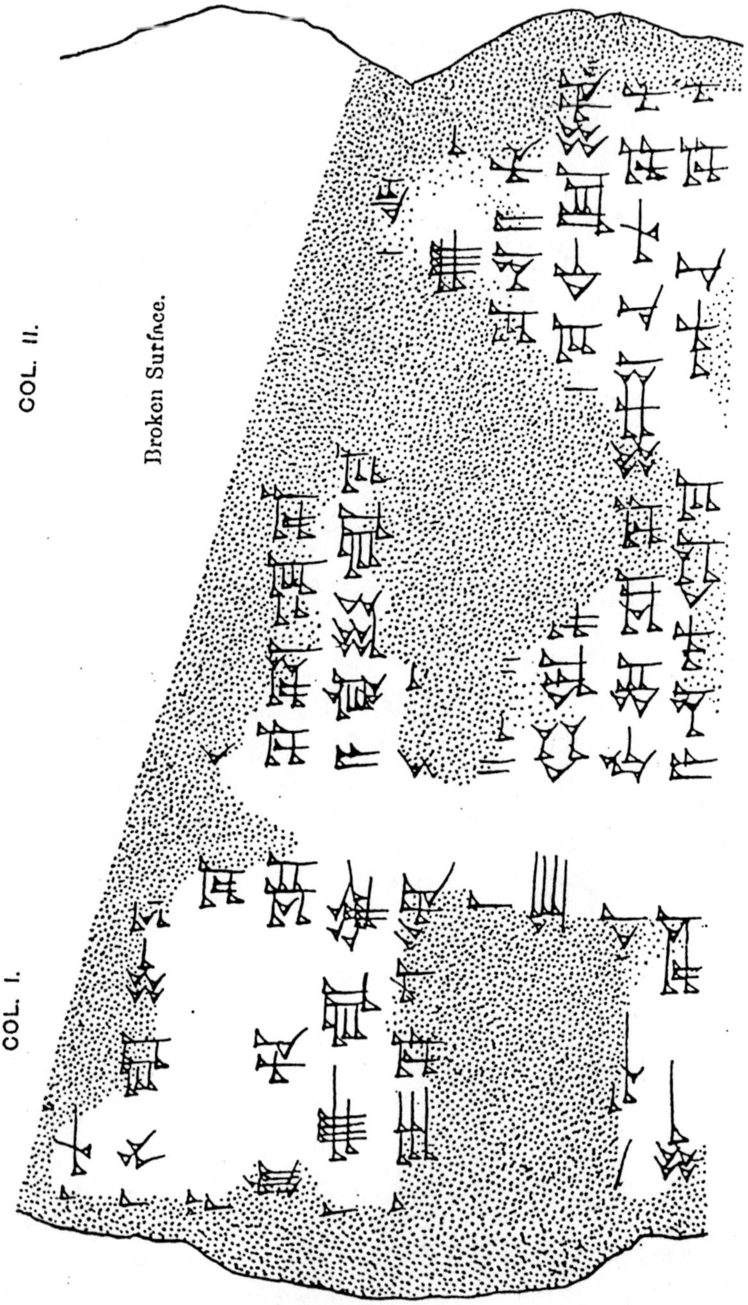

33851.

OBVERSE (Cont.).

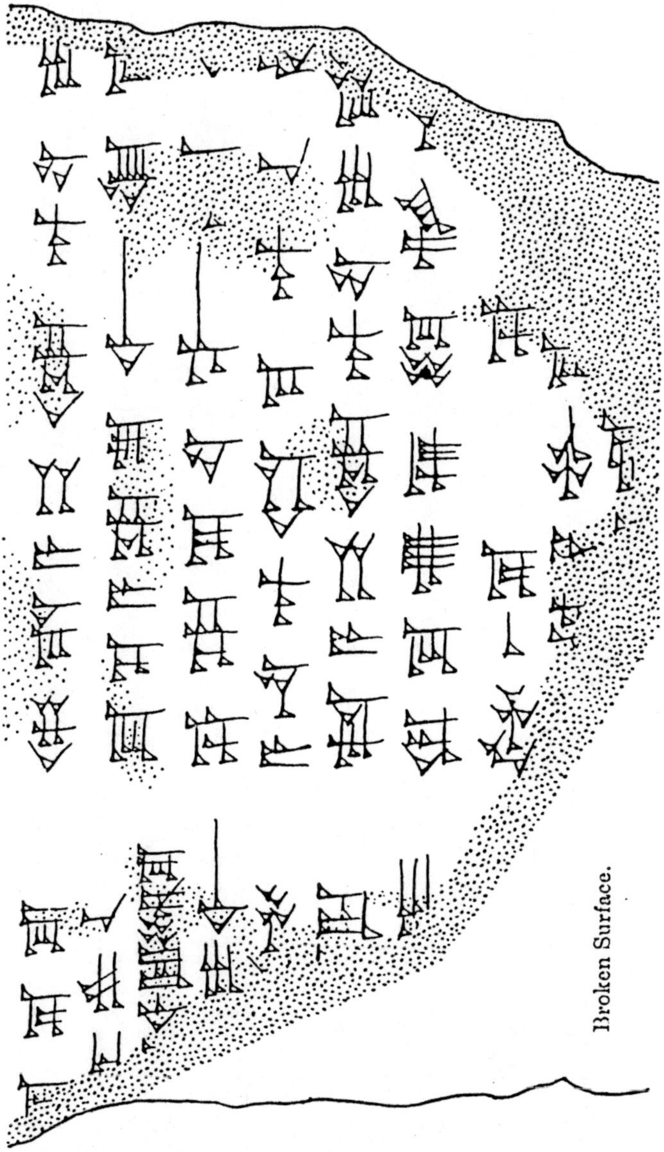

COL. II.

COL. I.

33851.

REVERSE.

COL. III.

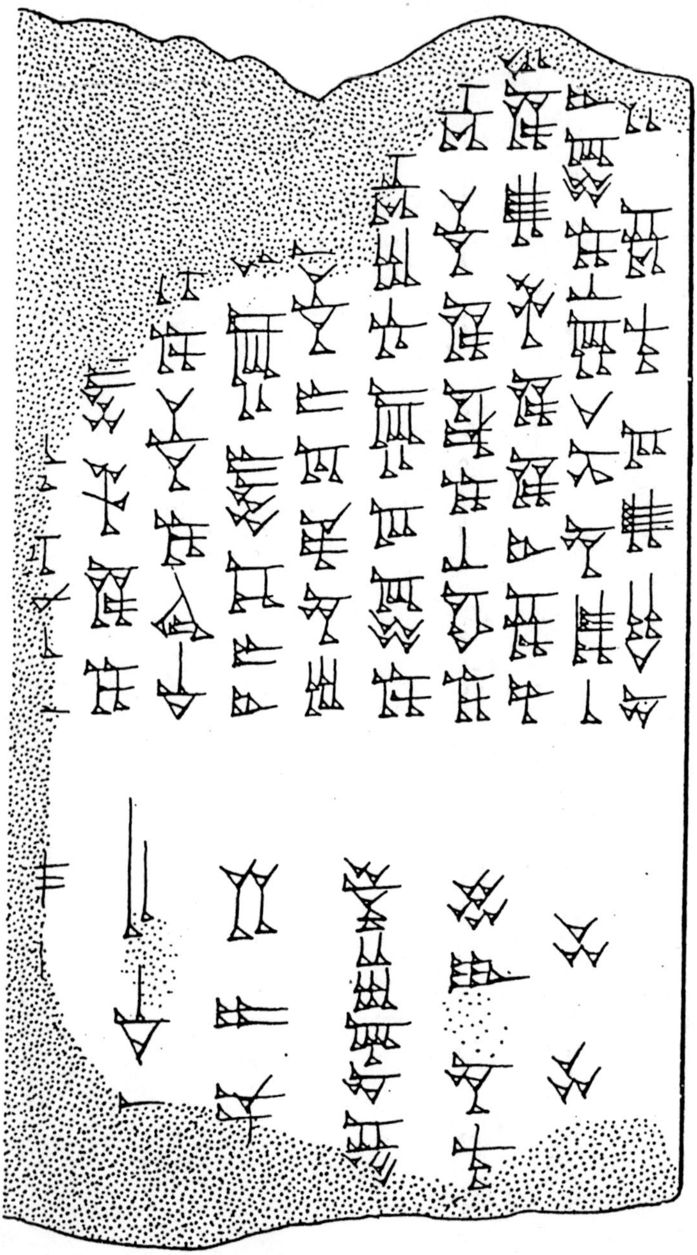

COL. IV.

55466+55486+55627.

OBVERSE.

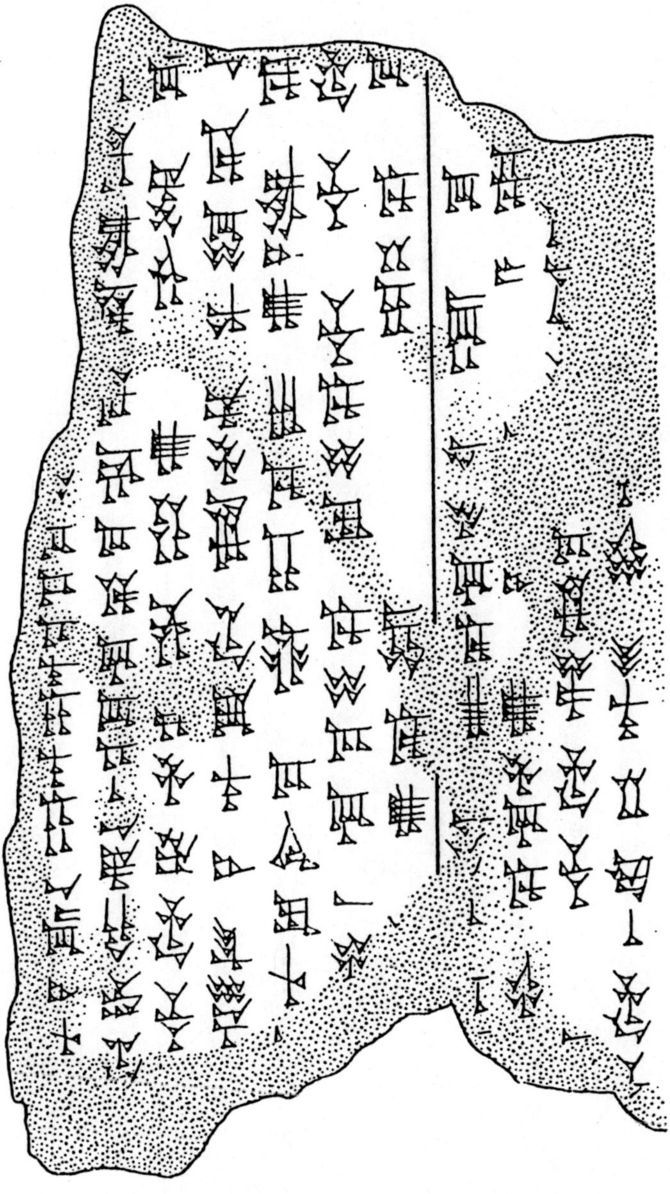

55466+55486+55627.

OBVERSE (Cont.).

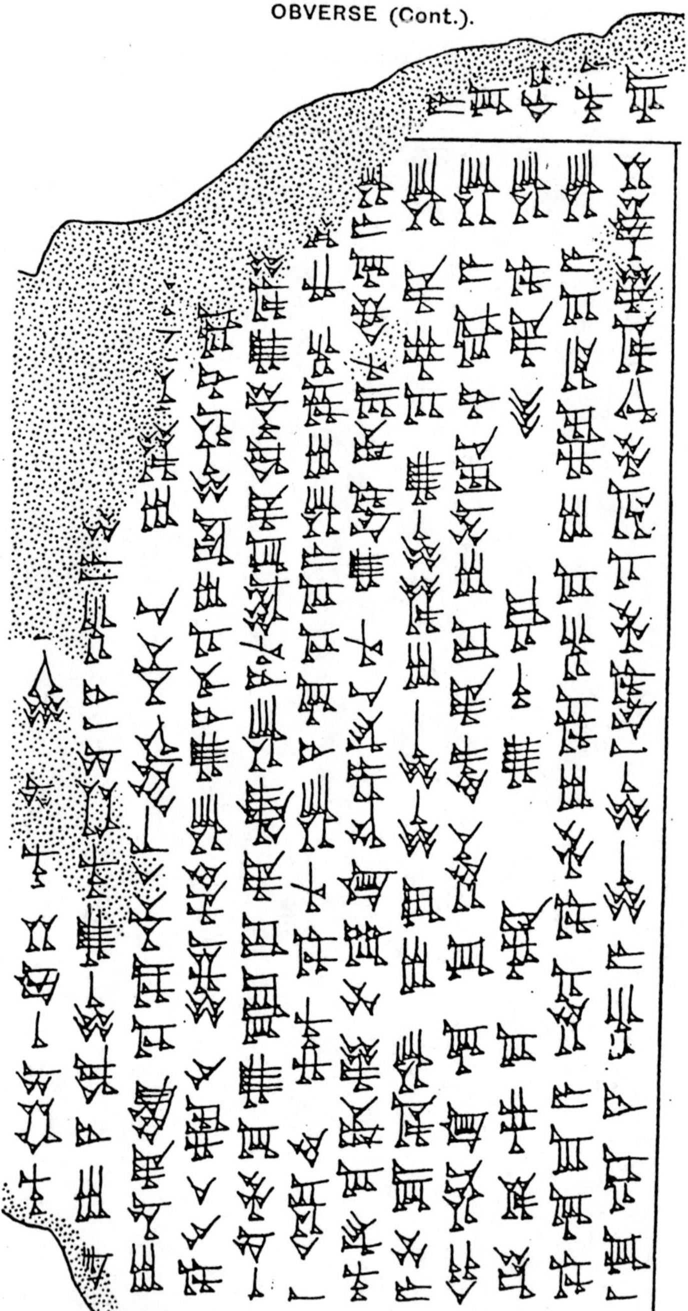

55466+55486+55627.

OBVERSE. (Cont.).

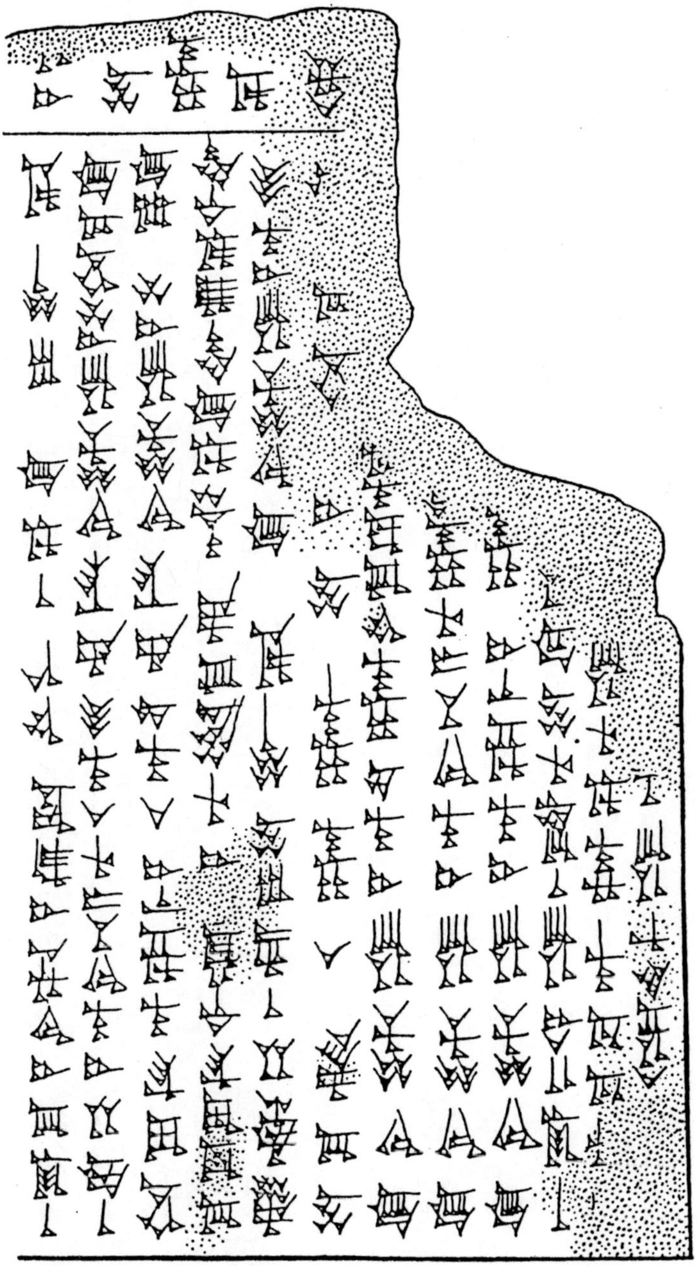

55466+55486+55627.

REVERSE.

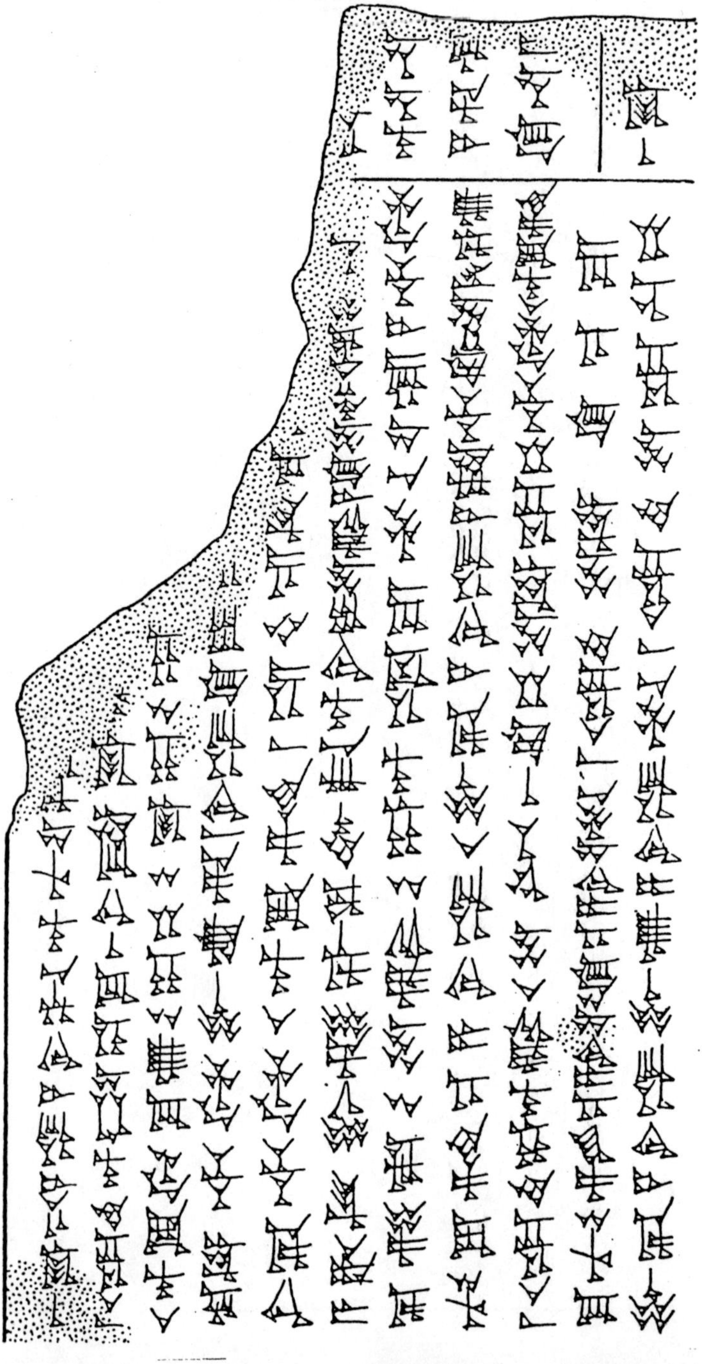

55466+55486+55627.

REVERSE (Cont.).

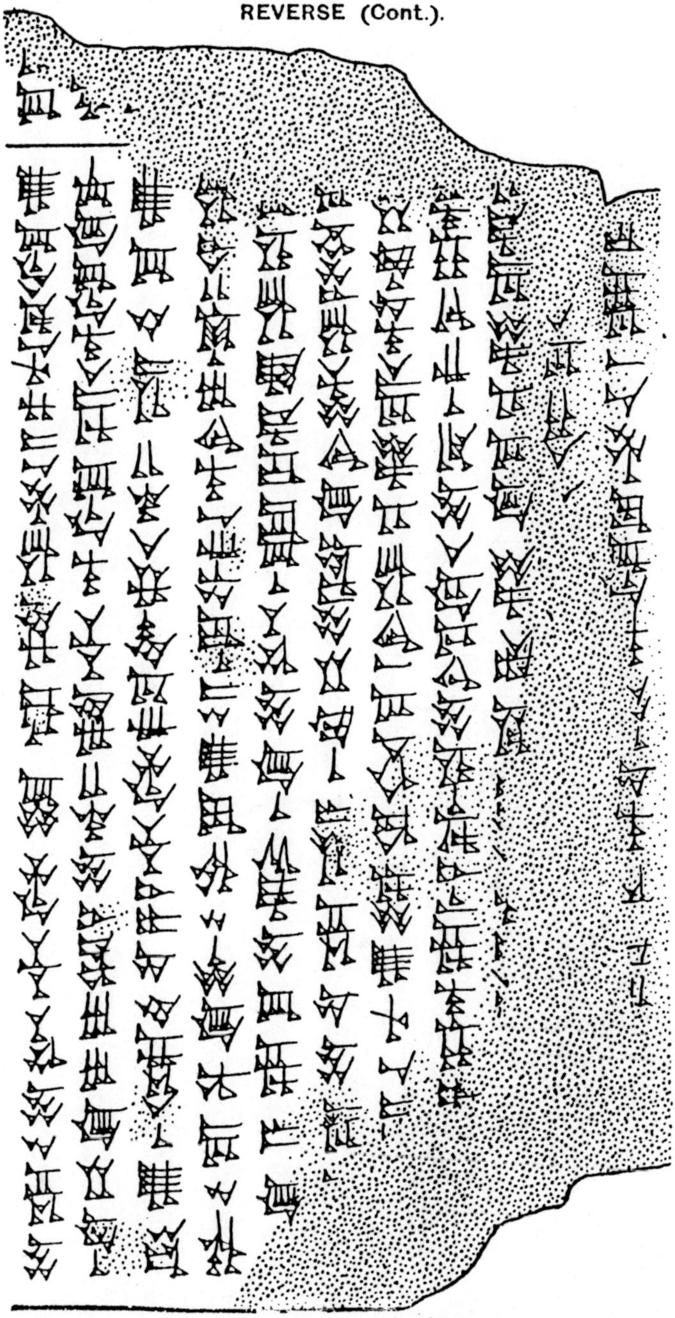

55466+55486+55627.

REVERSE (Cont.).

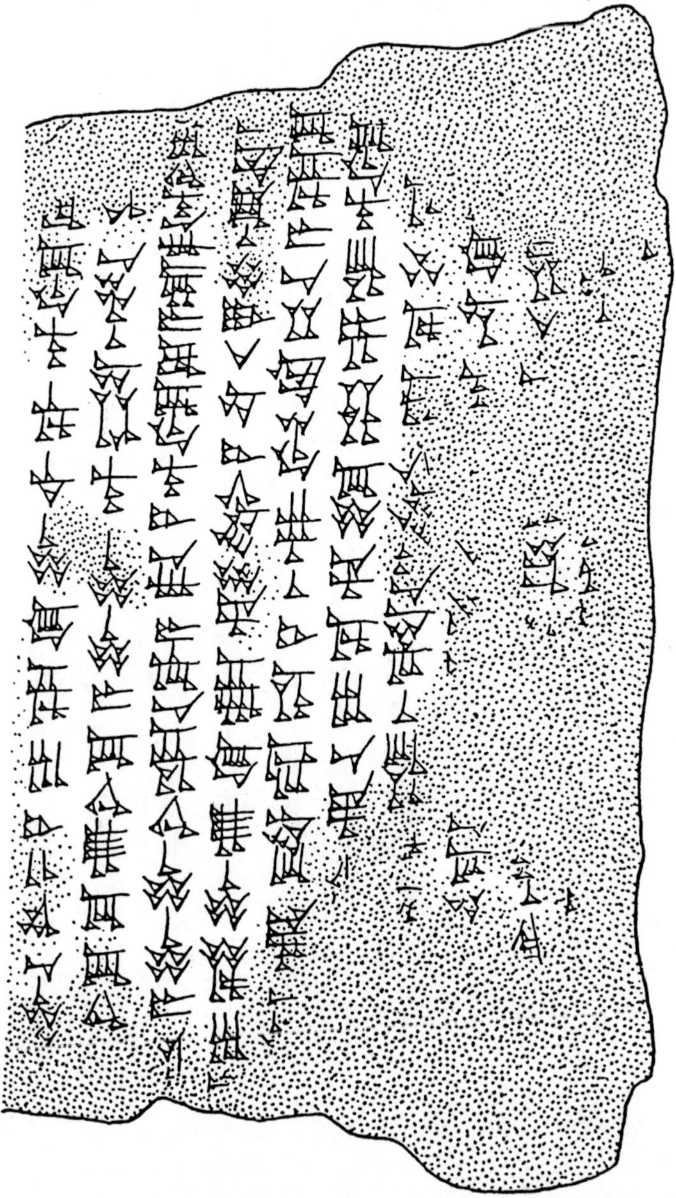

K. 3657.

OBVERSE.

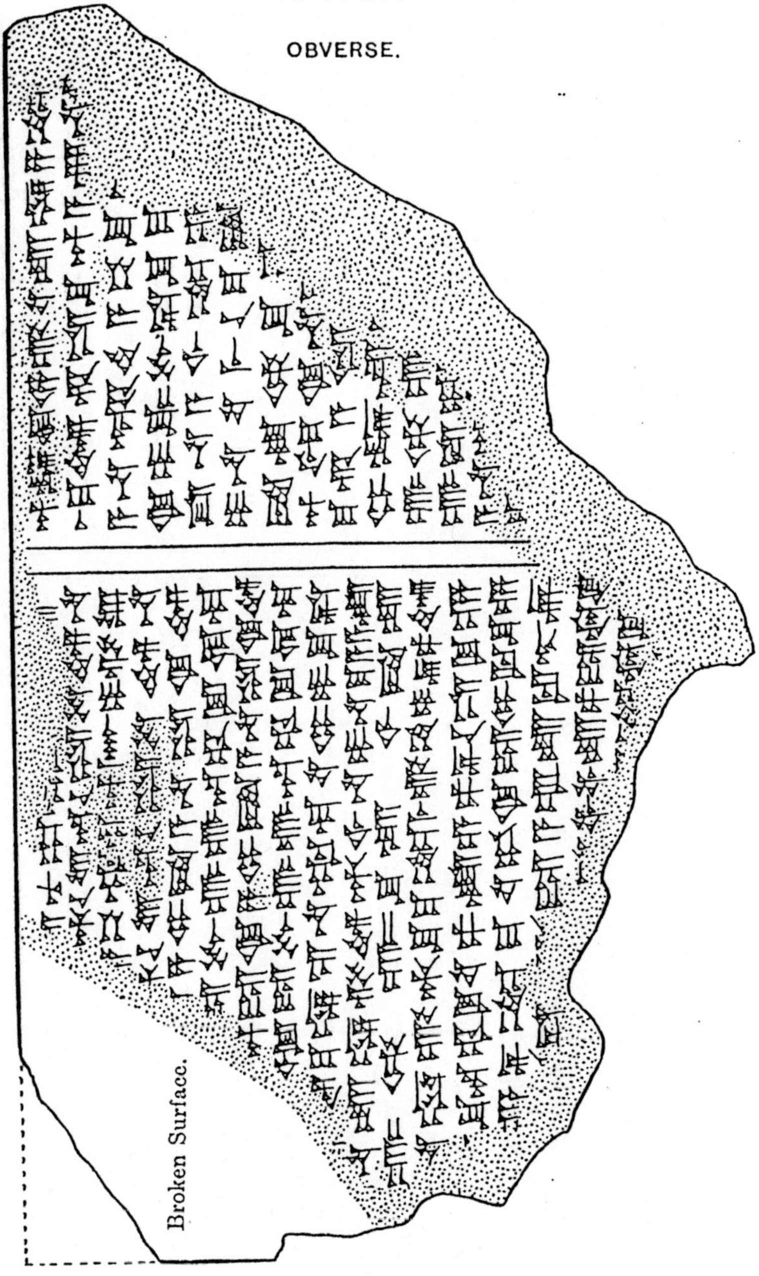

K. 3657.

REVERSE.

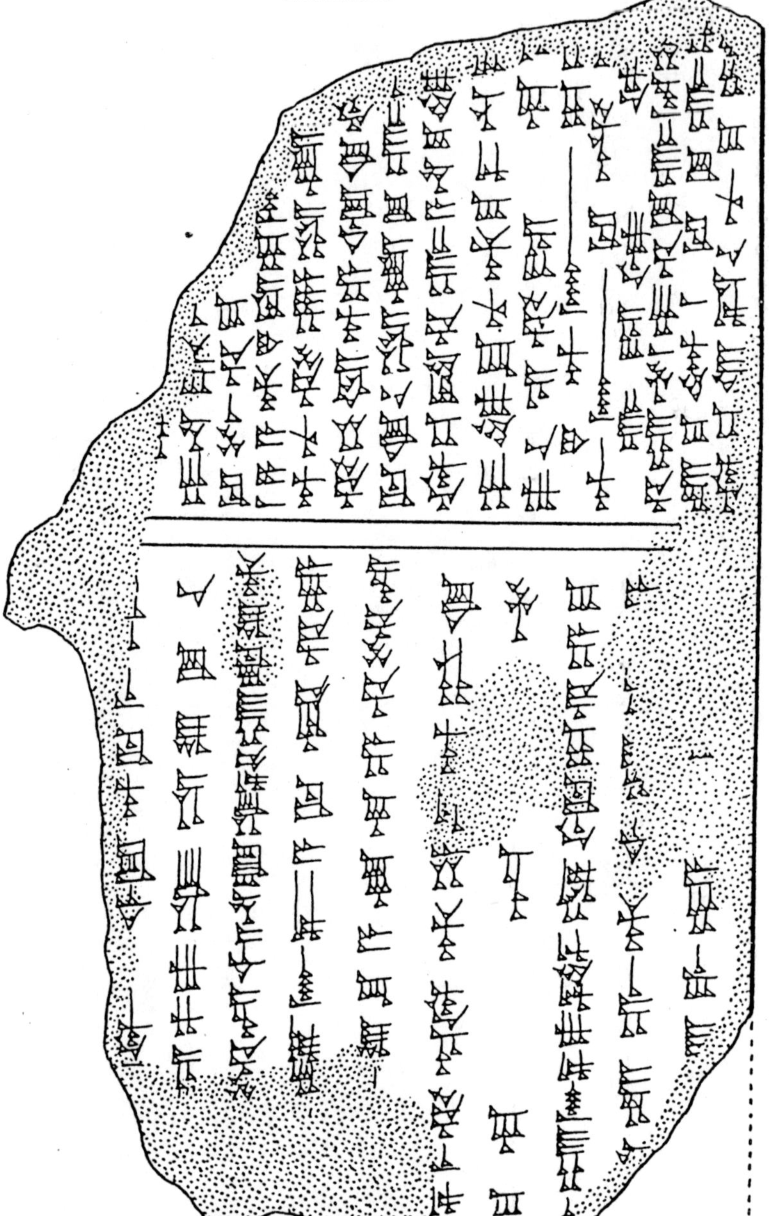

26187.

OBVERSE

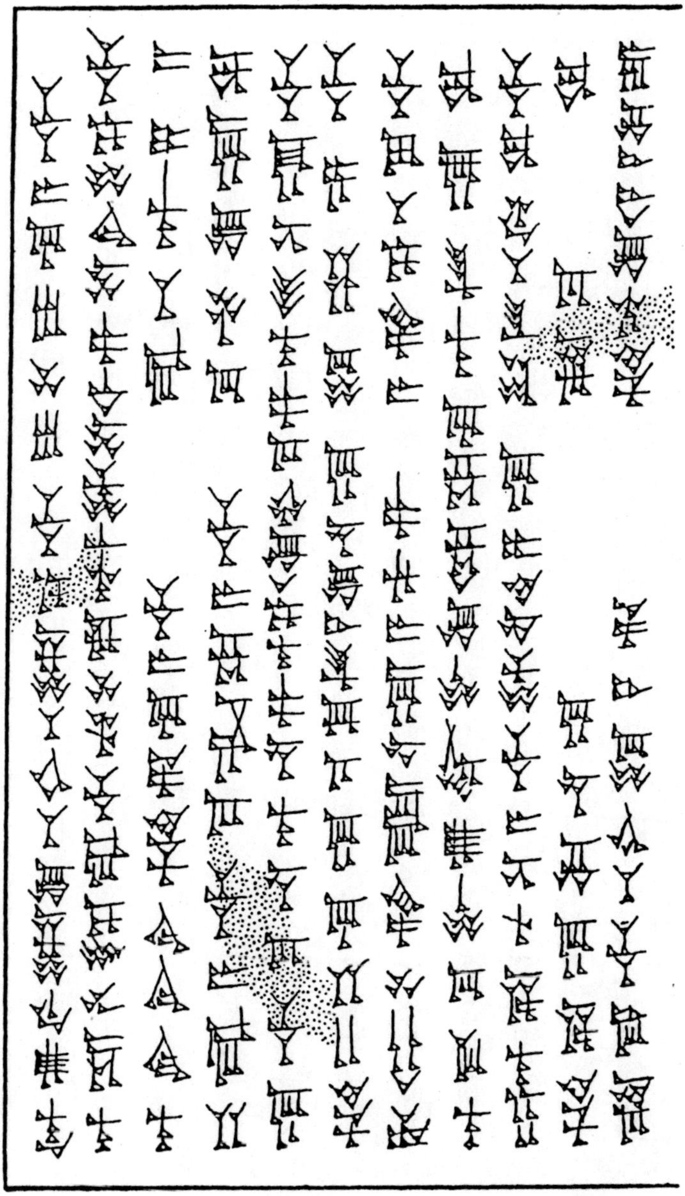

26187.

OBVERSE (cont.).

26187.

OBVERSE (Cont.).

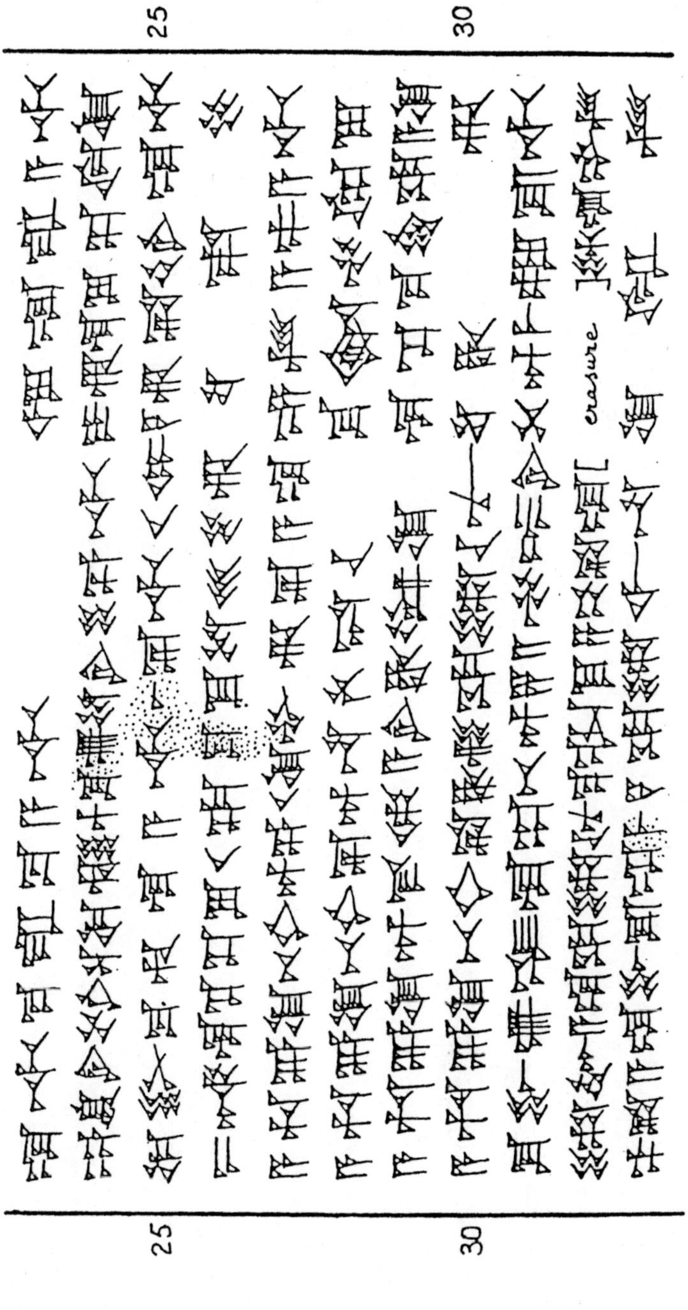

26187.

OBVERSE (cont.).

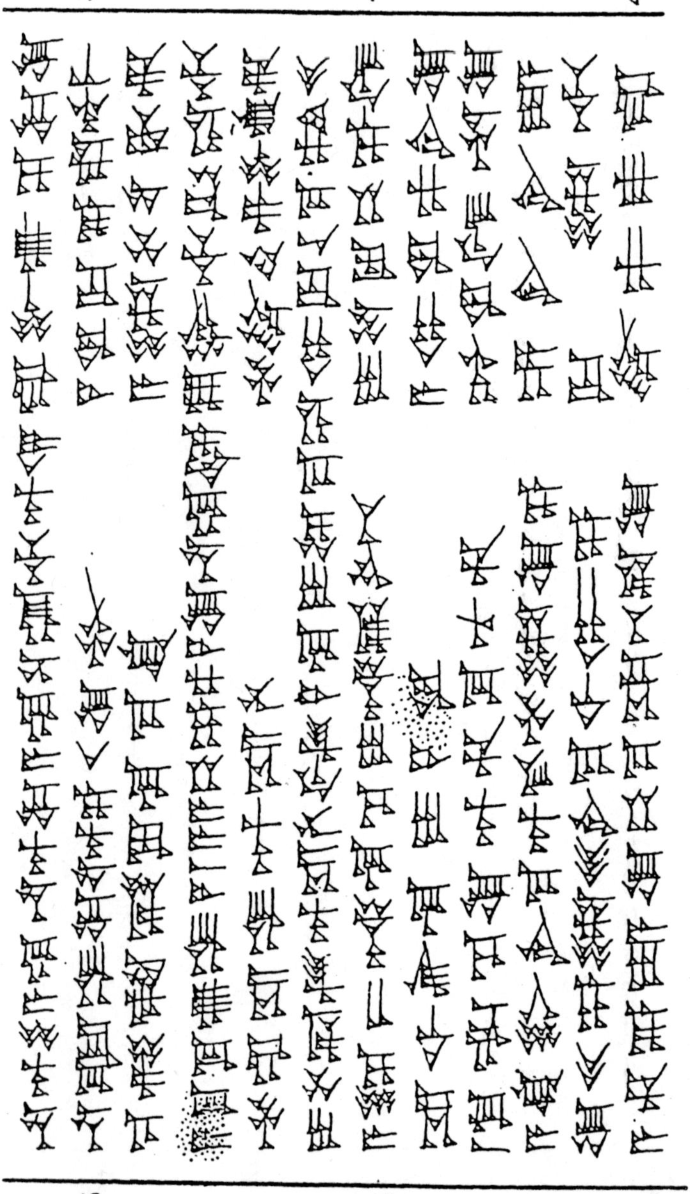

26187.

OBVERSE (cont.).

1. One sign erased by the scribe.

26187.

REVERSE.

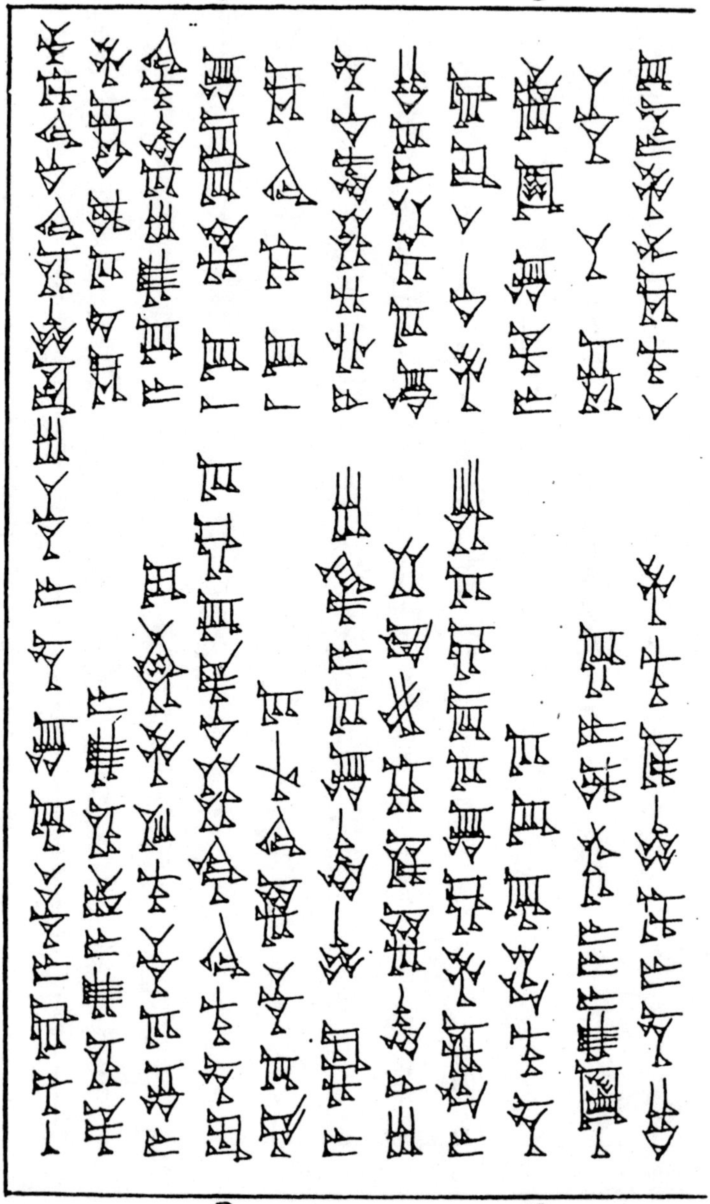

26187.

REVERSE (Cont.).

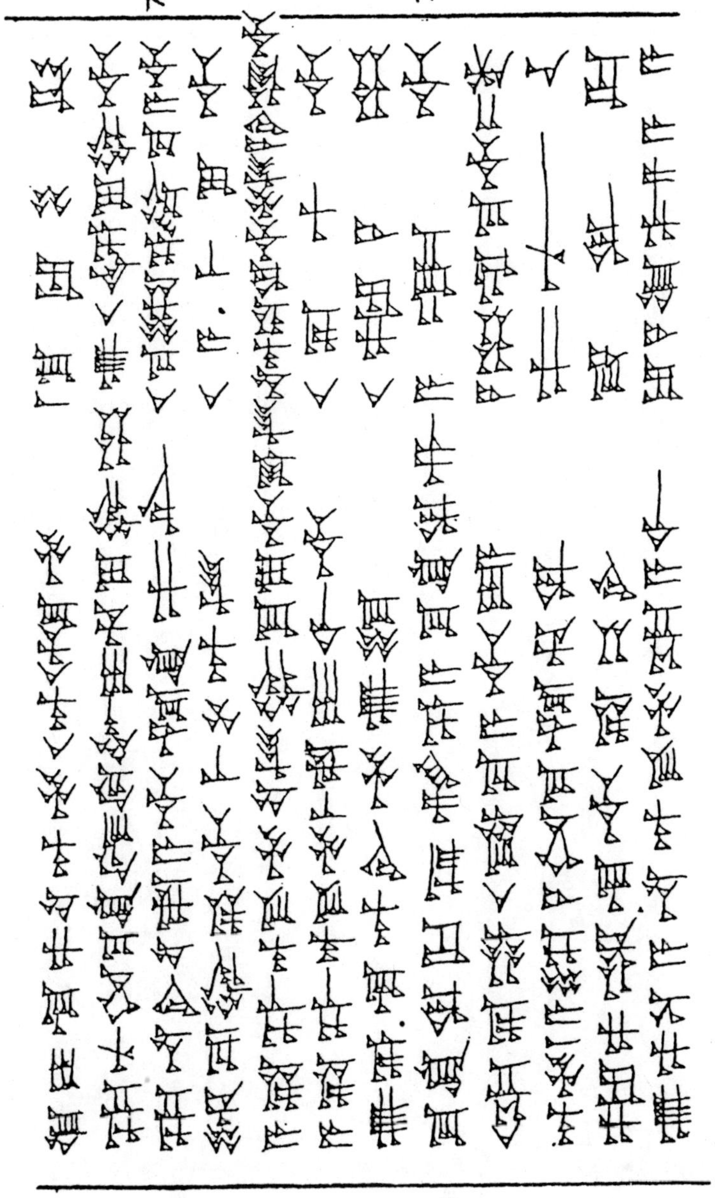

26187.

REVERSE (Cont.).

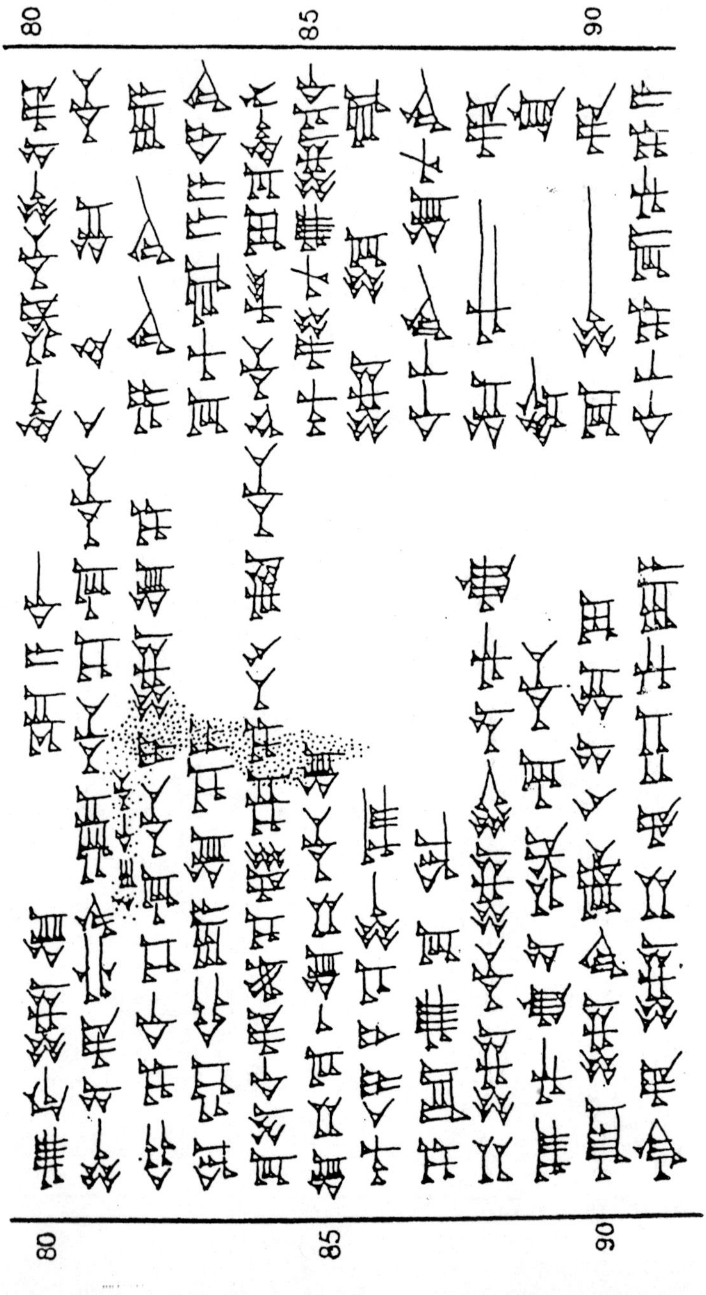

26187.

REVERSE (Cont.).

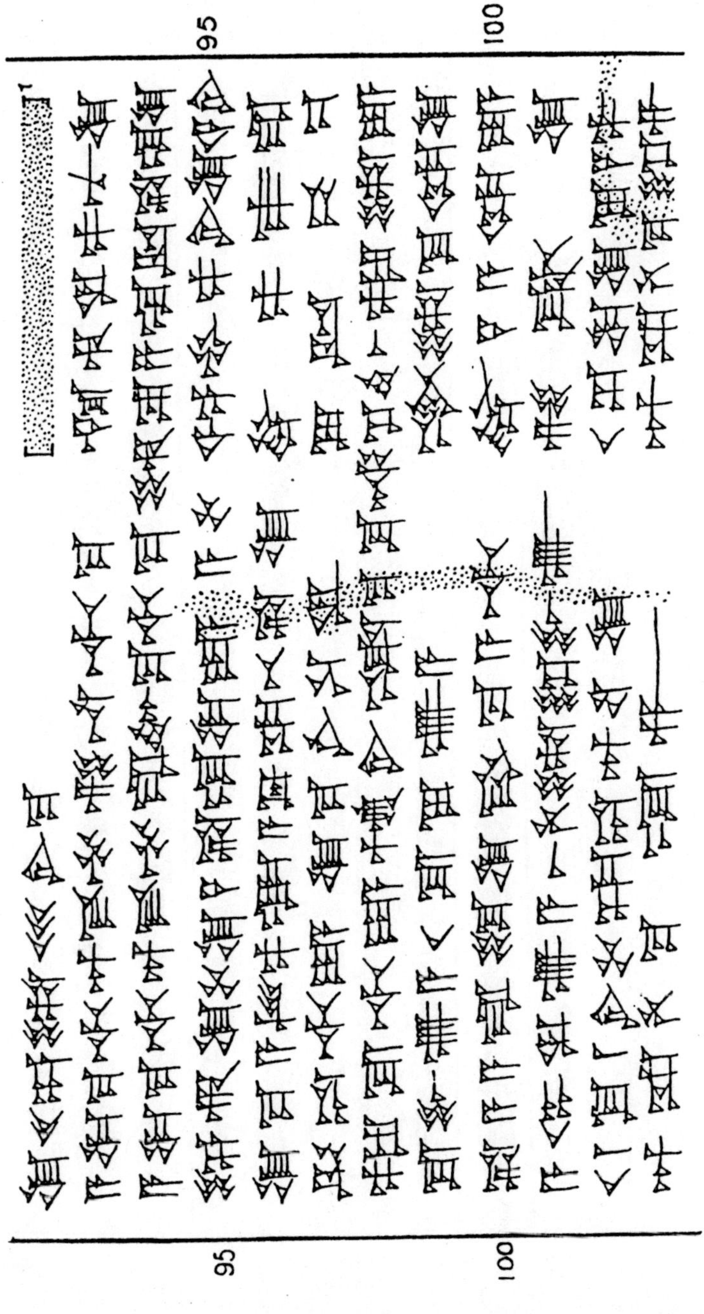

1. The second half of the line has been deeply erased by the Scribe.

26187.

REVERSE (Cont.).

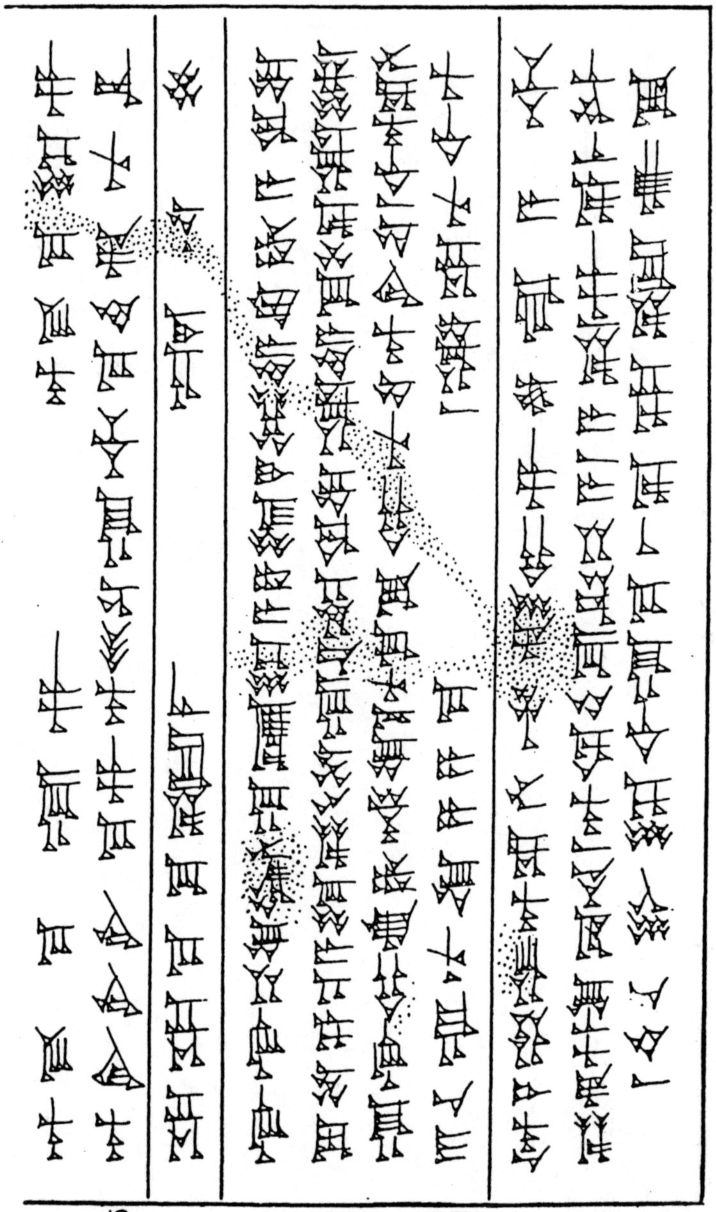

Index to Plates.

Index to Plates—*continued.*

9 781585 090426